BEST RECIPES

FROM THE LOS ANGELES TIMES

BEST RECIPES

FROM THE LOS ANGELES TIMES

Edited by Betsy Balsley,
Food Editor

HARRY N. ABRAMS, INC., PUBLISHERS, NEW YORK

Project Director: Darlene Geis
Editor: Ruth Peltason
Designer: Rhea Braunstein

Library of Congress Cataloging-in-Publication Data

Best recipes from the Los Angeles times / [compiled] by
Betsy Balsley.
p.   cm.
ISBN 0–8109–1237–6
1. Cookery.   I. Balsley, Betsy.   II. Los Angeles times.
TX714.B46   1989
641.5—dc19   89–6457

Harry N. Abrams, Inc., offers a varied selection of
calendars and desk diaries. For information, write to:
Harry N. Abrams, Inc., Attention Special Sales
Department, 100 Fifth Avenue, New York, N.Y. 10011

CONTENTS

ACKNOWLEDGMENTS

The question I'm most frequently asked as a newspaper food editor is, "Where do you get your recipes?" The answer is, "From everywhere." Readers, professional chefs, home cooks, home economists, and many others contribute to our weekly food section in the *Los Angeles Times*. And it is these contributors, among others, who have made this book possible. To them go my grateful thanks.

I especially want to thank Minnie Bernardino and Donna Deane for their expertise in both testing the recipes and styling many of the photographs in this book. Robin Tucker, creative food director for the *Los Angeles Times Magazine*, who also styled a number of the photographs, and Joan Drake, who helped me survive the vagaries of a new word processor and assisted in the initial proofing of the recipes, deserve a special vote of thanks.

Thanks also to others on the *Times* food staff—Rose Dosti, Barbara Hansen, Marge Powers, Greg Sokolowski, Dan Puzo, Dan Berger, Nancy Farr, and Toni Tipton—for without them there would be no book.

I am most grateful to Angela Rinaldi of the *Los Angeles Times Syndicate,* who held my hand through it all, while urging me to meet my deadlines.

And I could not, of course, have ever completed this project without the understanding and guidance of my editors at Abrams, Darlene Geis, and especially Ruth Peltason, who so ably made sense of the material they received.

I also want to thank all of the *Times* photographers, copy editors, editors, and librarians who, knowingly or unknowingly, contributed so much to this book's existence.

B.B.

INTRODUCTION

The recipes in this book reflect our changing dining habits during the 1980s, a remarkable period in American culinary history. They came from trendy young American chefs who became superstars and changed the way we ate and cooked. And they came from good home cooks as talented in their way as the professionals. Many of these recipes reveal our fascination with an ever-changing array of ethnic foods and, of course, a number of them show our increasing awareness of the need for, and a desire to follow, a more healthful diet.

It is hard to believe that a single decade could have changed our eating habits so much. But that's exactly what happened. And nowhere was that more apparent than in Los Angeles, where new food trends were legion during this single ten-year period. It was here that culinary artists responded quickly to the advent of the yuppies, who with their small, two-income households and their tendency to dine out many nights a week gave bright, creative young chefs the chance to break the bounds of tradition and do it "their way."

And it was here that home cooks took advantage of the ever-widening array of new produce and fresh herbs to create meals as innovative and exciting as those created by professional cooks.

The eighties have truly provided a grand culinary tour as we have progressed from rich, multicourse meals to simpler menus based on lighter foods and served in smaller portions. For anybody who flipped on a burner on a range, whether at home or in a restaurant, this has been an intriguing decade. In the years to come, the eighties will have to be acknowledged as a remarkable period in America's culinary history.

The recipes in this tribute to the eighties have been printed as they originally appeared in the *Times'* food pages, although they are not in chronological order. More importantly, they have not been adapted to today's lighter dining style. This has been done for two reasons. First, recipes that have withstood the vagaries and tastes of time deserve to be recognized as they are. And second, although we do tend to be considerably wiser in how and what we eat at the end of the decade, we still seem to be able to find a spot in our hearts and stomachs for old favorites on our dining table.

Betsy Balsley

APPETIZERS

Remember how it was ten years ago? Appetizers were something served with drinks or enjoyed as the first course of a leisurely dinner. Chips and dips were in their heyday. Satays and sushi were exotic, and stuffed mushrooms and pâtés were the glamour foods of the hour. No cocktail buffet was complete without cold shrimp or crab with a dip, usually a red one. And there was always a chafing dish or two filled with sweet-and-sour meatballs or tiny hot dogs.

How we've changed!

At some point in the mid- to late eighties, we moved appetizers out of the realm of snacks and turned them into mini meals. When we went out to dinner, we ate our collective way through the appetizer listing and ignored the rest of the menu.

We have become much more health conscious. We choose artichokes with a vinaigrette rather than with a butter sauce. Eventually we came to scorn cheese dips and fall in love with anything made with yogurt. There was great virtue in this; obviously we were eating far more sensibly and in a much lighter fashion.

We followed this same trend at home, too. Although we didn't totally give up dips and dunks, we began to make them with yogurt in place of cream cheese and we served them with crudités, not chips. And we cut back in other ways. Now if we have snacks with our white wine before dinner, we see to it that the rest of our meal has something low in calories and fat. And desserts are saved for special occasions, or so we say.

By the end of the eighties it has become difficult to tell the difference between appetizers and dinner. Most of us indulge in one or the other— but not both. The move to lighter dining has become a way of life, one that appears destined to be around for a while.

As for the future of dips and dunks, it looks as if they're going to stick around. They may be made with seafood mixed with yogurt, and vegetables may have replaced the chips, but dips, good or bad, seem to survive all fads or trends.

BELGIAN ENDIVE WITH SALMON DIP

Looking for a simple dip that would complement the slight bitterness in Belgian endive, we came up with this light yogurt-salmon mixture.

□

Wash the endive and pat dry. Trim root ends and separate leaves. Combine the yogurt, celery, shallots, pimiento, dill, and lemon peel. Gently stir in the salmon. Season to taste with hot pepper sauce. Mound mixture in a shallow bowl and tuck the endive leaves around the edges.

MAKES ABOUT 2 CUPS

4 heads Belgian endive
½ cup yogurt
¼ cup minced celery
2 tablespoons minced shallots
2 tablespoons minced pimiento
2 tablespoons minced fresh dill
1 teaspoon grated lemon peel
½ pound cooked salmon, chilled and flaked
Few drops hot pepper sauce

TUNA DIP

Sometimes the simplest recipes are the best, such as this dip from the Carlos 'n' Charlie's chain of restaurants. They serve it with tortilla chips, but any crisp chip or cracker would be equally good.

□

Combine the tuna and the chopped jalapeño chiles in their liquid. Add the onion. Stir in the mayonnaise until consistency is smooth. Sprinkle with cilantro and serve with the tortilla chips.

MAKES 6 SERVINGS

1 (14-ounce) can tuna
1 (6-ounce) jar or can jalapeño chiles, chopped
1 onion, minced
½ cup mayonnaise
Chopped cilantro
Tortilla chips

PAPAYA AND ASPARAGUS WITH SHRIMP DIP

This is one of those elegant appetizers that has everything—exotic fruit, superb color and texture, and a perfect blend of flavors. It also can be made in no time flat, but looks as though it took the entire day. Serve this as a first course if you want to make an impression on guests.

Blanch asparagus in boiling salted water, drain, and refresh in ice water. Reserve. Melt the butter in a skillet and sauté the garlic until lightly golden. Add shrimp and cook until pink, about 3 minutes.

Place about 5 shrimp in a food processor and process until smooth. Reserve remaining whole shrimp. Add skillet drippings, cream cheese, mayonnaise, serrano chile, cilantro, lime juice, and mustard, and process to blend. Season to taste with salt. Chill dip until ready to serve.

To serve, spoon shrimp dip into papaya shells and serve with the asparagus and shrimp.

MAKES ABOUT 6 SERVINGS

1 pound slender asparagus, trimmed and halved

2 tablespoons butter or margarine

1/2 teaspoon minced garlic

1 pound large shrimp, peeled and deveined

1 (8-ounce) package cream cheese, softened

1/2 cup mayonnaise

1 red serrano chile, minced

1 tablespoon chopped cilantro

1 tablespoon lime juice

1 tablespoon Dijon mustard

Salt

3 small papayas, halved crosswise and seeded

HOT CRAB DIP

Creamed horseradish and toasted almonds add flavor and texture to this hot crab dip.

Blend the cheese, mayonnaise, milk, horseradish, and lemon juice until well mixed and smooth. Stir in the green onions, almonds, and crab meat. Season to taste with salt and white pepper. Spoon the mixture into a shallow, ovenproof, 2- to 3-cup serving dish and bake at 375 degrees for 20 to 25 minutes or until heated through. Stir lightly and serve hot.

MAKES 1¾ CUPS DIP

1 (8-ounce) package Neufchatel or other low-calorie cream cheese

¼ cup light mayonnaise

2 tablespoons low-fat milk

2 teaspoons creamed horseradish

2 tablespoons lemon juice

¼ cup chopped green onions

¼ cup chopped, toasted, slivered almonds

½ pound cooked crab meat or surimi, flaked

Salt, white pepper

Belgian endive or crisp, raw vegetables cut into bite-size pieces

DRIED SPLIT PEA DIP

When Michael Roberts, the innovative chef-owner of Trumps in Los Angeles, decided to see if he could come up with an acceptable, less caloric version of guacamole, he chose fresh peas as a replacement for the traditional avocados. His efforts were a smashing success. So when we were looking for something new to do with split peas, we adapted his idea and the result was this unusual dip that, unlike true guacamole, retains its color for hours.

Sauté the onion in 2 tablespoons of the oil in a 1½- to 2-quart saucepan until tender but not browned. Stir in the water and split peas and bring to a boil. Boil 2 minutes, remove from heat, cover, and let stand 30 minutes.

Return the pan to the heat and bring to a boil. Cover, reduce heat, and simmer about 20 minutes, or until peas are tender. Cool slightly, drain peas; reserve any liquid. Purée the peas in a food processor or blender, adding enough reserved liquid to reach desired consistency.

Place the puréed peas in a bowl and stir in the chiles, garlic, lemon juice, tomatoes, cilantro, cumin, and remaining 1 tablespoon oil. Season mixture to taste with a few drops chili oil and salt. Cover and chill well.

Split pita rounds and cut each half into 6 to 8 wedges. Place on baking sheet and bake at 350 degrees for 5 to 10 minutes or just until crisp and wedges are light brown.

Place the dip in a serving bowl, with the crisp pita bread wedges for dipping.

MAKES ABOUT 3 CUPS

1 onion, chopped

3 tablespoons oil

3½ cups water

8 ounces green split peas

¼ cup finely chopped green chiles

2 cloves garlic, minced

Juice of 1 lemon

2 tomatoes, peeled, seeded, and chopped

2 tablespoons chopped fresh cilantro

½ teaspoon ground cumin

Chinese chili oil

Salt

6 (6-inch) pita breads

ARTICHOKE BOTTOM FILLED WITH WHITE EGG SALAD

With everyone trying to reduce their intake of cholesterol-laden foods, we came up with this simple appetizer that fits most of the requirements as an ideal snack. It's low in cholesterol and calories, but we left the flavor intact.

Trim the top leaves and sharp points of remaining artichoke leaves. Trim stem end even with the base of the artichoke. Cook in boiling water to which lemon juice has been added until the stem end of the artichoke can easily be pierced with a fork, about 30 to 40 minutes.

Pour off water and set the artichokes aside, upside down, to drain thoroughly. Remove the leaves and chokes; trim any uneven areas around the bottoms. Seal in plastic wrap and chill.

While the artichokes are cooking, separate egg whites from yolks, reserving yolks for another use. Chop whites coarsely and combine with mayonnaise, curry powder, celery, and chutney. Cover and chill mixture well.

To serve, mound egg white mixture onto artichoke bottoms. Garnish with parsley sprigs.

MAKES 2 APPETIZER SERVINGS

2 large artichokes
2 teaspoons lemon juice
4 hard-cooked eggs
2 tablespoons light mayonnaise
½ teaspoon curry powder
2 tablespoons finely diced celery
2 tablespoons chutney
Parsley sprigs

GRILLED FIGS STUFFED WITH TRIPLE CREAM

Staff writer Rose Dosti wrote a story on how to use specialty cheeses, providing the ultimate recipe for using fresh figs. The marrying of the ultra-creamy cheese and the luscious fruit makes one understand why fruits and cheeses have always been superb companions.

Split figs, but do not cut entirely through. Brush with melted butter. Grill with skin side toward heat source until the skin is roasted. Fill each center with 1 heaping tablespoon cheese and close part way. Sprinkle with sesame seeds. Serve 1 to a plate and garnish with crackers and edible flowers.

MAKES 6 APPETIZERS

Note: Packaged edible flowers may be purchased at specialty food stores.

6 fresh figs
1 tablespoon butter, melted
6 ounces ricotta, double or triple cream cheese, or other soft cheese, approximately
Sesame seeds, toasted
Crackers, for garnish
Edible flowers, for garnish

TRUFFLED BRILLAT-SAVARIN LOAF

Ken Frank, chef-owner of La Toque in Hollywood, served this far from inexpensive truffle-flavored cheese loaf with toasted brioche slices and fresh pear wedges. If the cheese and truffles are beyond your budget, try the version calling for fried sage leaves and a wheel of Brie. Both versions are outstanding.

Slice cheese wheel horizontally into 2 equal layers, using cheese wire or heavy thread. Sprinkle cut sides of each layer with truffle shavings. Stack the layers and wrap airtight in plastic wrap. Store in the refrigerator about 3 days to flavor the cheese.

When ready to serve, slice into 16 wedges and serve on a platter with sliced pears and toasted brioche slices.

MAKES 16 SERVINGS

Variation: Substitute 8-inch wheel Brie for the Brillat-Savarin and sliced stuffed olives or fried sage or spinach leaves for the truffles.

1 (8-inch) Brillat-Savarin wheel
1 or 2 fresh truffles, shaved
Sliced pears
Toasted brioche slices

Clean and pat dry the sage leaves. Dust lightly with flour. Add oil to a depth of 1 inch in a skillet. Cook the sage in the hot oil a few seconds until crisp. Remove immediately with a slotted spoon. Drain on paper towels.

FRIED SAGE LEAVES
1 bunch fresh sage leaves or young spinach leaves
Flour
Oil

PISTACHIO-STUFFED MUSHROOMS

Time was when pistachios were for the most part imported, expensive, and destined to leave your fingers stained with red dye. No more. Now there are huge groves of pistachio trees in the San Joachin Valley, and good cooks have found the readily available nuts excellent as ingredients in hot dishes such as this mushroom appetizer.

Preheat broiler. Remove stems from mushrooms and chop finely. Reserve caps. Sauté the stems and onion in ¼ cup butter until tender. Stir in the bread crumbs, pistachios, parsley, marjoram, and salt, mixing well. Remove from heat. Place the mushroom caps, stem-side up, on a baking sheet. Fill the centers with the stuffing and sprinkle with about 3 tablespoons melted butter. Broil about 6 inches from heat source for 5 minutes or until browned and heated through.

MAKES 20 APPETIZER SERVINGS

20 medium mushrooms
3 tablespoons minced onion
Butter or margarine
⅓ cup fine dried bread crumbs
¼ cup chopped pistachios
2 tablespoons chopped parsley
¼ teaspoon dried marjoram, crushed
¼ teaspoon salt

ONION MARMALADE TOAST

This onion marmalade from Claude Alrivy of Le Chardonnay in Los Angeles would make a marvelous hostess gift if packed in sterilized jars.

Spread both sides of each bread slice with butter. Toast both sides until golden. Spread with the onion marmalade. Garnish each slice of toast with half a quail egg and a watercress leaf.

MAKES 24 APPETIZERS

Melt the butter in a sauté pan. Add the onions and sauté until tender, but not brown. Add the wine vinegar, red wine, sugar, salt, and pepper. Simmer for 5 minutes. Add the grenadine. Cook until reduced to a thick marmalade consistency, about 45 minutes. Add more wine or water if necessary to keep marmalade from scorching.

MAKES ABOUT 1 CUP MARMALADE

24 French bread slices, cut ½-inch thick
Butter, softened
Onion Marmalade (recipe follows)
12 quail eggs, cooked
24 large watercress leaves

ONION MARMALADE
¼ cup butter
2½ to 3 cups minced onions
½ cup red wine vinegar
1 cup red wine
5½ tablespoons sugar
2 teaspoons salt
1 teaspoon white pepper
¼ cup grenadine syrup

ONION CAKES

When we heard about the unusual onion cakes prepared at the Hunan Restaurant in San Francisco, we expected some sort of typical dim sum appetizers. Were we ever wrong! In place of the traditional Chinese pancake, Henry Chung, who shared the recipe, suggested using flour tortillas.

Brush four of the tortillas with sesame oil, then some egg. Sprinkle each with about 2 tablespoons green onions. Cover with the remaining 4 tortillas and press firmly around the edges. Cover with plastic wrap; let stand until ready to deep fry.

Heat the oil in a wok or deep-sided pan to 400 degrees. Using tongs, slip the tortilla cakes, 1 at a time, into the hot oil. Cook, turning with tongs, to brown the other side. When done, drain off the oil, holding the tortillas vertically over the pan. Drain again on paper towels. Cut the tortillas into 4 to 8 wedges each while hot. Sprinkle lightly with salt.

MAKES 16 TO 32 SERVINGS

8 flour tortillas
2 tablespoons sesame oil
1 egg, lightly beaten
½ cup finely chopped green onions
Oil for deep frying
Salt

GARLIC FESTIVAL WOWCHOS

This redolent snack won second prize at the annual Gilroy Garlic Festival one year for Leonard Brill of San Francisco. It's not for the fainthearted.

Coat the garlic cloves with oil and bake at 375 degrees for 30 minutes or until soft and golden. Cover a 13 × 9-inch foil-covered metal pan with tortilla chips. Mash the garlic; mix with the onion, chiles, and olives, and distribute evenly over the chips. Cover with cheese and bake at 400 degrees for 5 minutes or until cheese has melted. Top with cilantro and green onion.

MAKES 4 APPETIZER SERVINGS

2 large heads garlic, separated into cloves and peeled
2 tablespoons oil
Tortilla chips
¼ cup chopped red onion
1 (4-ounce) can chopped green chiles
⅓ cup sliced pimiento-stuffed olives, optional
1½ cups shredded jalapeño Jack cheese
Chopped cilantro
Chopped green onion tops

PUERTO VALLARTA NACHOS

Times food writer Barbara Hansen acquired this recipe for nachos from Joe Ramirez of Mexican Joe's restaurant when she was on an assignment in Puerto Vallarta, Mexico. He used a blowtorch to melt the cheese, but an ordinary oven will do the trick more easily. The sauces range from mild (the guacamole) to fiery (the green sauce) in flavor.

Cut each tortilla into 6 wedges. Deep-fry the wedges in oil until crisp. Drain on paper towels. Paint each wedge with about 1 teaspoon refried beans. Arrange on a heatproof serving platter. Top with shredded cheese. Place in a hot oven or under the broiler just long enough to melt the cheese. Do not allow tortilla chips to burn.

Top each chip with 1 heaping teaspoon guacamole, then about ½ teaspoon sour cream. Top with a few pieces of diced tomato. Place more guacamole in the center of the platter. Serve the green and red sauces on the side.

MAKES 4 SERVINGS

Peel avocados. Place in a bowl and mash coarsely. Add the onion, lime juice, chiles, milk, olive oil, and season to taste with salt.

MAKES ABOUT 2½ CUPS

Place the chiles, tomatoes, onion, and garlic in a saucepan. Add water almost to cover, bring to a boil, and cook until vegetables are softened, about 10 minutes. Drain. Turn into a blender. Add the cloves, cumin, salt, and pepper, and blend. Heat the oil in a skillet. Add the sauce and bring to a boil. Simmer for 2 or 3 minutes, until cooked. Remove from heat and cool.

MAKES ABOUT 1⅓ CUPS

Note: Sauce will be very hot. Reduce quantity of chiles, if desired.

4 corn tortillas
Oil for deep frying
½ cup refried beans
1½ cups shredded Jack cheese
Guacamole (recipe follows)
Sour cream
1 small tomato, seeded and diced
Green Sauce (recipe follows)
Red Sauce (recipe follows)

GUACAMOLE
4 avocados
½ medium onion, finely chopped
2 teaspoons lime juice
2 small serrano chiles, finely chopped
2 tablespoons evaporated milk
1 teaspoon olive oil
Salt

GREEN SAUCE
¼ pound serrano chiles
1½ large tomatoes
¼ large onion
1 small clove garlic
2 whole cloves
¼ teaspoon cumin seeds
½ teaspoon salt
Pinch white pepper
1 tablespoon oil

Combine the tomatoes, onion, chile, cilantro, vinegar, lime juice, and season to taste with salt.

MAKES ABOUT 1½ CUPS

RED SAUCE

2 medium tomatoes, chopped

¼ medium onion, chopped

1 serrano chile, chopped

¼ cup chopped cilantro

1 teaspoon vinegar

½ teaspoon lime juice

Salt

CROUTONS WITH THREE CHEESES AND SUN-DRIED TOMATOES

When a group of Los Angeles chefs pooled their talents to raise money at a local benefit, Ken Frank of La Toque prepared this palate-pleasing hot canapé. The croutons can be prepared ahead and refrigerated until serving time. They are particularly good with a fruity California sparkling wine.

Place the bread slices on a large baking sheet; brush with olive oil on 1 side. Bake at 300 degrees until golden brown. Mound 1 teaspoon cheese topping on each toasted bread slice, top with sun-dried tomato, and cover with another teaspoon cheese topping. Bake at 350 degrees until cheese begins to melt.

MAKES 2 DOZEN

1 narrow baguette, cut into ¼-inch slices

Olive oil

Cheese Topping *(recipe follows)*

24 small sun-dried tomatoes

Combine the goat cheese, ricotta, mozzarella, garlic, and pepper to taste in a mixing bowl until blended and smooth.

CHEESE TOPPING

8 ounces California goat cheese with herbs

8 ounces ricotta cheese

8 ounces shredded mozzarella cheese

1 teaspoon chopped garlic, approximately

Freshly ground white pepper

FRIED ZUCCHINI, NEW YORK STYLE

Zucchini is a favorite vegetable with local home gardeners. The only drawback is that it is also an unbelievably prolific vine. So when a reader requested we ask for this deliciously crisp version of one of our favorite finger foods from Perretti's Italian Cafe in New York back in 1983, we happily did so. Needless to say, requests for a repeat of the recipe surface annually as backyard zucchini crops begin to overpower unsuspecting home farmers.

Peel the zucchini and cut into 1- to 2-inch strips, about ¼-inch wide. Beat the eggs in a large bowl. Mix the bread crumbs, garlic, and pepper in a large bowl. Place the flour in a bowl or on a plate. Dip the zucchini strips in the eggs, then in the flour, once again in the eggs, and lastly in the bread crumbs.

Meanwhile, heat the oil to 400 degrees. Add the zucchini strips, a few at a time, to prevent crowding. Cook until golden brown and crisp on all sides. Serve at once with lemon wedges and sprinkle lightly with freshly grated Parmesan cheese, if desired.

MAKES 8 APPETIZER SERVINGS

3 or 4 zucchini
3 or 4 eggs
2 cups dried bread crumbs
½ teaspoon granulated garlic
¼ teaspoon black pepper
1 cup flour
Oil for deep frying
Lemon wedges, for garnish
Grated Parmesan or Romano cheese, optional

CHICKEN WINGS PACIFICA

Some recipes enjoy a brief popularity and fade into oblivion. Not this one. Long before chicken wings became a familiar item in chafing dishes at cocktail parties, this recipe for chicken wings had earned D. J. McClary, who submitted it to our "My Best Recipe" column in 1964, a reputation as an imaginative cook. It is one of the most requested recipes we have ever printed.

Arrange the drumettes in a shallow baking pan. Combine the soy sauce, brown sugar, butter, mustard, and water, and heat until the sugar and butter dissolve.

Cool and pour over the wings. Marinate for 2 hours in the refrigerator, turning occasionally. Bake in the marinade at 350 degrees for 45 minutes, turning once. Baste with marinade occasionally. Drain on paper towels. Serve hot or cold.

MAKES 6 TO 8 SERVINGS

24 to 30 chicken wing drumettes
1 cup soy sauce
1 cup packed brown sugar
½ cup butter or margarine
1 teaspoon dry mustard
¾ cup water

GLAZED CHICKEN WINGS

Still another popular chicken wing appetizer is this spicy version from the Red Onion restaurant chain. We found the wings delicious when baked in the sauce, although the restaurant bakes the chicken wings first, and then brushes them with the spicy sweet-sour glaze; additional glaze is served on the side as a dipping sauce.

Combine the rice vinegar and both sugars in a saucepan. Bring to a boil. Continue to boil about 30 minutes until mixture is reduced by ⅓ to the consistency of pancake syrup. Add chili sauce and simmer 5 minutes. Remove from heat.

Stir in the hot pepper sauce and liquid smoke. The glaze may be stored at cool, dry room temperature or in the refrigerator in a covered container at this point. Place the chicken wings in a baking pan. Pour the sauce over the wings and bake at 350 degrees for 1 hour or until the chicken wings are tender.

MAKES 8 APPETIZER SERVINGS

2 cups rice wine vinegar
2 cups packed light brown sugar
½ cup granulated sugar
¼ cup chili sauce
1½ tablespoons hot pepper sauce
1½ tablespoons liquid smoke
2 dozen chicken wings, or more

CACAHUATES PICANTES

When Sheila Thompson sent in this recipe for chile-spiced peanuts to our "My Best Recipe" column, our tasters found it memorable. Do be sure to remove the chiles after a couple of days, or only the heartiest palate will be able to survive its zesty flavor.

Heat the olive oil in a skillet. Add the chiles and garlic, and sauté 1 to 2 minutes, stirring constantly to avoid scorching. Stir in the peanuts and transfer to a foil-lined baking sheet. Bake at 350 degrees for 5 to 8 minutes. Sprinkle with salt and chili powder and toss well. Cool. Transfer to glass jars, cover, and let mellow at room temperature about 24 hours.

After 2 days, remove the chiles, which continue to intensify the flavor of the peanuts.

MAKES 5 CUPS

Note: For longer storage, keep in the freezer or refrigerator up to 3 months.

3 tablespoons olive oil
16 small dried hot chiles
2 cloves garlic, pressed
24 ounces dry-roasted peanuts
Salt, optional
1 teaspoon chili powder

LIVER TERRINE

The smooth creamy texture of City Restaurant's elegant pâté makes it a welcome addition to any cocktail buffet spread. And the fact that it travels well means it turns up often at picnics, patio parties, and other alfresco celebrations.

Skin the fatback and cut into 1-inch cubes. Blanch in rapidly boiling salted water until the water returns to a boil. Drain. Rinse with warm water and reserve.

Combine the brandy and bay leaves in a small saucepan. Cook over low heat until warm, about 5 minutes. Set aside to cool, then remove the bay leaves.

Soak the white bread in water just long enough to soften, then squeeze out excess moisture.

Combine the fatback, bread, livers, eggs, and cream in a large mixing bowl. Set the bowl over a saucepan of simmering water and stir until the mixture is room temperature, about 2 minutes. Remove from heat.

Add cooled brandy, Madeira, salt, pepper, nutmeg, and thyme. Purée in blender until smooth. Pass the mixture through a medium strainer into a large bowl and stir to combine.

Pour the purée into an ungreased 9 × 5-inch glass or ceramic loaf dish. Cover with 2 layers foil, tucking edges under to completely seal. Place the dish in a roasting pan and pour enough boiling water into pan to come halfway up the sides of the terrine.

Bake at 325 degrees for 1 hour, or until center is slightly wobbly. Set aside to cool, then refrigerate at least 6 hours or up to 1 week.

To serve, dip the bottom of the pan into warm water to loosen. Run a knife along the inside edges and invert onto a large serving platter. Cut into ½-inch slices and serve on lettuce leaves.

MAKES ABOUT 12 SERVINGS

2 pounds, 3 ounces fatback
½ cup brandy
3 bay leaves
2 slices day-old white bread, crusts removed
14 ounces duck or chicken livers, trimmed
2 eggs
3 tablespoons whipping cream
¾ cup Madeira
2 teaspoons salt
½ teaspoon white pepper
⅛ teaspoon freshly grated nutmeg
3 sprigs thyme, leaves only
Lettuce leaves

PORK SHUI MAI WITH MUSTARD-SOY VINAIGRETTE

The restaurant 385 North in Los Angeles is now defunct, but when Roy Yamaguchi was there he served this version of pork shui mai with a wonderful mustard-soy vinaigrette at a special function. The little dumplings were so good that we asked for and received the easy recipe.

Grind the pork through a meat grinder or in a food processor. Place in a bowl and combine with soy sauce, sugar, ginger, and garlic.

Place 1 teaspoon of the mixture in the center of each wonton skin. Bring the edges together and twist to seal the mixture inside, using water to adhere the skin.

Bring a large pot of water to a boil. Drop the dumplings into the boiling water and cook about 5 minutes. Remove from pan. Sauce the bottom of a platter with the mustard-soy vinaigrette. Arrange the dumplings on the sauce. Sprinkle with chives and garnish with watercress.

MAKES 20 DUMPLINGS

1 pound pork butt
1 cup soy sauce
½ cup sugar
2 tablespoons grated ginger root
1 tablespoon grated garlic
20 wonton skins
Mustard-Soy Vinaigrette *(recipe follows)*
1 tablespoon minced chives
1 bunch watercress, for garnish

Place the mustard in a bowl. Dilute with a small amount of rice wine vinegar to form into paste. Add the remaining rice wine vinegar and soy sauce. Let stand for 1 hour to blend flavors before using.

MAKES ABOUT 2 CUPS

MUSTARD-SOY
VINAIGRETTE
½ cup dry mustard
1 cup rice wine vinegar
1 cup soy sauce

SOUPS

Soups have always been popular in Southern California, and the decade of the eighties was no different from any other in that respect.

Hot soups, cold soups, sturdy soups, light soups . . . all have been equally welcome on our tables. A significant, general change was that we lightened some cream-based soups by reducing the amount of cream called for, or substituting other liquids, or using puréed vegetables as a base.

Beyond that, our tastes have remained largely the same. We continue to serve fresh chilled vegetable soups such as tomato-rich gazpacho and creamy cucumber soups during the hot summer. And on cooler days hot onion soup topped with cheese-covered croutons or a rich black bean soup topped with a dollop of sour cream and a sprinkling of fresh and spicy salsa still suits our palate.

If there has been anything truly different in soup in the 1980s, it was its place at our tables: now we serve soup more often, and usually as the main dish. We like them served simply—with crunchy hot breads and crisp salads. We turn them into portable lunches, and we even serve soup as the main course at parties.

Chilled fruit soups are treated as appetizers and served on the patio; on occasion soup becomes dessert. The variety has broadened too—from the late Rudi Gernreich's Red Pepper Soup made with sweet red peppers to a Poblano chile soup from Dallas that is guaranteed to open one's sinuses.

Our tastes have become eclectic, and we're open to new ideas, but as for letting go of long-favored classics—that doesn't seem likely.

CUCUMBER SOUP

We like soups any time of year in Southern California, hot in winter and cold in summer. This summertime chiller from the Velvet Turtle restaurant chain has practically become a local classic. Its tart flavor makes it most welcome when the temperature rises.

Reserve ½ cup diced cucumber. Sauté the remaining cucumber, onion, and leek in 2 tablespoons butter until the onion is transparent. Season to taste with salt and pepper.

Cook, stirring, until mixture is blended. Add the wine, water, and chicken base, and bring to a boil. Melt 2 tablespoons butter in a small pan and blend in the flour. Stir into the onion mixture and simmer 1 hour.

Put the soup in a blender container and spin about 15 seconds, then strain through a fine sieve. Stir in the whipping cream, lemon juice, hot pepper sauce, dill, and reserved diced cucumber.

Cool the soup completely, correct seasonings, and add half and half if the soup becomes too thick when chilled. Serve in chilled soup cups. Garnish with ½ teaspoon sour cream, lemon wedge, and parsley if desired.

MAKES 6 SERVINGS

1 large cucumber, peeled, seeded, and diced

1 onion, chopped coarsely

1 cup chopped leek (white part only)

Butter or margarine

Salt, pepper

2 tablespoons dry white wine

2 cups water

1½ teaspoons chicken stock base

2 tablespoons flour

½ cup whipping cream

½ teaspoon lemon juice

5 drops hot pepper sauce

Pinch chopped fresh or dried dill

½ cup half and half, optional

Sour cream, lemon wedges, parsley, for garnish, optional

FRESH PEA SOUP

Pea soups are always popular with soup lovers. Although most are made from dried split peas, this recipe from Gulliver's restaurant in Marina del Rey is made with fresh or frozen sweet peas. It makes a nice change from the traditional recipe.

Melt the butter and stir in the flour in the top of a double boiler. Cook, stirring constantly until a golden paste is formed. Combine the onion, bay leaf, nutmeg, and oil in a large saucepan over medium heat. Bring to a boil, reduce heat, and simmer 10 minutes. Add the peas and and stock and return to a boil. Reduce heat and simmer 45 minutes.

Add white pepper, hot pepper sauce, Worcestershire, salt, and sugar to the soup and simmer 5 more minutes. Pass the soup through a fine sieve or purée in a food processor. Return to the saucepan and bring to a boil. Add the roux, stirring until smooth. Simmer 20 minutes longer. Add whipping cream and bring to a simmer. Do not boil. Ladle soup into bowls and add croutons to each dish.

MAKES 8 SERVINGS

3 tablespoons butter

3 tablespoons flour

1 cup chopped onion

¼ bay leaf

½ teaspoon ground nutmeg

1 tablespoon oil

1 quart plus ¾ cup fresh peas, shelled, or 2 (10-ounce) packages frozen peas

2 quarts chicken stock

Pinch white pepper

¼ teaspoon hot pepper sauce

2 tablespoons Worcestershire sauce

½ teaspoon salt

½ teaspoon sugar

¾ cup whipping cream

2 cups croutons

GAZPACHO DE LOS ANGELES

We've run this chilled tomato soup recipe from the Velvet Turtle chain so many times over the years that the original file card is yellowed with age. Gazpacho is the perfect choice for something cool and refreshing on a warm summer day.

Combine the tomato juice, green pepper, onion, cucumber, chiles, Worcestershire, olive oil, garlic, chives, herbs, and hot pepper sauce. Season to taste with salt and white pepper. Chill thoroughly. Serve with lemon wedges.

MAKES 6 TO 8 SERVINGS

Note: For smooth gazpacho served with vegetable garnishes, spin the tomato mixture in a blender container until smooth. Serve with additional diced cucumber, green pepper, and croutons on the side.

1 (46-ounce) can tomato juice
1 medium green pepper, minced
1 small onion, minced
1 cucumber, peeled and minced
2 small canned green chiles, minced
1 tablespoon Worcestershire sauce
1 tablespoon olive oil
1/2 teaspoon minced garlic
1 tablespoon chopped chives
1 teaspoon herb-seasoning blend
2 drops hot pepper sauce
Salt, white pepper
Lemon wedges, for garnish

FRESH GARLIC SOUP GRATINÉE

The neighbors may know what you're having for dinner when you prepare this garlic lovers delight, but who cares? The recipe came from La Grange restaurant and it's as rich as it's aromatic.

Cut the bread into 1-inch slices. Place on a baking sheet and brush lightly with melted butter. Bake at 325 degrees for 15 minutes, or until lightly browned. Turn the bread slices, brush lightly with melted butter, and continue to bake until browned.

Separate the garlic into cloves and peel. Place in a blender container or food processor and process until garlic is puréed. Melt the butter in a large saucepan over low heat. Gradually add the puréed garlic. Cook, stirring, 2 minutes. Cover and simmer 20 minutes, stirring occasionally. Check to make sure garlic does not burn.

Gradually stir in the flour to form a smooth paste. Slowly stir in the chicken broth until the mixture is smooth. Bring to a boil and season with salt and pepper. Reduce heat and simmer over medium heat 30 minutes. Pour the hot soup into ovenproof individual soup crocks or casseroles. Flatten 1 or 2 slices of toast and place on top of the soup. Cover the surfaces completely with Swiss cheese. Bake at 350 degrees for 5 to 10 minutes until cheese melts. Then set the soup crocks under the broiler until the cheese browns lightly, if desired.

MAKES 6 TO 8 SERVINGS

1 loaf French bread
Melted butter or margarine
2 heads garlic
3 tablespoons butter
3 tablespoons flour
2 quarts chicken broth
Salt, pepper
2 cups shredded Swiss cheese

LEEK SOUP

When Mary Cox visited Montreal in 1983, her sister gave her this recipe for a leek and onion soup. The next year, Mary shared the recipe with our readers through the "My Best Recipe" column.

Melt the butter in a kettle over medium heat. Sauté the leeks and onions until lightly browned. Add the boiling water, potatoes, and season to taste with salt and pepper. Cook about 25 minutes.

Mix flour with milk until smooth. Stir into the vegetables and simmer until thickened. Add sour cream, if desired, and heat without boiling.

MAKES ABOUT 6 CUPS

3 tablespoons butter or margarine
2 leeks, cut in 1-inch pieces
3 cups chopped onions
4 cups boiling water
2 cups diced potatoes
Salt, pepper
3 tablespoons flour
½ cup milk
½ cup sour cream, approximately

BAKED ONION SOUP

Onion soup topped with cheese-laden croutons makes a perfect main dish for a soup supper on a cold night. This version is a quick and easy one so filled with flavor we chose it as one of the twelve best recipes of the year for 1987.

Sauté the onions and garlic in butter in a large Dutch oven over low heat until browned and tender. Stir occasionally to prevent scorching. Add the beef and chicken broths. Heat to boiling, reduce heat, and simmer about 5 minutes to blend flavors. Add sherry and season to taste with salt and pepper.

Toast the bread and sprinkle with Parmesan cheese. Ladle the hot soup into 4 individual ovenproof casseroles. Place 3 slices of the toasted bread over each. Sprinkle with Jack cheese. Bake at 375 degrees for about 30 minutes, or until soup is bubbly and cheese is browned.

MAKES 4 SERVINGS

4 cups sliced onions
3 cloves garlic, minced
¼ cup butter or margarine
2 (14½-ounce) cans clear beef broth
1 (14½-ounce) can clear chicken broth
¼ cup dry sherry
Salt, pepper
12 small slices French bread
Grated Parmesan cheese
½ pound Jack cheese, shredded

POTATO, LEEK, AND FENNEL SOUP

Christopher Blobaum, executive chef at Colette, the restaurant in the Beverly Pavilion Hotel in Beverly Hills, gave us the recipe for this interesting soup. In 1988 we chose it as one of the twelve best recipes for that year. It can be served hot one day and chilled the next.

Sauté the onion, leeks, potatoes, and fennel bulb in butter over medium heat, 8 to 10 minutes. Add stock and bring to a boil. Simmer 20 minutes.

Purée the potato-leek mixture in a blender, or pass through a food mill until smooth. Season to taste with salt and white pepper. Add half and half. Heat through before serving. Serve in warmed soup plates, and garnish with reserved fennel fronds if desired. Soup may be served chilled.

MAKES 6 SERVINGS

1½ cups coarsely chopped onion

4 cups sliced leeks, white part only

2 medium potatoes, peeled and diced

½ pound fennel, sliced (remove fronds and reserve for garnish)

3 tablespoons butter or oil

4 cups chicken stock

Salt, white pepper

1 cup half and half

SPINACH SOUP

This beautiful bright green soup would make a good first course for a dinner party. But don't save the recipe for company only; this soup is good anytime.

Put the spinach in a heavy pot or Dutch oven. Add the broth and bring to a boil. Reduce heat, cover, and simmer about 5 minutes or until spinach is completely thawed and tender.

Sauté the onion and garlic in butter in a skillet until tender but not browned. Stir in the flour until cooked through and smooth. Add 1 cup of the whipping cream and cook, stirring, until mixture is well blended. Stir the onion mixture into the spinach and broth. Blend in the remaining 2 cups whipping cream and bring just to a simmer.

Purée the mixture in 2-cup quantities in a food processor until smooth. Return to the pan, and add lemon juice and salt and pepper to taste. Garnish each serving with hard-cooked egg slices.

MAKES 4 TO 6 SERVINGS

2 (10-ounce) packages frozen leaf spinach

1 (14½-ounce) can chicken broth

1 cup chopped onion

2 cloves garlic, minced

¼ cup butter or margarine

3 tablespoons flour

3 cups whipping cream

1 tablespoon lemon juice

Salt, pepper

2 hard-cooked eggs, sliced crosswise, for garnish

RED PEPPER SOUP

A charity cookoff featuring celebrity cooks resulted in the addition of this recipe for a delightful chilled sweet red pepper soup to our files. It came from the late Rudi Gernreich, the fashion designer who gave us the bikini.

Melt the butter with the oil in a large saucepan. Add the leeks and red peppers. Reduce heat and cook, covered, for 20 minutes or until vegetables are soft. Check occasionally to prevent scorching. Add chicken broth and salt to taste. Simmer, partially covered, over low heat for 30 minutes, or until vegetables are very soft.

Blend pepper mixture in a food processor or blender until smooth. Strain into a large bowl. Stir in the buttermilk and white pepper to taste. Garnish with chives or a thin slice of lemon with a small scoop of caviar centered on the lemon slice, if desired. For single servings, dole the soup into green pepper shells.

MAKES 10 TO 12 SERVINGS

1 cup unsalted butter

2 tablespoons oil

4 cups chopped leeks

6 large red peppers, seeded and sliced

3 cups chicken broth

Salt

6 cups buttermilk

White pepper

Chives or lemon slices, for garnish

Caviar for garnish, optional

10 to 12 green peppers, hollowed out, or any combination of red, green, yellow, and purple peppers

Dried Split Pea Dip (page 13)

34

Papaya and Asparagus with Shrimp Dip (page 11)

Truffled Brillat Savarin Loaf (page 15)

Gazpacho de Los Angeles (page 28)

Potato, Leek, and Fennel Soup (page 31)

Baked Onion Soup (page 30)

Opposite: *Spinach Soup (page 31)*

Curried Squash Soup (page 41)

CURRIED SQUASH SOUP

Some soups need hours of simmering to fully develop their flavor. Not this one. From start to finish, it only takes about 45 minutes before it's ready to serve. And it freezes beautifully. Serve this with hot corn bread and a simple salad for lunch or supper on a crisp autumn day.

Melt the butter with the oil in a large saucepan, and add the onion. Sauté until the onion is tender but not brown. Stir in the curry powder, nutmeg, cumin, and sugar. Add the squash, tomatoes, and chicken broth. Bring to a boil. Reduce heat to medium, partially cover, and simmer 30 minutes. Season to taste with salt and pepper.

Blend in a food processor or blender until smooth. Return to the saucepan and heat through.

MAKES 10 TO 12 SERVINGS

Note: Garnish with thin slices of crookneck squash and wedges of tomato, if desired.

2 tablespoons unsalted butter

1 teaspoon oil

1 large onion, minced

4 teaspoons curry powder or 1 teaspoon hot curry powder

2 teaspoons ground nutmeg

2 teaspoons cumin seeds

¾ cup packed brown sugar

8 large yellow crookneck squash, coarsely chopped

4 large tomatoes, peeled, seeded, and coarsely chopped

1½ quarts chicken broth

Salt, freshly ground black pepper

TOMATO-GINGER SOUP

This soup is the perfect answer for a backyard tomato patch that has gone wild producing tomatoes. The flavors of fresh ginger root and fresh tomatoes are most compatible. Domenico's on Fisherman's Wharf in San Francisco provided the recipe.

Purée the ginger and onion in a food processor. Set aside. Purée the tomatoes. Set aside.

Melt the fat over medium heat in a saucepan. Add the ginger and onion. Sauté until soft, but not brown, about 3 to 4 minutes. Add the puréed tomatoes (with their juice), consommé, sugar, and salt and pepper to taste. Bring to a boil. Stir in 1 cup whipping cream. Reduce heat and simmer 30 minutes.

Lightly beat the egg yolks in a small bowl. Gradually stir in about 1 cup hot soup to warm the egg yolks, then add the mixture to the soup in the saucepan. Cook, stirring over medium heat without boiling, until soup thickens slightly, about 2 minutes. Add more cream for thinner soup, if necessary.

MAKES 4 CUPS

3 ounces ginger root

1 medium white onion

4 tomatoes, peeled and seeded

4 ounces duck fat or ½ cup unsalted butter

½ cup chicken consommé

2 tablespoons sugar

Salt, white pepper

1 cup whipping cream, approximately

2 egg yolks

CANADIAN CHEESE SOUP

If you like vegetables and cheese, this is a soup worth making. The Fiddler's Three restaurant in Tustin shared the recipe with us years ago and it has since been reprinted at readers' requests many times.

Add the carrots, celery, and onion to the chicken soup base with the water. Cover and simmer 10 to 12 minutes, or until vegetables are tender.

Blend the flour and 1½ cups of the milk and add to vegetable mixture, stirring well. Add remaining milk and cook until thickened, about 15 minutes. Add cheese and stir just until melted. Season to taste with salt and pepper.

MAKES 4 TO 6 SERVINGS

1 cup shredded carrots

1 cup thinly sliced celery

⅔ cup thinly sliced onion

2½ tablespoons chicken soup base

2½ cups water

⅓ cup flour

3 cups milk

1 pound sharp natural Cheddar cheese, shredded

Salt, pepper

BACON, LETTUCE, AND TOMATO SOUP

When Bud's on Columbus Avenue in New York opened several years ago, it had marked Southern California ties. A spin-off of the very successful Jams, started by former Angelenos Jonathan Waxman and Melvin Masters, the restaurant offered foods with visible California overtones. We found this fresh tomato soup, served with crisp, thinly sliced and toasted walnut-onion bread, most refreshing.

Cook the bacon until crisp. Drain well, reserving fat, and crumble. Sauté the onion in a large, heavy saucepan with ¼ cup reserved bacon fat just until wilted. Add the garlic and cook briefly. (Do not let onions and garlic brown.) Add the tomatoes, tomato purée, and stock. Bring mixture to a boil, reduce heat, and simmer until the tomatoes begin to fall apart, about 15 minutes.

Press the mixture through a colander or food mill, discarding any remaining pulp. Season to taste with salt, pepper, and hot pepper sauce. Return to the pan, reheating if necessary.

Meanwhile, brush ¼-inch-thick slices of walnut-onion bread with reserved bacon fat and toast under broiler just until crisp and golden.

To serve, ladle the soup into shallow bowls and sprinkle lightly with crumbled bacon and shredded lettuce. Serve toasted walnut-onion bread on the side.

MAKES 8 SERVINGS

16 slices bacon

1 large white onion, diced

2 cloves garlic, minced

10 large very ripe plum tomatoes, peeled and seeded

2 cups canned tomato purée

1 quart unsalted chicken broth

Salt, pepper, hot pepper sauce

Walnut-Onion Bread (recipe follows)

1 cup finely shredded romaine lettuce

Stir the yeast into ¼ cup of the warm milk and let stand about 10 minutes. Add the butter to the remaining ¾ cup milk and stir to melt. Mix together the flour, sugar, and salt. Add the milk and butter to the flour mixture and let cool slightly. Add the yeast mixture and mix well.

Turn out onto a floured board and knead until elastic and soft. Sprinkle with additional flour while kneading, if needed, to keep dough from sticking. Place kneaded dough in a greased bowl, cover tightly with plastic wrap, and let rise in a warm draft-free place for 2 hours, or until doubled.

Punch down, return to floured board and knead in the onions and walnuts until evenly distributed. Cut in two, and shape into long, thin loaves (baguettes) about 1½ inches thick. Let stand 45 minutes uncovered in a warm draft-free spot.

Place the loaves on parchment paper on baking sheets and bake at 400 degrees about 25 to 30 minutes, or until loaves are golden brown and sound hollow when tapped. Serve warm, cold, or toasted.

MAKES 2 LOAVES

WALNUT-ONION BREAD

1 package dry yeast

1 cup warm milk

¼ cup butter

2¾ cups bread flour, approximately

1½ teaspoons sugar

1½ teaspoons salt

½ cup finely chopped red onions

¾ cup chopped walnuts

CLAM CHOWDER

The clam chowder served at the Legal Seafood restaurant in Boston has developed quite a following among Angelenos who visit that city. They very politely sent us the recipe, urging that home cooks who try it not cut down on either the amount of clams or cream. It just won't taste the same, they said. We concur.

Clean the clams and place in a large pot with the garlic and water. Steam clams just until opened, about 6 to 10 minutes, depending on size. Drain and shell the clams, reserving the broth. Mince the clam flesh and set aside. Strain the clam broth through coffee filters or cheesecloth and set aside. Liquid should measure about 4½ cups.

Render the salt pork in a large saucepan. Remove cracklings and set aside. Slowly cook the onions in remaining fat in the pan, stirring frequently, about 6 minutes or until tender but not browned.

Add the butter and melt through. Stir in the flour and cook, stirring, about 3 minutes. Add the reserved clam broth and fish stock. Whisk to remove any flour lumps. Bring liquid to a boil, add the potatoes, reduce heat, and simmer until potatoes are tender, about 15 minutes.

Stir in the reserved clams, salt pork cracklings, and half and half. Heat chowder through. Serve in large bowls with oyster crackers, if desired.

MAKES 8 SERVINGS

4 quarts littleneck clams

1 clove garlic, chopped

1 cup water

2 ounces salt pork, finely chopped

2 cups chopped onions

¼ cup butter

6 tablespoons flour

3 cups fish stock

1½ pounds potatoes, peeled and diced into ½-inch cubes

2 cups half and half

Oyster crackers, optional

CRAB BISQUE

We liked this Crab Bisque from Neiman-Marcus's restaurant so much we named it one of the year's twelve best recipes in 1987. It's an elegant soup from an elegant store.

Split crab legs down the middle and remove the meat. Reserve large pieces of crab shell. Set meat aside for garnish.

Sauté the carrot, onion, garlic, celery, leek, and tomatoes in oil until vegetables are tender. Stir in 3 tablespoons brandy and salt and pepper to taste. Cook over high heat until deglazed. Add the stock and crab shells and bring to a rolling boil. Reduce to a simmer and continue to cook 1 hour. Strain and discard crab shells and vegetables. Thicken soup with the roux and simmer over low heat for 20 minutes. Then add the tomato paste, half and half, cayenne, salt and pepper to taste, and additional brandy, if desired. Simmer 5 minutes and strain. Garnish with crab meat and parsley.

MAKES 4 SERVINGS

Melt the butter in a small saucepan. Stir in the flour and cook until pale golden in color.

¾ pound cooked snow crab legs in the shell
1 carrot, diced
1 onion, diced
4 cloves garlic, minced
1 stalk celery, diced
1 medium leek, diced
2 ripe tomatoes, diced
2 tablespoons oil
Brandy or dry sherry
Salt, pepper
2 cups fish stock or canned clam juice
Roux (recipe follows)
1 teaspoon tomato paste
1 cup half and half
Pinch cayenne pepper
Chopped parsley, for garnish

ROUX
6 tablespoons butter
1 tablespoon flour

ITALIAN SAUSAGE SOUP

*We heard about this soup from the One West California restaurant in Pasadena from a
reader. It's a sturdy, meal-in-one soup filled with spicy Italian sausages and noodles.
What's more, it doesn't take long to prepare.*

Combine the beef stock and brown cooking sauce in a large pot. Bring to a boil.

Meanwhile, heat the oil in a large skillet and add the sausage. Fry until browned on all sides, turning often. Remove from heat, and cut the sausages into ¼-inch-thick slices. Drain all but 2 tablespoons fat from skillet.

Add the sausage slices, onions, green pepper, and garlic. Sauté until onions are tender, but not browned. Combine the sausage mixture with the stock.

Add the wine to the skillet in which the sausage was cooked. Scrape any brown bits with a wooden spatula to loosen from the bottom of the skillet. Bring to a boil; boil until the wine is almost absorbed and pan is glazed. Add to the stock mixture. Skim fat from the stock mixture.

Add the tomatoes, zucchini, basil, oregano, and parsley. Bring to a boil again. Add the noodles. Simmer until noodles are tender, about 12 minutes, stirring soup occasionally. When serving, top soup with shredded cheese.

6 cups beef stock

2 teaspoons brown cooking sauce

1 tablespoon olive oil

1¼ pounds spicy Italian sausage
   links

2 onions, chopped

1 green pepper, chopped

2 cloves garlic, minced

1 cup Burgundy

¾ pound tomatoes, diced

1½ pounds zucchini, sliced

1½ teaspoons dried basil

1½ teaspoons dried Greek oregano

1 tablespoon minced parsley

4 ounces bowtie noodles

6 ounces shredded Jack cheese

MAKES 6 SERVINGS

Note: Add more beef stock if thinner soup is desired.

STEAK SOUP

The Clinker-Dagger restaurant in Cerritos is no longer there, but before it disappeared from view, we were fortunate enough to snare their recipe for steak soup. The recipe dates back to 1982, but we still get requests to print it again and again.

Melt the butter in a large saucepan. Add the onions, carrots, and celery. Sauté until the onions are tender, about 15 minutes. Add the flour and stir until well blended and smooth. Cook until mixture boils around edges, but do not overcook or roux will break down. Set aside.

Crumble the ground beef over a jelly-roll pan and pat into a layer 1 inch thick. Bake at 350 degrees for 15 to 20 minutes, or until meat is browned. The color of the beef will determine the color of the soup.

Drain. Break up the meat into ½-inch chunks. Add half of the water to the saucepan containing the vegetables and bring to a simmer. Add the tomatoes, beef chunks, and stock base. Season to taste with pepper. Cook, stirring, 10 minutes. Add remaining water and frozen vegetables. Cook 5 minutes longer or until vegetables are tender. Do not boil.

MAKES 4 QUARTS

1 cup butter or margarine

1½ cups chopped onions

1½ cups sliced carrots

1 cup diced celery

1 cup flour

1 pound ground beef

2½ quarts water

1 (8-ounce) can chopped tomatoes

⅓ cup beef stock base

Pepper

1 (10-ounce) package frozen mixed vegetables

SAN FRANCISCO BLACK BEAN SOUP

When Jeremiah Tower was consulting chef at San Francisco's Balboa Cafe in 1983 he added this soup to the menu. A dab of sour cream swirled around the top of the soup and a dollop of fresh salsa give the soup both a touch of class and extra flavor.

Combine the beans, onion, carrots, celery, garlic, ham bone, bay leaf, and parsley in a large heavy pan. Season with thyme. Cover the beans with stock and bring to a boil; reduce the heat and simmer until the beans are tender, about 1½ to 2 hours. Add more stock if necessary to keep the beans covered.

When the beans are tender, remove the bay leaf and discard. Purée the bean mixture using a meat grinder or food mill. (Texture should be slightly gritty rather than completely smooth.) Return the beans to a pan, add chile powder, and season to taste with cumin and salt. Add enough additional stock to get the consistency of pancake batter. Heat through gently, stirring often to prevent sticking.

Serve at once, or cool and refrigerate until ready to serve. Place the soup in the top of a double boiler to reheat. To serve, ladle soup into shallow bowls and swirl several tablespoons of sour cream thinned slightly with half and half over the surface. Spoon a dollop of Jeremiah's salsa in the center of each bowl.

MAKES 6 TO 8 SERVINGS

Note: If ancho chile powder is not available, substitute any pure ground chile powder, adjusting amount to taste.

2 pounds black beans, washed and drained

1 large onion, peeled

2 medium carrots, peeled

2 stalks celery

1 head garlic, separated into cloves and peeled

1 meaty ham bone or about ½ pound ham scraps

1 bay leaf

3 or 4 sprigs parsley, stemmed

Dried thyme

2 to 3 cups mixed-meat, chicken or duck stock

3 to 4 tablespoons ancho chile powder

2 tablespoons ground cumin, approximately

Salt

Sour cream

Half and half or milk

Jeremiah's Salsa *(recipe follows)*

JEREMIAH'S SALSA

2 tomatoes, peeled, seeded and chopped

2 medium red onions, cored and chopped

4 large cloves garlic, minced

2 serrano chiles

1 bunch cilantro

Juice of 3 or 4 limes

Combine the tomatoes, onions, and garlic. Split the chiles; remove the seeds and the thin edge of ribs. Julienne the chiles and mince. Chop the cilantro leaves finely. Add chiles and cilantro to tomato mixture. Stir in lime juice to taste. Chill well.

MAKES ABOUT 2 CUPS

LENTIL SOUP

The thing about this old-fashioned soup is that it's just plain good. The recipe came to us in 1986 from Orza's Romanian Restaurant in Hollywood, a popular hangout for many of the crew members who work at nearby Paramount Pictures.

Heat the oil. Add the onion and garlic and sauté until the onion is tender. Blend in the flour, stirring until browned. Add the water and bring to a boil. Add the lentils, celery, carrots, and parsley. Cover partially and simmer 45 minutes, or until lentils are tender and soup is slightly thickened. Add salt and pepper to taste. Serve with lemon wedges.

MAKES 8 SERVINGS

2 tablespoons oil
1 medium onion, chopped
1 clove garlic, minced
2 tablespoons flour
2 quarts water
1 pound lentils
1 stalk celery, sliced
3 medium carrots, sliced
½ bunch parsley, chopped
Salt, pepper
Lemon wedges

CREAM OF POBLANO SOUP

When a reader told us about a poblano chile soup she had eaten at the Tower Club in Dallas, we quickly requested the recipe. They complied, sending us the formula for a definitely spicy soup. If you prefer a milder bite, you would be wise to reduce the quantity of the chiles.

Remove the seeds from the chiles, wearing plastic gloves to avoid skin irritation. Cut the chiles into chunks. Sauté the chiles, onion, and carrot in butter about 5 minutes. Stir in the flour. Cook, stirring, 5 minutes over low heat. Whisk in the chicken stock and simmer 30 minutes.

Remove mixture from heat and purée in blender. Return to soup pot and continue to simmer. Add the cilantro and cream. Season to taste with salt.

Ladle the soup into 4 heatproof cups and top each with 2 tortilla chips and 1 slice cheese. Place under broiler until cheese melts.

MAKES 4 SERVINGS

3 medium poblano chiles
½ cup diced onion
¼ cup diced carrot
2 tablespoons clarified butter
2 tablespoons flour
4 cups chicken stock
1 tablespoon chopped cilantro
¾ cup whipping cream
Salt
8 tortilla chips
4 slices Jack cheese

TORTILLA SOUP

Tortilla soup is a fairly standard Mexican classic. At El Torito restaurant, however, they make it with fish stock, a change from the usual beef stock.

▫

Cut the tortillas into strips. Deep-fry in hot oil until crisp. Drain on paper towels and set aside.

Combine the fish stock, tomato sauce, celery, onion, green pepper, tomato, white pepper, garlic powder, oregano, and bay leaf in a saucepan. Season to taste with salt. Bring to a boil and simmer 20 to 30 minutes.

To serve, place tortilla strips in each bowl. Cover with shredded cheeses and add broth.

MAKES 4 SERVINGS

4 corn tortillas
Oil
2½ cups fish stock
¼ cup tomato sauce
2 tablespoons diced celery
2 tablespoons diced onion
2 tablespoons diced green pepper
2 tablespoons diced tomato
1 teaspoon white pepper
1 teaspoon garlic powder
1 teaspoon ground oregano
1 bay leaf
Salt
¾ cup shredded Jack cheese
¾ cup shredded Cheddar cheese

HAWAII BANANA BISQUE

At the Mauna Kea Beach Hotel in Kamuela, Hawaii, this simple cold soup is topped with cinnamon-sugar croutons. The chef suggested that the recipe would work well with almost any fruit in place of the bananas.

▫

Combine the bananas with half and half in a blender container until smooth. Serve the bisque chilled with generous amounts of cinnamon croutons on top.

MAKES 4 SERVINGS

4 ripe bananas, or more if desired
2 cups half and half
Cinnamon Croutons *(recipe follows)*

CINNAMON CROUTONS

2 slices white bread, crusts removed
¼ cup melted butter
1 tablespoon sugar
1½ teaspoons ground cinnamon

Cut the bread into small cubes and toss with the butter. Bake at 400 degrees, tossing frequently, until they are golden. Combine the sugar and cinnamon and sprinkle over the croutons. Mix well. Return the croutons to the oven and bake until the sugar has caramelized slightly.

COCONUT-LIME SOUP

When the Somerset Catering Service catered the opening of a special show at the Natural Science Museum in Los Angeles in 1987, they served this soup to delighted attendees. The lemon grass and fish sauce called for are usually available at Oriental markets or specialty food stores.

Crush and chop the lemon grass stalks and tie in cheesecloth. Put the coconut milk and lemon grass in a saucepan. Bring to a slow boil and simmer 10 minutes.

Add the chicken, ginger, and cinnamon and simmer, uncovered, until chicken is tender.

Add the green onions, cilantro, and chiles; bring soup just back to the boil. Remove from heat. Discard cheesecloth bag. Stir in the fish sauce and lime juice.

Taste to adjust seasoning by adding more lime juice, cilantro, or seasonings, if needed.

MAKES 6 TO 8 SERVINGS

Note: Lemon grass and fish sauce are available at most Oriental food stores. If lemon grass is not available, substitute thinly peeled rind of 1 lemon. Discard before serving.

4 stalks lemon grass

4 (14-ounce) cans coconut milk

12-ounces boneless chicken, diced

1¼ teaspoons ground ginger

Generous pinch ground cinnamon

½ bunch green onions, minced

1 tablespoon chopped cilantro

2 to 4 serrano chiles, seeded and minced

4 tablespoons fish sauce (nam-pla)

1 tablespoon lime juice

WASHINGTON STREET CHILLED PEACHES AND CREAM SOUP

When peach season rolls around, this delicious fruit soup is a wonderful way to serve them. The recipe came from the Washington Street Restaurant in Yountville, and it could be served as an appetizer or even for dessert on a hot summer day.

Remove the peach pits and skins. Slice the peaches and add to a blender or food processor. Add whipping cream, cinnamon, nutmeg, and mace. Blend or process until smooth. Add honey to taste and blend. Strain and chill. Garnish each serving with slices of strawberry and sprig of mint.

MAKES 6 TO 8 SERVINGS

3 pounds peaches

⅔ cup whipping cream

Pinch ground cinnamon

Pinch ground nutmeg

Pinch ground mace

Honey

Strawberries or peach slices, for garnish

Mint sprigs, for garnish

VEGETABLE SALAD PLATTER

Next time you need a spectacular presentation of vegetables, try this. Just be sure not to overcook any of the vegetables as they should still be a bit crunchy. This salad tastes best when served at room temperature, so if you do it ahead and refrigerate the ingredients, remove them from the fridge about 20 to 30 minutes before serving.

Steam the vegetables, but do not overcook. They should be just tender-crisp. Slice the chayote in thin wedges. Julienne the carrots and cut the cauliflower and broccoli into florets. Slice the zucchini in thin rings. Marinate them in half the rosemary dressing overnight.

At serving time, arrange the marinated vegetables on a large platter and garnish with cherry tomatoes and black olives. Serve with additional rosemary dressing on the side.

MAKES 8 TO 10 SERVINGS

Combine the oil, vinegar, sugar, paprika, rosemary, and garlic in a small bowl or jar. Season to taste with salt. Shake vigorously and then refrigerate overnight to blend flavors.

MAKES ABOUT 2 CUPS DRESSING

1 chayote, peeled

2 carrots, peeled

1 cauliflower

½ bunch broccoli

2 to 3 zucchini

1 pint cherry tomatoes, halved, for garnish

Black olives, for garnish

Rosemary Dressing (recipe follows)

ROSEMARY DRESSING

1½ cups oil

½ cup red wine vinegar

2 teaspoons sugar

½ teaspoon paprika

1 tablespoon crushed dried rosemary leaves

2 cloves garlic, split

Salt

RED CABBAGE SLAW

For years readers have requested the red cabbage slaw recipe from a popular family restaurant, which preferred not to share it. Finally, we decided to see how close we could come to matching the recipe in our test kitchen. This is our version of their slaw.

Shred the cabbage irregularly so that shreds are both fine and coarse. Combine the oil, vinegar, sugar, salt, seasoned salt, pepper, and onion powder. Blend well. Place cabbage in a large bowl and toss with the dressing. Refrigerate several hours or overnight to allow the flavors to mellow and the slaw to achieve a deep red color.

MAKES 6 TO 8 SERVINGS

½ *head red cabbage*

½ *cup oil*

½ *cup plus 2 tablespoons red wine vinegar*

3 *tablespoons sugar*

4 *teaspoons salt*

1 *teaspoon seasoned salt*

¼ *teaspoon black pepper*

¼ *teaspoon onion powder*

K.C. DELI BROCCOLI SALAD

Whenever food writers get together they do two things. They eat too much . . . and they search out new recipes wherever they can find them. A visit to the Gourmet Grocery in Kansas City, Missouri, turned up this sprightly and decidedly offbeat salad. The deli manager said it came from the Deep South, but few of the many Southerners present had ever come across anything like it. Wherever it came from, it's a great addition to a buffet.

Blanch the broccoli in salted boiling water about 30 seconds. Drain; immediately rinse with cold water. Drain again and chill in refrigerator, covered.

Combine the salad dressing, milk, lemon juice, and honey, blending well. Chill. At serving time, add the raisins and peanuts to the dressing; toss with the broccoli or serve on the side. Serve on lettuce leaves.

MAKES 6 TO 8 SERVINGS

4 *cups broccoli florets*

½ *cup mayonnaise-type salad dressing*

¼ *cup milk*

1 *tablespoon lemon juice*

2 *teaspoons honey*

½ *cup raisins*

½ *cup salted peanuts*

Lettuce leaves, for garnish

SPINACH SALAD WITH HOT BACON-CALVADOS DRESSING

When in Richmond, Virginia, to judge a cookoff, we added this excellent spinach salad to our collection. It comes from the elegant, recently restored turn-of-the-century Jefferson Sheraton Hotel in Richmond.

Wash and pat dry the spinach and remove the stems. Combine the spinach, red pepper strips, mushrooms, eggs, and pine nuts in a large bowl. Add hot dressing to taste and toss to coat mixture lightly.

MAKES 6 SERVINGS

2½ *pounds fresh spinach leaves*

2 *small sweet red peppers, cored, seeded, and cut into thin strips*

1 *cup thinly sliced fresh mushrooms*

3 *hard-cooked eggs, chopped*

1 *cup pine nuts, lightly toasted*

Hot Bacon-Calvados Dressing *(recipe follows)*

HOT BACON-CALVADOS DRESSING

¼ *pound bacon, diced*

1 *cup diced onion*

1 *Granny Smith apple, peeled and thinly sliced*

¼ *cup Calvados (apple brandy) or other fruit brandy*

¼ *cup red wine vinegar*

¼ *cup apple cider*

1 *teaspoon cornstarch*

¼ *cup apple juice*

1 *clove garlic, crushed*

Salt, pepper

Cook the bacon in a skillet until crisp. Drain off fat. Add the onion and apple slices to the bacon and cook, stirring occasionally, until the apples are tender. Stir in the brandy. Add the vinegar and cider, and heat until mixture begins to simmer. Dissolve the cornstarch in the apple juice and add to the skillet, stirring until mixture thickens slightly. Add the garlic and season to taste with salt and pepper. Remove from heat but keep warm.

MAKES ABOUT 1¾ CUPS

EGGPLANT SALAD

When reader Nitza Ben-Zvi sent us the recipe for this eggplant salad, we were eager to try it. This colorful salad will keep in the refrigerator for several days.

Peel the eggplant and dice in ½-inch cubes. Heat the oil and deep-fry the eggplant until golden brown. Drain well on paper towels. Combine the eggplant with the tomatoes, olives, parsley, garlic, and cayenne. Season to taste with salt and pepper. Mix the tomato paste and catsup and add to the eggplant mixture. Toss gently. Cover and chill overnight to blend flavors. Serve on a lettuce leaf-lined platter garnished with tomato wedges and whole olives.

MAKES ABOUT 8 SERVINGS

1 large eggplant

Oil for deep frying

2 medium tomatoes, diced

15 to 20 pitted green olives, quartered

¼ cup finely chopped parsley

2 cloves garlic, crushed

Pinch cayenne pepper

Salt, pepper

2 tablespoons tomato paste

2 tablespoons catsup

Lettuce leaves, tomato wedges, and whole, pitted green olives, for garnish

ZUCCHINI SALAD WITH HOT BACON DRESSING

Deciding how to use up all your home-grown zucchini can be a challenge. Mrs. T. Johnson solved part of the problem by creating this salad recipe. It won a weekly "My Best Recipe" award and delighted other gardeners inundated with too much squash.

Fry the bacon in a small skillet until crisp. Drain on paper towels; reserve 1 tablespoon drippings in skillet. Blend the sugar and cornstarch into the drippings. Stir in the vinegar, water, soy sauce, and pepper. Cook until mixture boils and thickens, stirring constantly. Set aside and let cool slightly.

Crumble cooked bacon. Combine in a bowl with the zucchini and onion. Season to taste with salt, and toss with the dressing. Arrange on a serving platter or individual salad plates with tomato slices and mushrooms.

MAKES ABOUT 4 SERVINGS

2 slices bacon

2 tablespoons sugar

2 teaspoons cornstarch

⅓ cup cider vinegar

⅓ cup water

1 teaspoon soy sauce

¼ teaspoon black pepper

4 cups (about 4 medium) shredded zucchini

¼ cup finely chopped onion

Salt

Tomato slices or cherry tomatoes, for garnish

Mushroom slices, for garnish

HAM-VEGETABLE SALAD IN CHEESY PUDDING PUFF

The next time you're looking for a showy presentation to serve for lunch or your bridge group, give this one a try. The pudding puff is a variation on Yorkshire pudding, and makes an unusual and delicious edible bowl for a crisp salad. The puff can be made several hours ahead, but don't refrigerate it.

Combine the oil, vinegar, rosemary, sugar, and garlic in a large bowl. Add the ham, onion, and celery, and toss to coat well. Let stand about 30 minutes.

Prepare the pudding puff, adding cheese to the batter. Bake as directed, remove from oven, and cool in the pie plate on a rack. At serving time, transfer to a serving platter.

Toss the endive, spinach, and cherry tomatoes with the ham mixture. Season to taste with salt and pepper. Just before serving, drain well. Fill the pudding puff with the salad.

MAKES 6 TO 8 SERVINGS

⅓ cup oil

⅓ cup Champagne vinegar

1 teaspoon crushed dried rosemary

2 tablespoons sugar

1 teaspoon minced garlic

6 ounces cooked ham, julienned

1 red onion, sliced in thin rings

½ cup chopped celery

Basic Pudding Puff (recipe follows)

¼ cup shredded Cheddar cheese

1 small head Belgian endive, optional

1 bunch spinach leaves, washed, dried, and stems removed

12 cherry tomatoes, halved

Salt, pepper

Beat the eggs until frothy. Gradually beat in the flour until smooth. Add milk, butter, and salt, and blend well.

Pour the batter into a well-greased 9-inch glass pie plate or divide among 3 well-greased 4-inch glass baking dishes. Bake at 425 degrees for 15 minutes, then reduce heat to 350 degrees and bake until puff is golden brown, 10 to 15 minutes longer for large puff or 5 to 10 minutes longer for smaller ones.

Remove from the oven to a rack and cool in the pie plate away from any drafts. As it cools, the puff will fall in the center, forming a bowl-like shape. When used to serve salads, it should be completely cooled. When used for hot fillings, serve the pudding warm.

Variations: Flavor the basic pudding batter with any of the following:
   ¼ cup chopped fresh basil
   1 teaspoon fresh dill
   1 teaspoon Chinese 5-spice powder
   1 tablespoon chopped onion and 1 tablespoon canned diced green chile

BASIC PUDDING PUFF

2 eggs

½ cup flour

½ cup milk

2 tablespoons butter or margarine, melted

Pinch salt

COBB SALAD

If ever there was the quintessential Los Angeles salad, it has to be the old Brown Derby's famous Cobb Salad. In the original salad, all the ingredients are chopped very finely or practically minced.

Chop lettuce, watercress, endive, and romaine in very fine pieces using knife or food processor. Mix together in 1 large wide bowl or individual wide shallow bowls. Add chives. Arrange tomatoes, chicken, bacon, avocado, and eggs in narrow strips or wedges across top of greens. Sprinkle with cheese. Chill. At serving time toss with ½ cup special French dressing. Pass remaining dressing.

MAKES 6 SERVINGS

½ head iceberg lettuce

½ bunch watercress

1 small bunch curly endive

½ head romaine

2 tablespoons minced chives

2 medium tomatoes, peeled, seeded, and diced

1 whole chicken breast, cooked, boned, skinned, and diced

6 strips bacon, cooked and diced

1 avocado, peeled and diced

3 hard-cooked eggs, diced

½ cup Roquefort cheese, crumbled

Special French Dressing *(recipe follows)*

Combine the water, vinegar, sugar, lemon juice, salt, pepper, Worcestershire, mustard, garlic, and oils. Chill. Shake well before using.

MAKES ABOUT 1½ CUPS

SPECIAL FRENCH DRESSING

¼ cup water

¼ cup red wine vinegar

¼ teaspoon sugar

1½ teaspoons lemon juice

½ teaspoon salt

½ teaspoon black pepper

½ teaspoon Worcestershire sauce

¾ teaspoon dry mustard

½ clove garlic, minced

¼ cup olive oil

¾ cup vegetable oil

SALADE POULET

The Redwood House restaurant in downtown Los Angeles is a hangout for newspaper people, city employees, and lawyers. During the busy lunch hour at the restaurant in the late eighties, Arnold Jewell, the chef, would serve this interesting chicken salad with a hot basil dressing. Be aware, however, that although the Redwood serves this as a salad for one, it really is ample for two or more people.

Place the salad greens on a large plate. Slice the chicken breast in ½-inch strips and place in the center of the greens. Arrange the olives, mushrooms, avocado, and tomato around the chicken breast. Serve with hot basil dressing.

MAKES 1 SERVING

Note: Poached salmon may be substituted for chicken.

Melt the butter in a saucepan. Add the vinegar, oil, garlic, basil, parsley, salt and pepper, and capers. Heat, but do not boil.

MAKES ABOUT 1 CUP

3 *cups mixed salad greens*

1 *broiled boneless chicken half breast*

½ *cup sliced black olives*

½ *cup sliced mushrooms*

1 *medium avocado, diced*

1 *medium tomato, diced*

Hot Basil Dressing *(recipe follows)*

HOT BASIL DRESSING

¼ *cup unsalted butter*

¼ *cup red wine vinegar*

½ *cup oil*

¼ *clove garlic, minced*

1 *teaspoon chopped fresh basil*

½ *teaspoon minced fresh parsley*

Pinch salt, black pepper

¼ *teaspoon capers*

CHICKEN-CELERIAC-POTATO SALAD

Celeriac is a vegetable that just isn't used enough. In a story on root vegetables, we combined it with potatoes and chicken to make a salad that was a real winner. We selected the recipe as one of the twelve best of 1988.

Combine the potatoes, celeriac, and chicken in a bowl with the pickles, pickle juice, mayonnaise, Chinese pea pods, and green onions. Season to taste with salt and pepper. Cover and refrigerate overnight. Mound on lettuce and garnish with red radishes.

MAKES 8 TO 10 SERVINGS

1 pound yellow or red potatoes, cooked, peeled, and diced

2 cups peeled and finely diced celeriac, parboiled until crisp-tender

4 cups cubed cooked chicken

½ cup chopped sweet pickles

¼ cup sweet pickle juice

1 cup mayonnaise

1 cup julienned Chinese pea pods

½ cup chopped green onions

Salt, pepper

Bibb lettuce, for garnish

Red radishes, for garnish

ORIENTAL CHICKEN SALAD

Few department stores have real tearooms anymore, but a number of them do serve lunch. One of the most popular luncheon salads at Bullock's is this chicken salad with Oriental flavorings and ingredients. We first printed the recipe in 1984, and it has been repeated numerous times since.

Deep-fry the rice sticks, a small handful at a time, in hot oil for 1 to 2 minutes, or until puffed. Drain.

For each serving, place 1 cup chopped lettuce in a bowl and toss with 1 tablespoon dressing. Add 2 cups cooked rice sticks and toss again. Top with ½ cup of the chicken and 1 tablespoon almonds. Or, combine everything in a large bowl and toss with dressing to taste.

MAKES 6 SERVINGS

Combine the mayonnaise, Worcestershire, soy sauce, oil, mustard, and lemon juice, and blend well.

MAKES ABOUT 2 CUPS

1 (6¾-ounce) package rice sticks

Oil for deep frying

1 head lettuce, chopped

Dressing *(recipe follows)*

3 cups diced or shredded cooked chicken

6 tablespoons toasted sliced almonds

DRESSING

2 cups mayonnaise

1¼ teaspoons Worcestershire sauce

2 teaspoons soy sauce

2 teaspoons oil

1 tablespoon plus 1 teaspoon prepared mustard

⅛ teaspoon lemon juice

ORIENTAL CHICKEN AND SHRIMP SALAD

Crisp bean sprouts are mixed with ginger, green onions, chicken, and shrimp in this easy salad. A Lompoc reader sent us the recipe some years ago.

Cover the bean sprouts with cold water. Drain well and chill. Combine the chicken, shrimp, green onions, ginger, and garlic in a large bowl. Cover and chill until serving time. When ready to serve, add the sprouts and toss with the chicken and shrimp mixture. Place in a lettuce-lined serving bowl and serve with the dressing on the side.

MAKES 4 TO 6 SERVINGS

¼ pound bean sprouts

1 whole chicken breast, cooked, skinned, boned, and cubed

1 cup shrimp, cooked, peeled, and chilled

4 small green onions, including green part, julienned

3 or 4 thin slices ginger root, minced

1 clove garlic, minced, optional

Lettuce, optional

Oriental Dressing (recipe follows)

ORIENTAL DRESSING

3 tablespoons soy sauce

1 tablespoon rice vinegar

1 teaspoon sesame oil

½ teaspoon hot pepper sauce

Combine the soy sauce, vinegar, oil, and hot pepper sauce in a small bowl or jar. Blend well.

MAKES ABOUT ¼ CUP DRESSING

ORANGE SOUFFLÉ RING WITH CHICKEN SALAD

This orange-flavored gelatin ring served with chicken salad at Neiman-Marcus in Newport Beach would make an attractive addition to any party.

Combine the gelatin, sugar, and salt in a saucepan. Set aside. Beat the egg yolks with 1 cup of the orange juice. Stir into the gelatin mixture. Cook over medium-low heat, stirring constantly, just until mixture comes to a boil. Remove from heat. Stir in the remaining 1½ cups orange juice, grated orange and lemon peels and lemon juice. Chill, stirring occasionally, until mixture mounds when dropped from a spoon.

Stir in the orange sections. Fold in the whipped cream. Pour into a 2-quart ring mold, and chill until set. At serving time, unmold onto a platter. Fill the center of the ring with chicken salad. Garnish with sliced almonds.

MAKES 8 TO 10 SERVINGS

2 envelopes unflavored gelatin

2 cups sugar

Pinch salt

4 egg yolks

2½ cups freshly squeezed orange juice (about 10 medium oranges)

1 teaspoon grated orange peel

1 teaspoon grated lemon peel

3 tablespoons lemon juice

1 cup orange sections, cut in halves

2 cups whipping cream, whipped

Chicken Salad (recipe follows)

Toasted sliced almonds, for garnish

CHICKEN SALAD

1 cup mayonnaise

Dash wine vinegar

½ cup whipping cream

3 cups diced cooked chicken

½ cup diced celery

Salt, pepper

Mix together the mayonnaise, vinegar, and whipping cream. Add the chicken and celery, and season to taste with salt and pepper.

MAKES 4 CUPS

SMOKED TURKEY SALAD

To serve at a party, heap the salad in the middle of a platter and surround it with Belgian endive.

Place the egg, mustard, lemon juice, salt, garlic, and rosemary in a food processor or blender container. Process or blend. With the motor running, gradually add the olive oil, blending until mixture is thickened and smooth. Stir in the green onions. Toss together the turkey, apple, and water chestnuts; fold in the rosemary mayonnaise. Chill until ready to serve.

MAKES 4 TO 6 SERVINGS

1 egg

1 teaspoon Dijon mustard

1 tablespoon lemon juice

½ teaspoon salt

1 clove garlic, crushed

1 teaspoon fresh rosemary leaves

1 cup olive oil

½ cup sliced green onion tops

4 cups diced smoked turkey

1 Red Delicious apple, diced

1 (8-ounce) can sliced water chestnuts

DUCK-NOODLE SALAD

This recipe came about when we were looking for some sort of new and different pasta salad to serve at the height of the pasta craze in the mid-eighties. It turned out to be a perfect choice for an alfresco buffet.

Cook the noodles in boiling salted water just until tender; they should still be firm. Drain and rinse in cold water. Cut into 3-inch lengths with scissors. Drain well.

Combine the duck meat, green onions, noodles, vinegar, and ginger root. Blend in the mayonnaise and sesame oil. Add water chestnuts, season to taste with salt and pepper, and toss until well blended. Chill until ready to serve.

To serve, mound the duck salad on a large platter and surround with the red lettuce and enoki mushrooms. Sprinkle the salad with crisp duck skin.

MAKES 6 TO 8 SERVINGS

Note: To prepare crisp duck skin, remove the skin from the roasted ducks, cut into small pieces, and pan-fry in a small amount of duck fat until well browned and crisp.

2 ounces cellophane noodles

Shredded meat from 2 (5-pound) roasted ducklings

¼ cup finely sliced green onions

1 tablespoon rice vinegar

1 tablespoon minced ginger root

¾ cup mayonnaise

1 teaspoon sesame oil

1 (8-ounce) can water chestnuts, drained and sliced

Salt, pepper

Red leaf lettuce, romaine, or bibb lettuce

Enoki mushrooms

Crisp-cooked duck skin

STEAK SALAD

Barbecue season often means that bits and pieces of steak are left over. Next time that happens to you, start freezing the leftovers and before you know it you'll have enough good beef to duplicate this recipe from Carlos 'n' Charlie's in West Hollywood.

Tear the romaine into larger than bite-size pieces and place in a large bowl. Cut the American cheese into bite-size pieces. With a vegetable peeler or very sharp knife, shave or cut the carrot in bite-size pieces. Peel the avocados and halve, and cut into thin 1-inch-long slices. Slice the steak into thin 1-inch-long strips. Combine the lettuce, cheese, carrot, avocados, onion, steak, and Parmesan. Toss with the vinaigrette.

MAKES 6 SERVINGS

12 to 15 romaine lettuce leaves

6 slices American cheese

¾ large carrot

3 avocados

1 medium onion, sliced and cut into thirds

1 pound filet mignon steak, cooked to desired degree of doneness

2 tablespoons grated Parmesan cheese

Vinaigrette (recipe follows)

VINAIGRETTE

Combine the vinegar, oil, Worcestershire, and Maggi seasoning in a small bowl or jar. Season to taste with salt and pepper and blend thoroughly.

MAKES ABOUT ¾ CUP DRESSING

3 tablespoons red wine vinegar

6 tablespoons olive oil

3 tablespoons Worcestershire sauce

3 dashes Maggi seasoning

Salt, pepper

WARM SWEETBREAD AND OYSTER MUSHROOM SALAD

Elegant is the only way to describe this imaginative salad from Le Chardonnay restaurant in Los Angeles. It's rich enough to be a luncheon main dish salad, and romantic enough to serve at an intimate candlelight supper.

Soak sweetbreads for 3 hours in cold water to remove any residue. Peel, then carefully remove all membranes. Place the lobes in a saucepan with cold water to cover and 1 tablespoon salt. Bring to a boil and drain immediately. Rinse under cold water and drain well.

String the pea pods and cook 2 minutes in boiling salted water. Rinse under cold water and drain again. Peel the oyster mushrooms, if desired. Sauté the mushrooms with 3 tablespoons peanut oil in hot pan for 3 minutes. Drain well.

Sprinkle the pea pods with the vinaigrette. Melt 2 tablespoons butter in a nonstick pan, and sauté the pea pods for 3 minutes. Season to taste with salt and pepper.

Slice each sweetbread lobe into 4 slices. Heat another skillet until very hot. Add 3 tablespoons peanut oil, then add the sweetbreads. Brown 1 to 3 minutes, being careful not to overcook sweetbreads. Place some oyster mushrooms in the center of each plate and surround them with 8 pea pods. Place 2 slices of sweetbreads on top of the mushrooms.

MAKES 8 SERVINGS

2 lobes sweetbreads

Salt

32 Chinese pea pods

1½ pounds oyster mushrooms, sliced

Peanut oil

Vinaigrette (recipe follows)

Butter

Pepper

Combine the vinegar, peanut oil, sugar, and salt and pepper to taste. Blend well.

VINAIGRETTE

1 tablespoon wine vinegar

¼ cup peanut oil

Pinch sugar

Salt, pepper

COLLEGE PASTA SALAD

Don't ever let anyone tell you that students don't eat well at Southern California schools. We are often asked to get recipes from the city schools or colleges in the area, and they are always happy to comply. This pasta and vegetable salad was served with a white wine dressing at the Center for Continuing Education at Cal Poly in Pomona in 1986.

Cook the rotelli in boiling salted water until tender, then drain. Rinse in cold water and drain well. Cool.

Mix the cooled pasta with the pepperoni, celery, red and green peppers, olives, red onion, and mushrooms. Add the chablis dressing. Toss and let stand 10 minutes to blend flavors. Drain in a colander to remove excess dressing. Chill.

MAKES 6 TO 8 SERVINGS

½ *pound rotelli (small wheels)*
½ *pound sliced pepperoni*
4 *stalks celery, sliced*
½ *cup chopped sweet red pepper*
½ *cup chopped green pepper*
½ *cup sliced black olives*
½ *cup chopped red onion*
½ *cup sliced mushrooms*
Chablis Dressing *(recipe follows)*

Combine the oil, vinegars, chablis, sugar, basil, pepper, salt, lemon pepper, garlic, rosemary, paprika, celery seeds, oregano, marjoram, and dry mustard. Blend well.

MAKES ABOUT 2½ CUPS

CHABLIS DRESSING

1⅓ *cups oil*
¼ *cup red wine vinegar*
¼ *cup cider vinegar*
⅔ *cup chablis*
⅓ *cup sugar*
2 *teaspoons chopped fresh basil*
¼ *teaspoon coarsely ground black pepper*
½ *teaspoon salt*
½ *teaspoon lemon pepper*
1 *teaspoon granulated garlic*
1 *teaspoon ground dried rosemary*
¾ *teaspoon paprika*
1 *teaspoon celery seeds*
1 *teaspoon ground dried oregano*
1 *teaspoon ground dried marjoram*
1 *teaspoon dry mustard*

WALNUT PASTA SALAD

When combined with sour cream and milk, blue cheese blends easily with walnuts. This is an especially creamy dressing for colorful pasta.

Cook noodles in boiling salted water until al dente. Drain well. Toss with walnut oil. Cover and chill.

Combine the cheese, milk, and sour cream in a blender until creamy. Stir in garlic salt, if using, and lemon juice. Toss with the noodles. Add walnuts and toss again. Season to taste with salt and pepper. Mound on a large serving platter or individual salad plates, and garnish with Belgian endive and watercress, if desired.

MAKES 4 TO 6 SERVINGS

½ pound red, green, and white spiral noodles

1 tablespoon walnut oil

3 ounces Saga blue cheese

¼ cup milk

½ cup sour cream

½ teaspoon garlic salt, optional

1 teaspoon lemon juice

¼ to ½ cup chopped walnuts

Salt, freshly ground pepper

Belgian endive, watercress, optional

CHICKEN-STUFFED SHELL SALAD

This type of salad is perfect for a picnic or a supper at the Hollywood Bowl. The shells can be finger food as easily as fork food, and they make great snacks when you're looking for something to assuage your hunger.

Cook the shells in boiling salted water until barely tender, following the package directions. Rinse and drain well. Combine the chicken, celery, green pepper, almonds, and pickle relish. Toss with the curry dressing. Stuff the shells with the chicken salad. Cover and chill until serving time.

MAKES ABOUT 6 SERVINGS

Mix together the sour cream, mayonnaise, curry powder, lemon juice, and coriander. Season to taste with salt and pepper.

1 (12-ounce) package jumbo shells

3½ cups diced cooked chicken

1 cup finely diced celery

¼ cup finely diced green pepper

¼ cup finely chopped toasted almonds

1 tablespoon pickle relish

Curry Dressing *(recipe follows)*

CURRY DRESSING

¼ cup sour cream

½ cup mayonnaise

1 teaspoon curry powder

1 tablespoon lemon juice

¼ teaspoon ground coriander

Salt, pepper

SUMI SALAD

Recipes for this salad have been changing hands around Los Angeles for years. It's unusual in that the noodles are not cooked, which gives the salad a nice extra crunch.

Break the noodles into 1-inch pieces and set aside. Heat the oil in skillet and sauté the almonds and sesame seeds until lightly browned. Combine with the onions, cabbage, and noodles. Toss with the dressing to taste. Cover and chill several hours for the flavors to blend.

MAKES 8 TO 10 SERVINGS

Note: Reserve any flavor packet in noodle package for another use.

2 (3-ounce) packages ramen (Japanese-style instant vermicelli) noodles
2 tablespoons oil
1/4 cup sliced almonds
1/4 cup sesame seeds
8 green onions, finely sliced
1 head cabbage, finely chopped
Sumi Dressing (recipe follows)

SUMI DRESSING
1/4 cup sugar
1 teaspoon black pepper
1 teaspoon salt
1 cup oil
6 tablespoons rice vinegar

Combine the sugar, pepper, salt, oil, and vinegar in a small bowl or jar and blend well.

MAKES ABOUT 1½ CUPS DRESSING

CURRIED RICE AND GREEN SPLIT PEA SALAD

Rice salads have become increasingly popular in recent years. This very pretty dish would make a good choice for a potluck or buffet supper.

Bring 1 quart water to a boil. Stir in 1 teaspoon salt, the split peas, and rice. Reduce heat and simmer mixture, covered, until rice is completely cooked and peas are crisp-tender, about 25 to 30 minutes. Drain mixture and set aside to cool.

Combine the oil, vinegar, curry powder, garlic, and pepper, beating lightly to blend. Season to taste with salt. Combine the dressing with the rice mixture, red pepper, and onions. Chill until serving time.

MAKES ABOUT 6 SERVINGS

Salt
1 cup green split peas, rinsed and drained
1 cup rice
1/3 cup oil
1/4 cup rice vinegar
1 tablespoon curry powder
1 clove garlic, minced
1/4 teaspoon black pepper
1 cup diced sweet red pepper
1 cup thinly sliced green onion

Chicken-Stuffed Shell Salad (page 71)

Spinach Salad with Hot Bacon-Calvados Dressing (page 57)

Ham-Vegetable Salad in Cheesy Pudding Puff (page 60)

Marinated Squid Salad (page 85)

LOBSTER SALAD

This particular salad is a fine example of how easily and perfectly culinary cultures can blend. Shigefumi Tachibe, chef at Chaya Brasserie in West Los Angeles, combined Mediterranean, French, and California tastes in a remarkable lobster salad with a red pepper dressing.

Cut the lobster horizontally in 4 or 5 pieces. Drop into boiling salted water and boil 1 to 2 minutes, or until shells turn bright red in color. Remove with a slotted spoon and plunge at once into ice water.

Drain the lobster, place in a bowl, and toss with the red pepper dressing. Chill thoroughly.

When ready to serve, toss the frise, endive, watercress, and radicchio in a bowl. Divide lettuce mixture among 4 large salad plates. Using the pieces of lobster, reconstruct 1 whole lobster in the center of each plate. Add any remaining dressing over the lobsters.

MAKES 4 SERVINGS

4 (1-pound) whole lobsters
Red Pepper Dressing (recipe follows)
1 head frise (curly endive)
2 Belgian endive, sliced
¼ bunch watercress, leaves only
½ radicchio, sliced

Combine the red pepper, red onion, capers, cornichon, egg, both vinegars, olive oil, mixed herbs, and salt and pepper to taste. Mix well.

MAKES ENOUGH DRESSING FOR 4 SALADS

RED PEPPER DRESSING

½ sweet red pepper, finely diced
½ red onion, finely diced
2 teaspoons capers
1½ teaspoons minced cornichon or sweet pickle
White of ½ hard-cooked egg, minced
1 teaspoon tarragon vinegar
⅓ cup rice wine vinegar
½ cup olive oil
1 tablespoon mixed fresh herbs (tarragon, basil, chervil, Italian parsley, chives)
Salt, pepper

ASPARAGUS CRAB SALAD

The Grand Hyatt Hotel served this appetizing asparagus and crab combination as a first course appetizer in 1983, but we like it as a light main dish salad today. The dressing, a creamy pale pink, is made with crème fraîche, Cognac, and fresh tomato.

Peel the asparagus spears starting about 1 inch below the bud. Blanch in rapidly boiling salted water for 30 seconds. Immerse in ice water until cold. Drain and pat dry on paper towels. Cut away the bottoms from the asparagus 3 inches below the bud. Dice the usable portions of the bottom stems and mix with the crab meat.

Place shredded lettuce in the bottoms of 4 saucer-type champagne glasses or any large bowl-stemmed glasses. Set 8 cut asparagus spears, bud side up, around the rim of each glass. Fill the center with crab meat mixture. Spoon over the dressing and chill the prepared salads thoroughly. At serving time, sprinkle walnuts over the crab meat.

MAKES 4 SERVINGS

32 green or white asparagus spears

6 ounces cooked and chilled crab meat

¼ head iceberg lettuce, finely shredded

Crème Fraîche Dressing *(recipe follows)*

2 tablespoons chopped walnuts

Combine the crème fraîche, horseradish, tomato, and Cognac in a bowl. Season to taste with salt and pepper. Whip mixture lightly until it starts to thicken. Chill until ready to use.

MAKES ABOUT 1½ CUPS DRESSING

CRÈME FRAÎCHE DRESSING

1 cup crème fraîche or sour cream

1 tablespoon prepared horseradish, preferably freshly grated

1 large tomato, peeled, seeded and puréed

2 tablespoons Cognac

Salt, pepper

FLORES'S SPICY CRAB SALAD

Surimi, the imitation crab usually made from haddock and shaped and colored to look like crab legs, has found a following among those for whom real crab can be too expensive. That was the case with Esther Flores and her husband, Richard, who started experimenting with the ersatz shellfish when they found it in their market. This chile-laden result of one of their experiments is delicious as a salad or as a spread for crackers.

In a large bowl, shred the surimi into bite-size pieces. Add the tomatoes, chiles, cilantro, green onions, and cucumber. Toss to blend. Sprinkle with lemon juice and chill 10 minutes. Fold in the mayonnaise. Chill again until serving time.

MAKES 4 TO 6 SERVINGS

½ pound surimi (imitation crab)

2 small firm tomatoes, diced

3 to 5 jalapeño chiles, seeded and finely chopped

1 bunch cilantro, chopped

1 bunch green onions, very thinly sliced

1 cucumber, seeded and cubed

Juice of 1 large lemon

2 tablespoons mayonnaise

SPICY SHRIMP SALAD

With more and more Thais and other Far Easterners moving to Southern California, we have access to many ingredients most of us had never heard of until recent years. This recipe from Aranya Harper, formerly a Thai citizen, is a traditional shrimp dish called pla kung. *It's pleasantly spicy, but not as hot as many Thai foods are.*

Wrap the shrimp in foil. Place on a hot grill and cook 2 minutes. Unwrap, and combine the shrimp with the fish sauce, lime juice, and cayenne.

Add the lemon grass, onion, garlic, green onion, cilantro, and mint leaves. Toss lightly. Chill until serving time. Serve on a bed of lettuce.

MAKES 2 SERVINGS

1 cup shelled and cleaned small to medium shrimp

1 tablespoon fish sauce (nampla) or ½ teaspoon salt

2 tablespoons lime juice

¼ teaspoon cayenne pepper

1 tablespoon finely chopped lemon grass

1 tablespoon thin strips onion

½ teaspoon finely chopped garlic

1 tablespoon chopped green onion

1 tablespoon chopped cilantro

20 mint leaves

Lettuce leaves, for garnish

ABALONE SALAD

After Wolfgang Puck opened Spago, but before he opened Chinois on Main, we challenged the famous chef to show us how he would cook in his own home. This was back in 1983, long before Puck had multiple restaurants and his frozen pizzas and desserts. If the fresh abalone isn't available, sea scallops make an excellent substitute.

Wash and dry the lettuce, arugula, and radicchio. Discard the mushroom stems and slice the tops in thin vertical slices. Rinse and dry the pea pods.

Remove the abalone from their shells, using the handle of a heavy spoon to break the muscle attachments. Reserve the shells. Clean the abalone well, discarding undesirable parts. Clean the shells thoroughly, dry, and set aside. Using a meat slicer, slice the abalone muscle crosswise into tissue-thin pieces. If the abalone can't be sliced tissue-thin, slice as thin as possible and pound each slice on a flat surface with a mallet or the flat end of a cleaver until tender and almost transparent but not shredded.

Combine the juice of 1 lime, 1 tablespoon grated ginger, and a grind or two of fresh pepper in a bowl. Add the abalone slices and toss to coat well. Marinate 15 to 20 minutes, stirring occasionally.

Combine the remaining lime juice, remaining ginger, vinegar, soy sauce, and 3 tablespoons olive oil in a small bowl. Tear the lettuce, arugula, and radicchio into coarse pieces and place in a large bowl; toss with the lime juice-olive oil dressing. Arrange the greens in the abalone shells or on serving plates. Set aside.

Heat the remaining 1 tablespoon olive oil in a skillet or sauté pan, add the mushrooms and pea pods, and season to taste with salt and pepper. Stir-fry briefly, just until the pods turn bright green. Remove from heat and toss to mix well. Pile hot mixture on top of greens in abalone shells. Top with the abalone slices. Garnish with lime or lemon wedges if desired.

MAKES 4 SERVINGS

Note: If abalone is not available, substitute sea scallops cut into paper-thin slices.

2 small or 1 large head red leaf lettuce

1 bunch arugula or watercress

1 small head radicchio or red cabbage

12 fresh shiitake mushrooms

24 Chinese pea pods

4 fresh medium abalone

Juice of 2 or 3 limes

1 inch fresh ginger root, peeled and grated

Freshly ground pepper

1 tablespoon rice vinegar

2 tablespoons dark soy sauce

1/4 cup extra-virgin olive oil

Salt

Lime or lemon wedges, for garnish, optional

MARINATED SQUID SALAD

Although it isn't as popular as some of the other sea critters that grace our tables these days, by the mid-eighties squid was becoming a regular on restaurant menus. Now it has begun to appear on home menus too, often in salads.

Cut the squid into ½-inch rings. Combine the olive oil, lemon juice, and garlic in a glass bowl. Add the onion, cilantro, and sugar. Mix well with the squid. Season to taste with salt and white pepper.

Let stand in the refrigerator at least 4 hours or overnight. Serve the squid with the endive and tomato wedges. Garnish with green onion tops, if desired.

MAKES 4 TO 6 SERVINGS

2 pounds squid, cleaned

½ cup olive oil

2 tablespoons lemon juice

4 cloves garlic, crushed

½ cup chopped onion

1 tablespoon cilantro

¼ teaspoon sugar

Salt, white pepper

1 Belgian endive, for garnish

2 to 3 Italian plum tomatoes, cut into wedges, for garnish

Green onion tops, for garnish, optional

SPRING FRUIT SALAD

A salad of mixed spring fruits is always welcome. Here we combined fruit with a salad dressing seasoned with Chinese 5-spice powder and poppy seeds. The result—a delicious, sweet-tart mix of flavors and textures.

Prepare the strawberries, kiwi, oranges, red and green grapes, and pineapple one day before serving; store separately in sealed plastic bags. At serving time, pour any juices that have accumulated in bags into a small bowl for use in the fruit dressing. Toss the fruit together and spoon into a large lettuce leaf-lined serving bowl or arrange attractively on a serving platter. Serve with the dressing.

MAKES 8 SERVINGS

Combine the lemon juice and reserved fruit juices in a small bowl. Whisk in the 5-spice powder and sugar. Continue whisking while slowly adding oil. Whisk in poppy seeds and chill well.

MAKES ABOUT 1 CUP

1 cup strawberries, hulled

2 very ripe kiwi, peeled and sliced

2 oranges, peeled and sliced

1 cup red seedless grapes

1 cup green seedless grapes

1 small pineapple, peeled, cored, and cut into chunks, optional

Fruit Dressing *(recipe follows)*

Lettuce leaves

FRUIT DRESSING

2 tablespoons lemon juice

2 tablespoons reserved fruit juices

¼ teaspoon Chinese 5-spice powder

2 teaspoons sugar

⅔ cup oil

1 teaspoon poppy seeds

POT-OF-GOLD SALAD

When persimmon season hits, everyone gorges on the beautiful orange fruit while it's around.
This salad combines a collection of gold fruit—papayas, oranges, persimmons, and
pineapples—in a rich smorgasbord of fresh sweetness.

Combine the lime juice, wine, and honey. Bruise the chopped mint leaves with the back of a spoon and stir into juice mixture. Set aside.

Peel and core the pineapple, and cut into 1-inch chunks. Trim the persimmon ends and cut into 1-inch chunks. Peel and section the oranges. Cut away the pulp from the papayas, leaving ¼-inch shell. Reserve shells; cut the pulp into chunks. Combine the fruit and dressing and toss lightly. Cover and chill well. To serve, spoon the fruit onto salad greens or into reserved papaya shells and garnish with whole mint leaves.

MAKES 6 SERVINGS

2 tablespoons lime juice
2 tablespoons dry white wine
1 tablespoon honey
2 tablespoons chopped fresh mint leaves
1 small pineapple
3 or 4 ripe Fuyu persimmons or combination of Fuyu and Hachiya persimmons
2 small navel oranges
3 papayas, halved and seeded
Salad greens, optional
Whole mint leaves, for garnish

MANDARIN ORANGE SALAD

This interesting fruit and nut salad from a reader makes a superb addition
to any holiday buffet.

Wash the lettuce and drain. Tear into bite-size pieces and store in a plastic bag. Refrigerate.

Caramelize the sugar in small heavy skillet until golden. Stir in the pecans and continue cooking until lightly browned. Pour onto a wax paper-lined tray or oiled pan. Cool; break apart into small bite-size pieces. Just before serving, toss the lettuce with the pecans, green onions, oranges, and parsley. Toss again with the dressing.

MAKES 4 SERVINGS

Combine the oil, sugar, vinegar, salt, and pepper. Stir well. Chill until ready to serve.

MAKES ABOUT ½ CUP

1 head lettuce
2 tablespoons sugar
¼ cup chopped pecans
4 green onions, chopped
1 (11-ounce) can mandarin oranges, drained
1 tablespoon chopped parsley
Dressing *(recipe follows)*

DRESSING
¼ cup oil
2 tablespoons sugar
2 tablespoons vinegar
¼ teaspoon salt
Pinch black pepper

SANDWICHES

◻

The art of making sandwiches is a simple one, yet it takes a bit of creativity to do it well. Unusual breads, new seasonings added to ordinary fillings, and ingredients not normally found in sandwiches all whet our appetite.

Again, chefs have led the way for creative sandwiches: Italian focaccia bread topped with the standard ingredients found in a club sandwich mix with crisp alfalfa sprouts, or chicken breasts grilled over grapevine branches and served with tarragon mayonnaise dress up homemade hamburger buns.

Sandwiches in all forms shaped up at home, too. Parties for football or softball games feature long, well-stacked heros. We dress up hamburgers and grill them on our patios; lobster salad in individual brioches are fine for bridge clubs. Picnics now include pita breads filled with unusual salads and meats. And Italian tortas and calzones are great for luncheon parties. Moreover, Mexican tacos and burritos, which never go out of favor in Southern California, are still devoured by the dozens.

GRILLED CHICKEN SANDWICH WITH TARRAGON MAYONNAISE

The Temecula district just north of San Diego has become quite a wine producing area. In 1988, Culbertson Winery, which specializes in sparkling wines, opened the charming Cafe Champagne where chef Dennis Barry had this tarragon-flavored chicken sandwich on the menu.

Combine the vinegar and tarragon in a small saucepan. Bring to a boil and cook until reduced by half. Melt the butter in a small skillet and sauté the shallots until tender.

Combine the mayonnaise, tarragon reduction, sautéed shallots, and white pepper, mixing well. Set aside.

Remove the skin and fat from the chicken breasts. Pound slightly with the fine side of a meat tenderizing mallet. Cut in half down natural seam, eliminating any cartilage at center. Season with salt and pepper.

Grill chicken over moderate heat until cooked through, turning once, and basting with about 1 tablespoon reserved mayonnaise mixture per side. Slice and warm the sandwich buns.

Spread the inside of the buns generously with the flavored mayonnaise. Place 2 chicken slices on the bun; top with the lettuce, tomato, and other bun half.

MAKES 6 SERVINGS

½ cup red wine vinegar

2 tablespoons crushed dried tarragon

2 tablespoons butter

4 teaspoons minced shallots

2 cups mayonnaise

½ teaspoon white pepper

6 (8-ounce) whole boneless chicken breasts

Salt, pepper

6 sandwich buns, preferably homemade

6 lettuce leaves

6 slices tomato, optional

FOCACCIA TURKEY CLUB SANDWICH

Don Ferch, chef at Highlands Inn in Carmel, chose Italian focaccia as the bread for this easy club sandwich. Homemade mayonnaise and alfalfa sprouts are added to the usual bacon, tomato, and turkey filling.

Cook the bacon until crisp. Drain on paper towels. Combine the mayonnaise with cilantro and parsley.

Cut each focaccia in half, forming 4 (8 × 4-inch) rectangles. Spread half of the mayonnaise on top of 2 of the focaccia halves. Layer half of the turkey, tomato, bacon, avocado, and alfalfa sprouts onto each.

Spread the bottoms of the focaccia with more mayonnaise and cover the sandwich fillings. Cut into halves or thirds.

MAKES 4 TO 6 SERVINGS

Note: Commercially produced mayonnaise may be substituted. Focaccia (round or square), purchased at Italian delicatessens, may be used.

8 slices bacon

½ cup Homemade Mayonnaise (recipe follows)

2 teaspoons minced cilantro

2 teaspoons minced parsley

2 (8-inch) squares Focaccia (recipe follows)

10 slices turkey breast

1 tomato, sliced

½ avocado, peeled and sliced

2 cups alfalfa sprouts

Combine the eggs, lemon juice, mustard, and hot pepper sauce in a food processor bowl fitted with the steel or plastic blade. Process 5 to 10 seconds. With the processor running, add the oil in a very slow stream through the feed tube. Process until smooth, scraping sides occasionally for even blending. Season to taste with salt.

MAKES ABOUT 2 CUPS

HOMEMADE MAYONNAISE

2 eggs

2 tablespoons lemon juice

2 teaspoons Dijon mustard

3 drops hot pepper sauce

1½ cups oil

Salt, optional

Allow the bread dough to thaw 2 to 4 hours or overnight in the refrigerator. Cut dough in half, and roll out each half to make an 8-inch square. If the dough pulls back, let rest 15 to 30 seconds and roll out again.

Place the dough in 2 greased 8-inch-square baking pans. Thoroughly pierce dough at 1-inch intervals with a fork.

Sauté the onion and garlic in olive oil until lightly browned. Add the seasoning and brush the mixture over the dough squares. Let rise 10 minutes.

Bake at 400 degrees for 15 to 18 minutes, or until golden brown. Let cool.

MAKES 2 (8-INCH SQUARE) FOCACCIA

FOCACCIA

1 (1-pound) loaf frozen bread dough

2 tablespoons finely chopped onion

1 clove garlic, minced

2 tablespoons olive oil

1 teaspoon Italian Seasoning

LOBSTER SALAD SANDWICH

This is not a sandwich to toss into a brown-bag lunch. It is, however, a little something that will impress luncheon guests. If you don't want to make your own brioches, buy them at a bakery.

Cook and chill the lobster. Extract the meat from the shell and shred or chop. (Lobster meat should measure about 1 cup.) Quarter the cucumber lengthwise, remove seeds, and slice thinly. Combine the lobster, cucumber, water chestnuts, green onions, egg, lemon juice, chili sauce, and mayonnaise. Season to taste with salt and pepper. Chill mixture well, covered.

At serving time, add shredded lettuce and toss to mix well. Split the brioches, cutting about ¼-inch below the top of bottom portions. Set aside the top knots. Scoop out the centers of the brioches and fill with the lobster salad. If desired, place tops gently over the lobster and fasten in place with long, fancy skewers.

MAKES 4 LOBSTER SANDWICHES

Note: One cup crab meat may be substituted for lobster.

1½ to 2 pounds fresh or frozen lobster in the shell

½ cucumber, peeled

¼ cup sliced water chestnuts

3 green onions, cut in 1-inch julienned pieces

1 hard-cooked egg, chopped

1 tablespoon lemon juice

1 tablespoon chili sauce

¼ cup mayonnaise

Salt, white pepper

1 cup shredded lettuce

Individual Brioches (recipe follows)

INDIVIDUAL BRIOCHES

½ package dry yeast

3 tablespoons warm water

¼ cup butter or margarine

2 tablespoons sugar

¼ teaspoon salt

Flour

¼ cup milk

3 eggs

Combine the yeast with 2 tablespoons warm water. Cream the butter, sugar, and salt in the bowl of an electric mixer until light. Beat in ½ cup flour and milk. Add 2 eggs, one at a time, beating until mixture is smooth. Stir in the softened yeast until blended. By hand stir in 1½ cups flour until well blended. Turn out onto a floured board and knead until smooth. Place in a greased bowl, turning to grease all sides. Cover and let rise in a warm spot until doubled, about 2 hours. Sprinkle the top lightly with flour, cover again, and refrigerate overnight.

Next day, punch down the refrigerated dough and divide into 5 equal portions. With floured hands, shape 4 portions into balls and place in the bottoms of 4 well-greased 4½-inch-diameter fluted brioche pans. Divide the remaining portion into 4 equal parts and shape each into a ball. Pinch 1 side of each, elongating it about ½ inch.

With a well-floured finger, poke a deep indentation in the tops of the large brioche balls in the pans and insert the tapered ends of the small balls into the indentations. Place the pans on a baking sheet, cover lightly with greased plastic wrap, and let rise in a warm place until doubled, about 40 to 45 minutes.

Stir together the remaining egg and 1 tablespoon water, and brush the top knots and tops of brioches with the mixture. Bake at

425 degrees for 5 minutes, reduce heat to 375 degrees and bake about 12 minutes longer. Lightly cover with foil if the brioches seem to be browning too much. Remove from the oven and cool to room temperature in the pans. Turn out and cool completely.

MAKES 4 BRIOCHES

YOSEMITE MONTE CRISTO SANDWICH

The Ahwahnee Hotel in Yosemite National Park dips its three-decker Monte Cristo sandwiches in a light crêpe batter before frying them. They're a little awkward to eat, but worth every bite.

Top 2 slices of bread with ham and turkey and a third one with cheese. Stack to make three-decker sandwiches. Cut in halves diagonally. Dip each sandwich half in the crêpe batter. Add enough oil in a skillet to measure ¼-inch-deep and heat to 375 degrees. Fry the sandwich halves until golden on both sides, using tongs to turn. Drain on paper towels and dust with powdered sugar.

MAKES 2 SERVINGS

6 slices white bread
2 slices ham
2 slices turkey
2 slices cheese
Crêpe Batter *(recipe follows)*
Oil for frying
Powdered sugar

CRÊPE BATTER
½ cup sifted flour
2 eggs
¼ cup milk
Salt

Combine the flour, eggs, milk, and salt to taste. Beat lightly. Mixture should be the consistency of buttermilk.

MAKES ENOUGH BATTER FOR 2 SANDWICHES

PITA POCKET SANDWICHES

Simple tuna salad sandwiches become more interesting when served in pita bread pockets.

Drain the tuna, and combine with the carrot, yogurt, water chestnuts, green onion, soy sauce, and ginger. Slice the pita breads in halves. Fill the pockets with the tuna salad and alfalfa sprouts.

MAKES 2 SERVINGS

1 (6½-ounce) can chunk light tuna in water

1 cup shredded carrot

⅓ cup plain yogurt

¼ cup sliced water chestnuts

1 tablespoon sliced green onion

1 tablespoon soy sauce

¼ teaspoon minced ginger root

2 (6-inch) pita breads

1 (3-ounce) package alfalfa sprouts

JOE'S SPECIAL BEEF BURGERS

Joe's Special, a classic old San Francisco dish, is a mixture of ground beef, spinach, and eggs all sort of stir-fried together. It's not a thing of beauty, but it tastes wonderful.

Slowly cook the onion in oil until transparent but not browned. Add the spinach and heat until any liquid cooks off. Cool. In a large bowl beat the egg with the oregano and season with salt and pepper. Add the beef and spinach mixture, mixing well with a fork. Shape into 6 patties about 4½ inches in diameter. Grill over hot coals to desired degree of doneness, turning once. Serve on toasted rolls.

MAKES 6 SERVINGS

¾ cup chopped onion

1 tablespoon oil

½ cup thawed and drained frozen chopped spinach

1 egg

1½ teaspoons chopped fresh oregano

Salt, pepper

1½ pounds ground beef chuck

6 buttered and toasted rolls

DRIVE-IN NUT BURGER I AND II

Often even we are astonished at how far back our recipe files go. When a reader wrote "Culinary SOS" and asked for a hamburger recipe topped with nuts from a drive-in that existed in the 1930s, the card file produced two recipes that purported to be from the popular teen hangout. So we printed them both. That caused quite a flood of mail, most of it contending that the second recipe, with the addition of some Russian dressing on the bottom half of the bun, was the real thing.

On the bottom of the bun place the hamburger, and sprinkle with chopped nuts. Serve with lettuce, tomato, and onion slices and Thousand Island dressing. If a cheeseburger is desired, partially grill the patty, top with nuts, 1 slice cheese, and finish grilling until cheese melts. Cover with top half of bun.

MAKES 1 SERVING

1 grilled hamburger patty
1 hamburger bun
Chopped salted peanuts
Lettuce leaves
Tomato slices
Onion slices
Thousand Island dressing
1 slice American cheese, optional

DRIVE-IN NUT BURGER II

Place the hamburger patty on the hamburger bun, and spread with the nut butter. Finish grilling until peanut butter melts slightly. Top with lettuce leaves and tomato slices. Cover with top half of bun.

MAKES 1 SERVING

1 grilled hamburger patty
1 hamburger bun
Chunky-style peanut butter, macadamia nut butter, pecan nut butter, or any other nut butter
Lettuce leaves, optional
Tomato slices, optional

MY BEST BURRITO

Burritos are messy, awkward, and utterly soul-satisfying when the craving hits. This simple version of the popular Mexican sandwich came to us from one of our readers.

Combine the beef with enough water to cover, and the onion and garlic in a large skillet. Season with garlic salt, salt, and pepper. Cover and cook until the meat is very tender and the water has been absorbed.

Pull the meat apart with a fork. Add the tomatoes, chiles, and hot tomato sauce. Simmer, uncovered, until liquids evaporate and meat mixture is just moist.

Spoon into hot, steamed flour tortillas. Sprinkle with shredded cheese. Serve with sour cream, guacamole, tomatoes, and lettuce.

MAKES ABOUT 8 SERVINGS

2½ to 3 pounds London broil

1 large onion, chopped

4 cloves garlic, minced

Garlic salt

Salt, pepper

1 (28-ounce) can plum tomatoes, chopped

1 (7-ounce) can green chiles, diced

1 (7¾-ounce) can hot tomato sauce

Flour tortillas, steamed

Shredded Cheddar or Jack cheese

Sour cream, guacamole, chopped tomatoes, and shredded lettuce, for garnish

FETTE DI MELANZANE RIPIENE (EGGPLANT SANDWICHES)

Carlo Middione, the genius behind a charming small neighborhood deli and restaurant called Vivande in San Francisco, gave us this superb eggplant "sandwich" recipe back in 1983. We served it as a hot appetizer, but it easily could double as a light luncheon entrée.

Cut the eggplant into an even number of ½-inch-thick crosswise slices. Set aside. Combine the bread crumbs, Parmesan, and parsley in a pie plate. Place 1 slice provolone and 1 slice mortadella (or more, if desired) on half of the eggplant slices. Top with remaining eggplant slices, forming individual eggplant "sandwiches."

Dip the sandwiches into the beaten eggs and then into the bread crumbs, making sure both sides are well coated with crumbs. Place on baking sheets and drizzle about 1 teaspoon olive oil over each. Turn, and drizzle other sides each with about 1 teaspoon oil. Bake at 375 degrees for 40 minutes, or until golden brown and tender, turning once during cooking.

MAKES ABOUT 6 SERVINGS

1 large eggplant

1 cup fine dried bread crumbs

⅓ cup grated Parmesan cheese

⅓ cup chopped fresh parsley

Sliced provolone cheese

Sliced mortadella

2 eggs, beaten

Olive oil

Lobster Salad Sandwich (page 92)

Bike Wheel Sandwich (page 107)

Torta Rustica (page 111)

Opposite: *Cheese and Lentil Quiche* (page 132)

Left: *Pesto Chicken Pasta* (page 148)

Below: *Layered Beer Bean Pot* (page 139)

Spinach Linguine with Tomatoes, Pine Nuts, and Olives (page 149)

SUPER-HERO SURPRISE

When Monday night football is in season or the weekends are taken over with games, requests pour in for foods suitable to the occasion. This sturdy sandwich will feed a crowd of hungry sports lovers.

Thaw the bread dough until pliable. Pinch off about ⅓ cup dough and set aside. Roll out the larger portion of dough to form a circle about 12 inches in diameter. Place the circle in a well-greased shallow 2-quart round casserole and pull and pat out until the dough completely lines the inside of the casserole.

Combine the ham, mayonnaise, bread crumbs, olives, nuts, pimiento, and parsley. The filling should be at room temperature. Spoon into the casserole. Roll the reserved dough into a circle large enough to fit the top of the casserole and cover the filling. Pinch the edges of the dough to seal in the filling. Cover, and let sit in a warm spot for 30 to 40 minutes.

Bake at 350 degrees for 40 minutes, or until well browned. (To prevent the top from becoming too brown, cover with foil after the first 10 minutes of baking.) Let the bread cool in the casserole about 5 minutes, then turn out onto a plate or board. Cut into wedges to serve. Serve warm or cold.

MAKES 8 TO 10 SERVINGS

1 (1-pound) loaf frozen bread dough
1 cup chopped cooked ham
½ cup mayonnaise
½ cup fine dried bread crumbs
½ cup sliced stuffed olives
¼ cup finely chopped nuts
¼ cup chopped pimiento
¼ cup minced parsley

BAKED HERO SANDWICH LOAF

Another type of hero sandwich, this one meant to be served hot, is ideal for a party for teenagers. Slice the sandwiches by cutting through the middle of the thick slices of bread from the top to the bottom. If you cut it differently, don't worry. It will still taste scrumptious.

Trim the crust from the top and sides of the bread. Slice the loaf in 8 slices almost through to the bottom. Place on a lightly greased baking sheet. Combine the butter, mayonnaise, mustard, chives, and parsley. Reserve ¼ cup butter mixture, and spread the remaining butter between the bread slices.

Insert the sliced meats and cheese between bread slices, using two slices for each opening. Tuck down the meat slices until level with the top of the loaf. Tie the loaf together near the top and bottom with heavy string. Spread the remaining ¼ cup butter mixture over the top and sides; bake at 350 degrees for 30 minutes, or until cheese melts and the loaf is golden brown. Let the loaf stand about 5 minutes. Remove the string and cut into sandwiches by cutting through the middle of the thick bread slices.

MAKES 8 TO 10 SERVINGS

1 (1-pound) day-old loaf, unsliced
½ cup butter or margarine, softened
¼ cup mayonnaise
1 tablespoon Dijon mustard
2 tablespoons minced chives
2 tablespoons minced parsley
14 slices assorted cold cuts
14 slices Swiss cheese

BIKE WHEEL SANDWICH

When we decided to do a story on theme picnics for the paper's Home *magazine in 1985, one of the picnics was designed for bicyclists. A package of hot roll mix and a good chicken salad turned this showy sandwich into a real winner with our readers.*

Soften the yeast from the roll mix in ½ cup hot water. Add eggs and oil. Gradually blend in the flour mixture to make a soft dough. Knead until smooth. Place in a mixing bowl, lightly oil the top of the dough. Let rest 10 minutes. Shape the dough into a circle and let rise in a warm place until doubled, about 1 hour.

Cook the chicken in 1½ cups water with 2 teaspoons salt, bay leaf, and Italian seasoning for 30 minutes, or until tender. Let stand until cool enough to handle. Bone and skin the chicken, and cut the meat into chunks. Stir the cornstarch into the chicken broth and cook in a small saucepan, stirring constantly, until thickened. Cool. In a large bowl combine the mixture with the mayonnaise, mustard, lemon juice, green onion, pimiento, remaining ½ teaspoon salt, and the chicken.

When the dough has doubled, divide in half for making 2 sandwich wheels. Pinch off about ⅛ of each half for the tops. Pat out a large piece of each dough half to fit the bottom of a greased 8-inch cake pan, building up the rim about ½ inch higher at the sides. Spread half the chicken mixture over each, and sprinkle each with ⅓ cup cheese.

Divide each reserved piece of dough into 2 or 4 portions, depending upon number of servings, and roll each into an 8½-inch strand. Place strands spoke-fashion over each pan, tucking the ends in the sides of the pan. Brush melted butter over the dough and "spokes." Let rise in a warm place about 30 minutes. Bake on lowest rack of oven at 375 degrees for 25 to 30 minutes, or until browned. Serve warm or cold, cut into wedges.

MAKES 2 SANDWICH WHEELS, 4 TO 8 SERVINGS

1 (13¼-ounce) package hot roll mix

2 eggs, beaten

2 tablespoons oil

1 (2¾-pound) frying chicken, cut up

2½ teaspoons salt

1 bay leaf

½ teaspoon Italian herb seasoning

2 teaspoons cornstarch

½ cup chicken broth

¼ cup mayonnaise

1 teaspoon prepared mustard

1 teaspoon lemon juice

2 tablespoons chopped green onion

1 tablespoon chopped pimiento

⅔ cup grated Cheddar cheese

1 tablespoon melted butter or margarine

SCHOOL DAYS PIZZA

*When pizzas began to be trendy, even the Los Angeles City Schools started serving them.
We knew they were doing a good job with the pizzas when we began to get
requests for their recipe.*

Brown the beef with the onion in a large skillet. Add the tomatoes, tomato paste, water, oregano, basil, garlic, luncheon meat, and season to taste with salt. Sauté until the mixture comes to a boil. Simmer a few minutes. Spread the sauce on prepared French-style pizza crust in pans. Sprinkle each pizza evenly with cheese. Bake at 400 degrees for 30 to 35 minutes, or until cheese layer is bubbly and browned.

MAKES ABOUT 24 SERVINGS

1 pound ground beef

1 tablespoon instant minced onion

1 (8-ounce) can tomatoes, drained and chopped

1 (6-ounce) can tomato paste

¾ cup water

¾ teaspoon dried oregano

¾ teaspoon dried basil

¼ teaspoon minced garlic

¾ pound ground or chopped luncheon meat

Salt

French-Style Pizza Crust *(recipe follows)*

1½ cups grated Parmesan cheese

FRENCH-STYLE PIZZA CRUST

2 packages dry or cake yeast

1 tablespoon sugar

3½ cups lukewarm water

9 cups flour

1 tablespoon salt

Dissolve the yeast and sugar in lukewarm water. Add the flour and salt. Knead until smooth. Cover and let rise until doubled. Cut into 2 portions. Let rest 15 minutes. Pat or roll to even thickness large enough to fit into two 15½ × 10½-inch jelly-roll pans.

THREE CHEESE AND MUSHROOM CALZONE

When staff writer Joan Drake did a story on shortcut single-serving savory pies, one of the easiest and tastiest of all the recipes developed was this one.

Unroll the pizza crust. Cut the rectangle crosswise in half to form 2 smaller rectangles. With a pastry wheel, cut a thin strip of dough from the short end of each. Set aside the strips.

Mound ½ cup Jack, ¼ cup scamorza, 1 tablespoon ricotta, 1 tablespoon green onions, 1 teaspoon oregano, and 1 tablespoon mushrooms on half of each rectangle. Fold over the top half and seal the edges. Cut the edges with a pastry wheel, rounding the corners.

Place on an oiled baking sheet. Seal the edges with the tines of a fork. Garnish with the reserved dough strips. Brush with olive oil. Bake at 400 degrees for 25 minutes, or until golden brown.

MAKES 2 SERVINGS

Note: Scamorza is available at Italian delicatessens, cheese shops, and specialty grocery stores.

1 (10-ounce) package refrigerated pizza dough

1 cup shredded Jack cheese

½ cup shredded scamorza (smoked mozzarella)

2 tablespoons ricotta cheese

2 tablespoons sliced green onions

2 teaspoons chopped fresh oregano

2 tablespoons sliced, sautéed mushrooms

Olive oil

PIZZA RUSTICA

The packed shelves and crowded aisles of Sorrento Italian Market in Culver City assure customers of Albert Vera and his family that a little patience will eventually reveal whatever it is they are looking for. Vera's mother, Lydia, told us how to make this sturdy pizza rustica with three cheeses.

Sift together the flour, baking powder, and salt into a large bowl. Work in butter as for pastry. Stir in 3 eggs just until mixed. Do not overmix or dough will become tough. Set aside.

Prepare cheese filling. Divide the dough in half. Roll out 1 portion to fit a greased 12-inch pizza pan, bringing up edges to form rim. Pour mixed cheese filling into the pie shell.

Roll out remaining dough to fit over filling, reserving a small portion of dough to decorate the top of the pie. Seal edges. Roll out small piece of reserved dough and cut into floral or geometric shapes. Beat remaining egg in a small bowl. Brush beaten egg over pastry. Arrange pastry cutouts over pie dough. Brush cutouts with egg wash. Bake at 350 degrees for 45 to 50 minutes, or until golden brown.

MAKES 8 TO 10 SERVINGS

3 cups flour

1 tablespoon baking powder

Pinch salt

¾ cup butter, softened

4 eggs

Mixed Cheese Filling *(recipe follows)*

Combine the ricotta, tuma, mozzarella, and pecorino cheeses. In a large bowl, mix the eggs, salami, prosciutto, sausage, parsley, oregano, basil, garlic, and pepper. Blend in the cheese mixture.

Note: Tuma cheese is a semisoft cheese often available in Middle Eastern as well as Italian grocery stores. Mexican panela cheese may be substituted.

MIXED CHEESE FILLING

1¼ cups ricotta cheese

1 (1-pound) package tuma cheese, diced (see note)

6 ounces mozzarella cheese, diced

⅓ pound grated pecorino or Romano cheese

5 eggs, lightly beaten

¼ pound diced dry Italian salami (soppressata)

¼ pound diced prosciutto

2 links fresh Italian sausage, skinned and crumbed

Pinch chopped fresh parsley

Pinch oregano

Pinch chopped fresh basil

2 cloves garlic, minced

Pinch pepper

TORTA RUSTICA

A visit to an Italian deli for most of the ingredients and a couple of loaves of frozen bread dough adds up to a spectacular Italian-style torta. This may seem a complicated recipe, but it actually is very easy. And it is also very adaptable; substitute meats and cheeses you like if you don't care for some of these ingredients.

Roll 1 loaf of thawed bread into a circle large enough to fit the bottom and up the sides of a 10-inch springform pan. (If the dough is too elastic to retain its shape when rolled out, let rest a few minutes and try again.) Press the rolled dough in the bottom and up the sides of the pan.

Arrange 7 slices of the provolone over the dough, overlapping slightly, then follow with 4 slices of the 7-inch mortadella with pistachios. Flatten the red peppers on paper towels to remove excess moisture, and arrange half of them over the meat. Add a layer of 7 slices of the mozzarella, and all the cappicola and 4-inch mortadella slices. Press down each layer firmly before adding the next.

Slide the omelet layer over the mortadella. Flatten the golden peppers on paper towels and arrange them over the omelet layer. Add 6 slices mozzarella. Spread with the collard greens. Press each layer down firmly while continuing to add layers of 6 slices provolone, prosciutto, 6 slices mozzarella, dry sausage slices, remaining half of the sweet red peppers, remaining 7 slices provolone, all the hard salami, the remaining 4 slices 7-inch mortadella, and the remaining 6 slices mozzarella.

Roll the other loaf of dough into a circle large enough to cover the torta. Pinch together the edges of the dough at the sides, sealing well. Brush with egg white mixed with water. Bake at 350 degrees for 1 hour, or until the bread is golden brown and pulls away from the sides of the pan slightly.

Completely cool in the pan set on a rack. Refrigerate and serve cold. Cut in wedges to serve.

MAKES 16 TO 20 SERVINGS

2 loaves frozen bread dough, thawed

20 slices provolone

8 (7-inch diameter) slices mortadella with pistachios

1 (1-pound) jar roasted sweet red peppers, drained, seeded, and halved lengthwise

25 slices mozzarella

10 slices cappicola

6 (4-inch diameter) slices mortadella

Omelet Layer (recipe follows)

1 (1-pound) jar Macedonian golden peppers, drained, seeded, and halved lengthwise

1 (10-ounce) package frozen collard greens, thawed and well drained

¼ pound thinly sliced prosciutto

1 (6-inch long) link Italian dry sausage, cut in thin diagonal slices

13 slices spicy, hard salami

1 egg white

1 tablespoon water

Melt the butter in a 10-inch nonstick skillet. Combine the eggs, garlic, and tarragon; season to taste with salt and pepper. Pour the egg mixture into the skillet and cook over medium heat, lifting edges to allow uncooked portion of eggs to flow underneath to cook. Cook until set. Slide onto plate and cool.

MAKES 1 10-INCH OMELET

OMELET LAYER

1 tablespoon butter or margarine

3 eggs, beaten

1 clove garlic, minced

¼ teaspoon dried tarragon

Salt, pepper

VEGETABLES

Vegetables had their ups and downs during the eighties. First they were puréed with great enthusiasm, but after a while they bored us. Then came the idea of steaming them. And, of course, this has been the decade of baby vegetables.

Baby vegetables became the rage in the early part of the decade, turning up on restaurant menus everywhere. Tiny pattypan squash, baby carrots, finger-length zucchini with the blossoms still attached, all were cooked al dente and served with foods and sauces of all kinds. Once these specialty vegetables hit the supermarket, they were eagerly snapped up by consumers. Either because we were not familiar with cooking these baby vegetables, or because they simply didn't have a very developed flavor, the lure of the produce soon became more of a trend than a staple.

Eventually, halfway into the eighties, meatless dinners centered around vegetable casseroles were served frequently, with vegetable salads and stuffed vegetables as the main dishes. Long-neglected varieties of squash appeared on the scene, and mushrooms took on new guises and application.

As vegetables became the all-around ingredient of any meal—as crudités, in salads, as main dishes and side dishes, in soups, and even as sandwiches—it seems dessert was about the only spot on the menu where vegetables had no business. For all their popularity, this makes good sense.

APPLE SAUERKRAUT

If you adore sausages, this dish is the perfect complement. The apple flavoring comes from three sources, apple juice, apple brandy, and a fresh apple. The secret to success here lies in making sure the sauerkraut is well rinsed of all salt and vinegar before the apple flavoring is added.

Fry the bacon in a large saucepan until golden and crisp. Drain fat, reserving about 1 tablespoon in pan. Add the garlic, celery, green onions, sauerkraut, apple juice, lemon zest, sugar, and caraway seeds. Simmer, covered, 20 minutes. Season with salt and pepper. Stir in the apple slices and Calvados. Simmer 5 more minutes. Serve hot with sausages.

MAKES 8 SERVINGS

4 slices bacon, diced

1 clove garlic, minced

1 cup chopped celery

2 green onions, chopped

1 (2-pound) jar sauerkraut, well rinsed and drained

1 cup apple juice

Zest of 1 lemon, cut in fine strips

1 tablespoon sugar

1 teaspoon caraway seeds, optional

Salt, pepper

1 red apple, cut in thin wedges

1 to 2 tablespoons Calvados

Cooked sausages

BROCCOLI-ONION DELUXE

Vegetable casseroles are as popular with meat eaters as they are with vegetarians in Southern California. Reader Stephanie Pendleton told us she often serves this as a main dish with some fresh fruit and homemade bread.

Steam the broccoli and onions until just crisp-tender, about 3 to 5 minutes. Drain. Melt 3 tablespoons of the butter in a heavy saucepan over low heat. Add the flour and stir until smooth. Cook 1 minute. Gradually add the milk and cook until thickened, stirring constantly. Remove from heat and add the cream cheese. Stir until melted. Add salt and white pepper.

Add the broccoli and onions, and stir gently. Spoon into a lightly greased 1½-quart casserole. Top with Cheddar cheese. Cover and bake at 350 degrees for 25 minutes.

Melt the remaining 2 tablespoons butter and add the bread crumbs. Uncover the baked casserole and sprinkle with the buttered bread crumbs. Bake an additional 5 minutes, or until golden brown.

MAKES ABOUT 4 SERVINGS

1 to 1½ pounds broccoli, cut into 1½-inch pieces

6 to 8 pearl onions, halved

5 tablespoons butter or margarine

3 tablespoons flour

1 cup milk

1 (3-ounce) package cream cheese, cubed

¼ teaspoon salt

⅛ teaspoon white pepper

½ cup shredded sharp Cheddar cheese

1 cup fresh bread crumbs

KOREAN BEAN SPROUTS

Rarely do we get recipes that call for cooked bean sprouts, so when Talitha Scheevel sent us this one, we just had to try it. We found it very different and very good.

Clean the bean sprouts. Drop into boiling water and boil 5 minutes. Drain well. Return to the pan. Stir in the salt, sesame seeds, sesame oil, garlic powder, cayenne, and green onions. Simmer 2 minutes. Serve hot or cold.

MAKES 4 TO 6 SERVINGS

½ *pound bean sprouts*

1 *teaspoon salt or to taste*

2 *tablespoons sesame seeds, toasted*

2 *tablespoons sesame oil*

½ *teaspoon garlic powder*

Pinch cayenne pepper, optional

¼ *cup finely chopped green onions*

CARROT RING

Filled with green peas or mixed vegetables, this carrot ring makes a great side dish for any kind of party buffet. Similar recipes have circulated the country for years. This one came from the Midwest.

In a large mixing bowl combine the carrots, milk, cracker crumbs, cheese, onion, butter, salt, pepper, and cayenne; do not overblend. Beat the eggs until frothy and blend into the carrot mixture. Pour into a greased 1½-quart ring mold and bake at 350 degrees for 30 to 40 minutes, or until a knife inserted near the center comes out clean. Turn out onto warm platter and fill the center with other cooked vegetables, if desired.

MAKES 6 TO 8 SERVINGS

2 *cups mashed cooked carrots*

1 *cup milk*

1 *cup cracker crumbs*

½ *cup shredded sharp Cheddar cheese*

¼ *cup minced onion*

⅓ *cup butter or margarine, softened*

½ *teaspoon salt*

¼ *teaspoon black pepper*

Pinch cayenne pepper

3 *eggs*

PARSNIP AND CARROT JULIENNE

This simple recipe from Jennifer Swift is a hit: the vegetables are greatly enhanced by the orange flavor of the liqueur and the fresh mint.

Slice the parsnip and carrot in 2-inch-long julienne strips. Melt 1 tablespoon butter in a skillet and add parsnip strips. Sauté, stirring occasionally, 1 minute. Add the carrot strips and sauté 2 minutes longer, adding more butter if needed.

Add ⅓ cup triple sec, lower heat, cover, and simmer 5 minutes, or until vegetables are tender. Uncover and reduce the triple sec to 1 tablespoon over high heat. Stir in the mint leaves to taste.

MAKES 3 TO 4 SERVINGS

1 large parsnip, peeled
1 large carrot, peeled
1 to 2 tablespoons butter or margarine
⅓ cup triple sec liqueur
Fresh mint leaves, minced

CAULIFLOWER SOUFFLÉ

This vegetable-based soufflé was a favorite at La Masia, a restaurant in West Hollywood that specializes in Spanish food.

Parboil the cauliflower in boiling salted water, covered, about 4 minutes. Drain and chop finely. Melt the butter in a large skillet. Gradually add the flour and stir until smooth. Slowly add the milk and cream. Cook, stirring, until slightly thickened. Cool.

Beat egg yolks. Add to the sauce, along with 2½ cups cheese, salt, and nutmeg, blending well. Fold in the cauliflower. Beat the egg whites until stiff, but not dry. Fold into the cauliflower mixture. Turn into a greased 1-quart soufflé or baking dish. Sprinkle with the remaining 2 tablespoons cheese. Bake at 325 degrees for 30 to 35 minutes, or until golden brown.

MAKES 6 TO 8 SERVINGS

1 head cauliflower
⅓ cup butter
⅓ cup flour
1⅓ cups milk
⅓ cup whipping cream
2 eggs, separated
2½ cups plus 2 tablespoons grated Parmesan cheese
Pinch salt
Pinch nutmeg

STUFFED CHAYOTES

In the west they're known as chayotes, in the South they're called mirlitons. By any name they're wonderful as a light entrée when served this way.

Cut the chayotes in halves lengthwise. Remove the seeds and cook in boiling salted water until tender but not mushy, about 20 minutes. Cook the ham in oil until lightly browned. Add the onion and garlic, and cook until tender but not browned. Stir in the cracker crumbs, capers, raisins, and olives. Carefully scoop out the chayote pulp, leaving the sturdy shells. Add the pulp, tomato juice, oregano, and vinegar to the ham, blending well. Season to taste with salt.

Stuff the shells with the ham. Place in a shallow baking dish, dot with butter, and bake at 400 degrees for 15 minutes, or until heated through.

MAKES 6 SERVINGS

3 chayotes
½ to 1 cup finely chopped ham
1 tablespoon oil
¼ cup minced onion
1 clove garlic, crushed
½ cup cracker crumbs
1 teaspoon capers
2 tablespoons raisins
½ cup sliced olives
¼ cup tomato juice
½ teaspoon ground oregano
½ teaspoon vinegar
Salt
2 tablespoons butter or margarine

CREAMED CORN

It would be impossible for any cookbook writer concentrating on Los Angeles food favorites to overlook the creamed corn served at the Gulliver's chain of restaurants. It's one of those simple, homey recipes that never goes out of style.

Cut the corn from the cobs and place in a saucepan with the whipping cream. Bring to a boil, reduce heat, and simmer 5 minutes. Stir in the salt to taste and sugar. Melt 2 teaspoons butter in a small pan and stir in the flour. Do not brown. Stir the butter-flour mixture into the corn and cook until slightly thickened. Turn the corn into an ovenproof dish, sprinkle with cheese, and dot with butter. Brown under the broiler.

MAKES 8 TO 10 SERVINGS

8 ears corn
1 cup whipping cream
Salt
1 teaspoon sugar
Butter or margarine
2 teaspoons flour
Grated Parmesan cheese

EGGPLANT-SPINACH CURRY

*Indian cuisine is growing in popularity in the West as the ingredients become more available.
This vegetable curry, from the Dhaba Cuisine of India restaurant in Santa Monica,
uses an authentic homemade curry mixture of spices and other seasonings rather
than the bottled mix.*

Heat the oil with half of the mustard seeds in a large saucepan. Add remaining mustard seeds when the cooked seeds begin to pop. Add the garlic and sauté until tender.

Add the spinach, a small amount at a time, stirring occasionally to keep the spinach from scorching. When the spinach wilts, add the eggplant, ginger, jalapeño chiles, turmeric, paprika, coriander, and cumin. Sauté to blend the flavors. Cover, and cook over medium-low heat for 15 minutes. Add the tomatoes and season to taste with salt. Cook, uncovered, 5 minutes longer. Garnish with cilantro.

MAKES 8 SERVINGS

¼ cup oil

1 teaspoon black mustard seeds

12 cloves garlic, minced

2 pounds spinach, rinsed, dried, and finely chopped

1 medium eggplant, cut into ½-inch cubes

1-inch piece ginger root, peeled and grated

¼ teaspoon jalapeño chiles, minced

¼ teaspoon turmeric powder

¼ teaspoon paprika

½ teaspoon ground coriander

½ teaspoon ground cumin

2 medium tomatoes, finely chopped

Salt

Cilantro sprigs, for garnish

MADDALENA'S EGGPLANT ALLA PARMIGIANA

The San Antonio Winery, located in the heart of downtown Los Angeles, is a local landmark. Owned and operated by the Riboli family, the winery has a restaurant that serves authentic home-style Italian food and draws huge crowds, particularly at lunch. Maddalena Riboli is the genius behind the menu at San Antonio, and she gave us her recipe for Eggplant alla Parmigiana.

Cut the eggplant into ½-inch-thick rounds. Let stand in a colander for 45 minutes. Beat the egg with the milk, then add the garlic powder, parsley, basil, salt and pepper. Place some flour in a shallow bowl or on a plate. Heat a small amount olive oil in a large, heavy skillet. Flour each slice of eggplant, dip it in the egg mixture, and sauté, a few pieces at a time, until lightly browned. Remove and set aside.

To assemble, line a 14 × 11-inch baking dish with 1 cup of the marinara sauce. Add a layer of the eggplant. Cover with the mozzarella. Sprinkle over ⅓ cup Romano cheese. Cover with 1½ cups marinara sauce. Repeat this step, two more times, ending with the cheeses. Cover with foil, supported with wood picks to form a tent so the foil does not touch the cheese.

Bake at 375 degrees for 20 to 25 minutes, until heated through and the cheese has melted. Cut into squares. Spoon additional marinara sauce over each serving.

MAKES 12 SERVINGS

Heat the olive oil in a Dutch oven. Add the vegetables and cook until lightly browned. Stir in the tomato purée, about 1⅔ cups water, basil, bay leaves, stock base, sugar, Worcestershire, and garlic powder. Season to taste with salt and pepper. Simmer, uncovered, 20 to 25 minutes.

MAKES 6 CUPS

3 medium-large eggplants, peeled

1 egg

1 cup milk

⅛ teaspoon garlic powder

½ teaspoon dried parsley

½ teaspoon dried basil

½ teaspoon salt

⅛ teaspoon white pepper

Flour

Olive oil

Maddalena's Marinara Sauce (recipe follows)

1½ pounds mozzarella cheese, thinly sliced

1 cup grated Romano cheese

MADDALENA'S MARINARA SAUCE

½ cup finely grated or ground carrot

½ cup minced or ground celery

½ onion, minced

2 tablespoons olive oil

2 (28-ounce) cans tomato purée

½ teaspoon dried basil

2 or 3 bay leaves

2 teaspoons beef stock base

2 teaspoons sugar

½ teaspoon Worcestershire sauce

Pinch garlic powder

Salt, white pepper

EGGPLANT WITH HOT GARLIC SAUCE

This Oriental treatment for eggplant is outstanding. The recipe came from the Maple Garden Restaurant in Honolulu.

Blend the ginger, garlic, sugar, soy sauce, vinegar, and hot pepper sauce in a bowl. Mix the cornstarch with the water in a small bowl. Blend into the soy mixture. Heat the oil to 360 degrees in a wok or deep-fryer. Add the eggplant and pork and deep-fry until the pork is tender and the eggplant is golden brown. Remove the eggplant and pork with a slotted spoon and drain on paper towels. Drain all but 1 teaspoon oil from the pan. Add the soy sauce to the pan and heat until slightly thickened. Combine with the eggplant and pork, tossing lightly.

MAKES 4 SERVINGS

Note: The pork is used mainly for flavoring, hence the small amount.

1 teaspoon minced ginger root
1 teaspoon minced garlic
1 teaspoon sugar
1 tablespoon soy sauce
1 teaspoon vinegar
1 teaspoon hot pepper sauce
1 teaspoon cornstarch
⅓ cup water
Oil for deep frying
¼ to ½ pound peeled eggplant, cut into 1-inch-long strips
2 tablespoons julienned pork

CIPOLLE ARROSTITE (ROASTED ONIONS)

Carlo Middione at Vivande in San Francisco gave us this simple onion side dish that can be served as a hot side dish with roasted meats, or at room temperature as an antipasto or with cold foods. Be sure to use the balsamic vinegar called for as other vinegars are too astringent.

Leave the outer brown skins on the onions. Rub well with olive oil and sprinkle all over with salt and pepper. Combine the vinegar and basil and set aside. Set the onions in a flameproof shallow baking pan and bake at 375 degrees for about 1 hour, or until onions are tender but not mushy.

Remove the onions to a serving platter, still leaving the brown skins attached. Cut in halves vertically through the stem-ends. Deglaze the baking pan with the vinegar mixture, scraping well to absorb brown caramelized onion juices. Cook over low heat 3 to 5 minutes, until mixture is reduced to 2 to 3 tablespoons liquid. (Push aside any large pieces of onion skin that may have stuck to the pan.)

With a pastry brush, brush the pan juices over the cut sides of the onions.

MAKES ABOUT 6 SERVINGS

6 yellow onions, about 3 inches in diameter
Olive oil
Salt, pepper
⅓ cup balsamic vinegar
½ teaspoon dried basil

SPECIAL SWEET POTATO CASSEROLE

This sweet potato recipe is often requested by readers when the holiday season approaches. It makes a pretty accompaniment to turkey.

Mix the sweet potatoes, ⅓ cup butter, and the granulated sugar. Beat in the eggs and milk. Pour into a greased 1½- to 2-quart casserole. Combine the pecans, coconut, brown sugar, and flour. Stir in 2 tablespoons melted butter. Sprinkle the mixture over the sweet potatoes. Bake at 325 degrees for 1 hour.

MAKES 6 TO 8 SERVINGS

4 cups hot mashed sweet potatoes
Butter or margarine
2 tablespoons granulated sugar
2 eggs, beaten
½ cup milk
⅓ cup chopped pecans
⅓ cup flaked coconut
⅓ cup brown sugar, packed
2 tablespoons flour

VEGETABLES IN CHESTNUT CREAM SAUCE

When we developed this recipe in our test kitchen for a feature on chestnuts during the holidays one year, a number of us seized on it as a perfect side dish for a Thanksgiving dinner.

Sauté the onion and 1 cup of the chestnuts in ¼ cup butter. Stir in the flour and cook, stirring, about 2 minutes. Remove from heat and gradually add the chicken broth and milk. Return to heat and cook, stirring, until thickened. Season to taste with salt and white pepper.

Cook the broccoli, cauliflower, and carrots in boiling water until crisp-tender. Drain. Combine with the cream sauce and spoon into a casserole dish.

Sauté the remaining ¼ cup chestnuts, rosemary, and bread crumbs in remaining 2 tablespoons butter. Sprinkle over the top of the casserole. Bake at 350 degrees for 30 minutes, or until heated through.

MAKES ABOUT 8 SERVINGS

2 tablespoons chopped onion
1¼ cups chopped roasted chestnuts
¼ cup plus 2 tablespoons butter
3 tablespoons flour
1 cup chicken broth
1 cup milk
Salt, white pepper
2 cups broccoli florets
2 cups cauliflower florets
2 cups sliced carrots
1 teaspoon minced fresh rosemary
½ cup fresh bread crumbs

Note: Can be prepared ahead, but sprinkle the casserole with bread crumbs just before baking. Increase the baking time if the vegetables have been refrigerated.

GARDEN PATCH CASSEROLE

This interesting broccoli and corn casserole was sent to us in 1984 by Rusty Greenlee, who was always on the lookout for good vegetable casserole ideas.

Peel the broccoli stems if using fresh, and cut in small pieces. Place the broccoli in the bottom of a 2-quart casserole. Mix the cottage cheese, sour cream, eggs, onion, corn, and flour. Season to taste with salt and pepper. Pour over the broccoli. Sprinkle with cheese. Bake at 325 degrees for 45 minutes to 1 hour, or until egg mixture is set and the top is browned slightly.

MAKES ABOUT 10 SERVINGS

Note: If using fresh broccoli, cover for about 20 minutes to speed the cooking. Cook, uncovered, for the remaining time to brown the casserole.

2 pounds fresh broccoli or 2 (10-ounce) packages frozen chopped broccoli, thawed

1½ cups cottage cheese

½ cup sour cream

3 eggs, lightly beaten

2 tablespoons minced onion

1 (16-ounce) can whole kernel corn, drained

1 tablespoon flour

Salt, pepper

½ cup grated Parmesan cheese

RATATOUILLE

Ratatouille is a terrific addition to any buffet or portable meal. It can be prepared ahead and it travels well. This particular recipe, which came from the Cafe Casino in Beverly Hills, is a favorite with our readers.

Heat the olive oil in a skillet. Add the onion and green pepper, and sauté a few minutes until the onion is wilted. Add the zucchini, eggplant, tomatoes, salt, pepper, tomato paste, cayenne, oregano, garlic, and parsley. Mix well and simmer over low heat 15 to 20 minutes, stirring occasionally, until vegetables are just cooked.

MAKES 4 TO 6 SERVINGS

½ cup olive oil

¼ medium onion, thinly sliced

1 large green pepper, cut into strips

1 medium zucchini, thinly sliced

½ large eggplant, diced

4 to 5 medium tomatoes, cut into chunks

1 teaspoon salt

¼ teaspoon white pepper

1 tablespoon tomato paste

Pinch cayenne pepper

Pinch dried oregano

1 clove garlic, minced

2 teaspoons chopped parsley

HURRY-UP VEGETABLE CHILI

Chili of any kind has great appeal for westerners, as do vegetables. So when we needed something special for a story on light, quick, and easy meals, we developed this vegetable chili. It's a wonderfully filling, light main dish.

Sauté the onions and garlic in olive oil in a large, heavy saucepan just until soft. Do not brown. Add the orzo and cook, stirring, 1 to 2 minutes, or until orzo is well coated.

Stir in the tomatoes and their liquid and 1 can of the broth. Bring the mixture to a boil and add the celery, carrots, chili powder, cumin, cayenne, oregano, marjoram, yellow and pattypan squash, zucchini, and tomato sauce.

Return to a boil, reduce heat, cover and simmer 20 minutes, adding additional chicken broth as needed. (Mixture should be thick rather than watery.) Add beans and season to taste with salt and pepper. Continue cooking until beans are heated through.

MAKES 8 SERVINGS

2 small red onions, diced

2 teaspoons minced garlic

2 tablespoons olive oil

½ cup orzo pasta

1 (1-pound) can tomatoes

2 (14½-ounce) cans chicken broth

½ cup chopped celery

½ cup chopped carrots

1 tablespoon chili powder

1 tablespoon ground cumin

½ teaspoon cayenne pepper

1 tablespoon chopped fresh oregano

1 tablespoon chopped fresh marjoram

1 yellow squash, cut in chunks

2 pattypan squash cut in chunks

1 large zucchini, cut in chunks

1 (8-ounce) can tomato sauce

1 (15- to 16-ounce) can chili beans with liquid

Salt, pepper

MICROWAVE VEGETABLE LASAGNA

For a story on quick cookery, we did as so many of our present-day readers do — we turned to the microwave for help. Fresh herbs, ricotta cheese, and two different kinds of squash were blended and turned into a delicious vegetable lasagna that needed no noodles.

Slice the zucchini and yellow squash lengthwise in halves and place cut side down in a microwave-safe baking dish. Cover the dish with plastic wrap, venting 1 corner. Microwave on HIGH (100% power) for 5 minutes or until vegetables are crisp-tender and have released excess water.

Add the mushrooms. Microwave on HIGH 3 more minutes. Drain the vegetables on paper towels and cut zucchini and squash into ¼-inch-thick slices lengthwise.

Spread ⅓ marinara sauce over the bottom of a 10-inch round, flat-bottomed glass baking dish. Top with a layer consisting of ⅓ mixed zucchini and squash slices arranged spoke fashion. Spread half the ricotta over the vegetables. Sprinkle with half each of onions, mushrooms, oregano, and marjoram.

Repeat layering. Cover second layer with remaining ⅓ zucchini and squash and top with remaining ⅓ marinara sauce. Sprinkle Jack and Parmesan cheeses over top. Season to taste with salt and pepper.

Cover the dish with plastic wrap, sprayed with nonstick spray, venting 1 corner. Microwave on HIGH for 6 to 8 minutes, or until mixture is bubbling and vegetables are cooked but still slightly crisp, turning dish after 3 minutes. Remove from the oven and let stand, covered, at least 5 minutes before serving.

MAKES 6 TO 8 SERVINGS

3 medium zucchini

3 medium yellow crookneck squash

1 cup thinly sliced mushrooms

1 (15½-ounce) jar thick vegetarian marinara sauce

½ pound ricotta cheese

1 small onion, diced

1 tablespoon minced fresh oregano leaves

1 tablespoon minced fresh marjoram leaves

½ cup shredded Jack cheese

½ cup grated Parmesan cheese

Salt, pepper

EGGS AND CHEESE

Quiches, omelets, soufflés, and other egg-based dishes were popular foods as we entered the eighties. So were cheeses of all types. Then came that dreaded word, cholesterol, *and everything changed. We began to eliminate eggs from our diet wherever we could, whether we needed to or not.*

With time—and more information—we again found a place for these foods on our tables; we simply indulged in them less often and were more selective in how we used them.

Oddly enough, cheese remained high in favor. We discovered double and triple creme cheeses and went wild about them, despite their high fat content. Fruit and cheese trays were served in place of dessert. And quiches, now made with fewer eggs and more vegetables, are ideal light suppers and luncheons. Where possible, low-fat, low-cholesterol cheeses were used. And late in the decade came news of a new, lower cholesterol egg. Fortunately, we can still eat our eggs and cheese—just with more care.

PINK PICKLED EGGS

*For some reason pink pickled eggs retain their popularity year after year. This version of this
age-old food is one of our most popular. Try slicing the eggs over the top of a spinach salad
for a touch of unexpected color.*

Place the eggs in a 1-quart jar. In a saucepan combine the beet juice, wine, vinegar, bay leaf, allspice, salt, pepper, and garlic. Heat, but do not allow to boil. Pour the hot liquid over the eggs. Cool, then cover and refrigerate overnight or longer, if desired.

MAKES 6 EGGS

6 hard-cooked eggs, shelled

¾ cup juice drained from canned or cooked beets

½ cup dry red wine

¾ cup vinegar

1 bay leaf

¼ teaspoon allspice

¾ teaspoon salt

Pinch black pepper

1 clove garlic, crushed

POPOVERS STUFFED WITH CREAMY EGG-SAUSAGE SCRAMBLE

For a leisurely weekend brunch serve your guests this easy, but spectacular looking popover-based entrée. Good hot coffee and a fruit platter will round out the menu nicely.

Beat the eggs in a deep bowl. Beat in the milk until well blended. Combine the flour and salt. Work the butter into the flour, then gradually add the flour to the egg mixture, blending well. Thoroughly grease 8 custard cups or popover cups.

Set the custard cups on a baking sheet. Fill three-fourths full with batter and bake at 400 degrees for about 1 hour, or until golden. Remove from oven and let stand about 5 minutes. Cut off the tops and scoop out any moist batter remaining in the centers. Fill with creamy egg-sausage scramble and replace the tops. Serve warm.

MAKES 8 SERVINGS

Mix half of the eggs and cream cheese. Heat half of the butter in a skillet over medium heat. Pour the egg mixture into the pan. As it begins to set, gently lift the cooked portions with a spatula to allow any uncooked portion to cook on the bottom. Avoid constant stirring.

When the eggs are thickened but still quite moist, lightly stir in half of the sausage. Sprinkle with half of the chives. Remove from heat and season to taste with salt and pepper. Repeat with the remaining ingredients.

MAKES ENOUGH EGGS TO FILL 8 POPOVERS

6 eggs
2 cups milk
2 cups flour
¾ teaspoon salt
6 tablespoons butter or margarine
Creamy Egg-Sausage Scramble (recipe follows)

CREAMY EGG-SAUSAGE SCRAMBLE

16 eggs, lightly beaten
2 (3-ounce) packages cream cheese, diced
¼ cup butter or margarine
1½ cups diced cooked link sausage
¼ cup chopped chives or green onions
Salt, pepper

MUSHROOM CRUST QUICHE

This simple quiche, which has a mushroom and crushed cracker crust, was a "My Best Recipe" winner in 1984.

Melt 3 tablespoons butter in a skillet over medium heat. Sauté the mushrooms until tender. Remove from the heat, and stir in the cracker crumbs. Press into the bottom and along the sides of a greased 9-inch pie plate.

Melt the remaining 2 tablespoons butter in a skillet. Add the green onions and sauté quickly. Spread over the crust. Sprinkle with Jack cheese. Combine the cottage cheese, eggs, and cayenne in a blender or food processor. Blend well. Turn into the prepared mushroom crust. Sprinkle with paprika. Bake at 350 degrees for 35 to 45 minutes. Let stand about 10 minutes before serving.

MAKES 6 TO 8 SERVINGS

5 tablespoons butter or margarine
½ pound mushrooms, coarsely chopped
½ cup finely crushed plain crackers (about 16)
¾ cup chopped green onions
2 cups shredded Jack cheese
1 cup cottage cheese
3 eggs
¼ teaspoon cayenne pepper
¼ teaspoon paprika

POLLY'S FIESTA QUICHE

If you're watching your cholesterol intake closely, this elegant and creamy quiche is not for you. But if your health is good and you can afford a caloric splurge now and then, don't pass this one up. The recipe came from Polly's in Huntington Beach.

In a bowl combine the eggs, salt, nutmeg, cayenne, and whipping cream. Whip until smooth and light in consistency. Spread the onions, tomatoes, and chiles on the bottom of the pie crust. Pour the egg-and-cream mixture over the filling. Sprinkle with Cheddar and Jack cheeses. Bake at 375 degrees for 60 to 70 minutes, or until wood pick inserted near center comes out clean. Allow to cool 10 to 15 minutes before cutting.

MAKES 1 (9- OR 10-INCH) PIE

5 to 6 medium eggs
¼ teaspoon salt
⅛ teaspoon ground nutmeg
¼ teaspoon cayenne pepper
2 cups whipping cream
⅓ cup finely diced onions
⅓ cup finely diced tomatoes
⅓ cup diced canned chiles
1 (9- or 10-inch) unbaked pie crust
1½ ounces shredded Cheddar cheese
1½ ounces shredded Jack cheese

CHEESE AND LENTIL QUICHE

When we developed this pretty quiche recipe for a story on lentils, we were amazed at how many readers were unaware that lentils come in a variety of colors. This particular recipe calls for red ones, but other kinds of lentils can be substituted.

Beat the eggs until frothy, then add the whipping cream and beat just until mixed well. Stir in the lentils and mixed vegetables. Season to taste with salt and pepper.

Pour the mixture into the cheese pastry shell and bake at 350 degrees for about 45 minutes, or until filling is set. Sprinkle cilantro over the quiche and serve warm or cold.

MAKES 6 TO 8 SERVINGS

Sift together the flour and salt. Cut in the shortening until the mixture resembles small peas. Lightly stir in the cheese. Add the water in small amounts, using only enough to form the pastry into a ball.

Roll out the dough on a floured board or pastry cloth; fit it into a 10-inch pie plate. Flute the edges and pierce the entire surface with the tines of a fork. Loosely press a piece of foil into the bottom and up the sides of the pastry shell. Weight the foil with dry beans or baker's beads and bake at 350 degrees for 15 minutes.

Remove from oven, remove foil and beans from the shell and set the shell aside.

MAKES 1 (10-INCH) PASTRY SHELL

3 eggs

1½ cups whipping cream

1 cup cooked and drained red lentils

1 (10-ounce) package frozen mixed vegetables, thawed and drained

Salt, pepper

Cheese Pastry Shell *(recipe follows)*

Minced fresh cilantro, for garnish

CHEESE PASTRY SHELL

1½ cups flour

¾ teaspoon salt

10 tablespoons shortening

½ cup shredded Cheddar cheese

4 to 5 tablespoons ice water

BRIE-FRESH STRAWBERRY FRENCH TOAST

The next time a yen for French toast strikes, treat yourself to this elegant version. We like it with a thickly cut homemade bread.

Slice about two-thirds of the strawberries, reserving nice whole ones for garnish. Spread 4 slices of bread with Brie. Top with sliced strawberries. Cover each with the second slice of bread.

Lightly beat the eggs with milk and nutmeg. Dip each sandwich in the egg mixture and cook in a buttered skillet until lightly browned on each side. Serve with reserved strawberries and warm syrup.

MAKES 4 SERVINGS

1 pint strawberries, washed and hulled

8 slices French bread

8 ounces Brie cheese

4 eggs

¼ cup milk

2 teaspoons freshly ground nutmeg, optional

Butter

Maple syrup, warmed

CHEESE FRITTERS

On a cool winter evening with a hot bowl of soup, or on a hot summer day with a crisp salad, it will be hard to beat these super double-cheese fritters from Houlihan's in Torrance. The recipe makes enough for a crowd, but could easily be halved.

Combine the butter, water, wine, garlic, nutmeg, white pepper, cayenne, and salt in a medium saucepan. Bring to a rapid boil over high heat. Add the flour all at once, stirring rapidly with a wooden spoon until the dough leaves the sides of the pan. Remove from heat and add the cheeses, stirring constantly until thoroughly blended. Beat in the eggs, one at a time.

While the batter is still warm, scoop balls, about ½ teaspoon for each fritter. Roll the dough into uniform round balls. Place the balls on a lightly floured baking sheet and chill 6 to 8 hours, or overnight. Do not cover while chilling.

Heat the oil to 360 degrees. Cook the cheese balls in the hot oil; fry until golden brown and crisp. Remove with a slotted spoon and drain well on paper towels.

MAKES ABOUT 10 DOZEN FRITTERS

¼ cup butter

½ cup cold water

½ cup chablis

¼ teaspoon minced garlic

⅛ teaspoon ground nutmeg

⅛ teaspoon white pepper

⅛ teaspoon cayenne pepper

¾ teaspoon salt

1⅛ cups flour

6 ounces shredded Cheddar cheese

¼ cup grated Parmesan cheese

2 eggs

Oil for deep frying

EASTER BRUNCH STRATA

Stratas are always in demand as the centerpiece for a brunch, probably because they not only can, but should, be made well ahead of time. This one, originally designed to be the mainstay of an Easter brunch, takes advantage of the availability of asparagus in the spring. Serve it with some seasonal fruit and Mimosas to drink for a deliciously easy meal for company.

Blanch the asparagus briefly in boiling water and drain well. Spoon 1½ cups of the bread cubes into the bottom of a greased 2-quart ovenproof casserole. Scatter ¾ cup asparagus over the bread cubes. Top with another 1½ cups bread cubes. Cover with the ham. Add 1½ cups bread cubes and top with the remaining ¾ cup asparagus. Cover the asparagus layer with the remaining 1½ cups bread cubes. Combine the eggs and milk, season with salt and pepper, and pour evenly over the strata. Cover and chill 3 or 4 hours or overnight.

Bake, uncovered, at 350 degrees for 1 hour and 15 minutes. Let stand 10 minutes; serve with the cheese sauce on the side.

MAKES 6 TO 8 SERVINGS

1½ cups diced asparagus
6 cups cubed sourdough bread
1½ cups diced ham
4 eggs, beaten
2½ cups milk
Salt, white pepper
Spicy Cheese Sauce *(recipe follows)*

Melt the butter in a heavy saucepan, then stir in the flour. Stir in the mustard and cook, stirring, about 1 minute or until the mixture forms a paste. Do not let brown. Add the milk and cook, stirring, until the mixture comes to a boil. Boil, stirring, 1 minute, then add the cheese and continue stirring until the cheese is melted. Season to taste with salt, pepper, and hot pepper sauce.

MAKES ABOUT 3 CUPS

SPICY CHEESE SAUCE
3 tablespoons butter or margarine
3 tablespoons flour
½ teaspoon dry mustard
2 cups milk
1 cup shredded Cheddar cheese
Salt, pepper
Hot pepper sauce

SEÑOR PICO CHILES RELLENOS

When Señor Pico, a longtime favorite Mexican restaurant in Los Angeles, closed, panic set in among the fans of the restaurant's chiles rellenos. Fortunately we have the recipe here.

Rinse the chiles and discard the seeds and ribs. Insert 1 strip Jack and 1 strip Cheddar cheese in each chile, cutting a slit in 1 side of the chiles if necessary. Dust the chiles with flour.

Beat the egg whites until stiff. Beat the egg yolks and fold into the whites. Add the melted butter to the egg mixture. (Butter should not be hot.)

Grease well 6 individual baking dishes. Pour a thick coating of batter into each dish. Place 1 stuffed chile in each dish, then spoon any remaining batter over them. Bake at 375 degrees for 15 minutes. To serve, turn out of baking dish and top with Señor Pico sauce.

MAKES 6 SERVINGS

6 canned long green chiles

6 (2-inch) strips Jack cheese, about ½ inch thick

6 (2-inch) strips New York Cheddar cheese, about ½ inch thick

Flour

1 cup egg whites (about 8)

½ cup egg yolks (about 6)

¼ cup melted butter

Señor Pico Sauce *(recipe follows)*

SEÑOR PICO SAUCE

Cook the onion and garlic in oil until the onion is transparent. Add tomato paste and chopped tomatoes and simmer a few minutes. Add the broth, sugar, salt, and vinegar. Simmer until the tomatoes are cooked, then purée in a blender.

Reheat and thicken lightly with flour mixed with 1 or 2 tablespoons cold water. Cook, stirring, until the sauce comes to a boil.

MAKES ABOUT 3 CUPS SAUCE

½ cup chopped onion

1 clove garlic, minced

1 tablespoon oil

2 tablespoons tomato paste

1 cup chopped peeled tomatoes

1 (14½-ounce) can chicken broth

1 teaspoon sugar

½ teaspoon salt

1 teaspoon vinegar

1 tablespoon flour

BEANS, GRAINS, AND PASTA

It could be said that the eighties is the decade in which we discovered pasta was something other than spaghetti covered with tomato sauce. Once discovered, we indulged in it with whole-hearted abandon.

We went wild over any trendy "new" ingredient that could be served on pasta: fresh basil was the herb of the day in the early eighties, and the joys of freshly grated Romano and Parmesan cheeses were not to be denied. Sun-dried tomatoes and extra-virgin olive oils were in great demand, to say nothing of balsamic vinegars.

Fresh pasta was the rage, so some of us made our own, but as the time crunch began to hit in the mid eighties, we put away our pasta machines and settled for some of the good commercial fresh pastas that were available by then.

As the eighties slip into the nineties, pasta has apparently settled into a niche as a less trendy but still popular menu item. It seems likely to play a major role in our meals for some time to come.

With the growth of our local Oriental population, we were introduced to Oriental noodles and along with them, we were reintroduced to rice. Mexican-style rice has always been a Southern California favorite, but now we were sampling it as it was prepared in other cuisines. And we were rediscovering how good it was when used in old-fashioned rice puddings.

Then, too, as California became a big source of wild rice, we began to find more uses for this nutty grass seed that really isn't rice at all. Grains of all types came into their own late in the decade as health authorities began to emphasize the need for more fiber in our diets. Oats and oat bran, barley, and some of the newer grains such as quinoa have found regular spots on our menus. And dried beans, especially black beans, remain popular as we enter the 1990s, probably because they too provide us with the fiber we need.

CHILI BEANS

There's great merit in adding a touch of chili powder to a bowl of beans when you serve it as an accompaniment to a beef or pork main dish. This recipe, which came from a restaurant called This Old House in San Luis Obispo, is a good example of western-style chili beans.

Sauté the onion in butter until tender. Stir in the brown sugar until well mixed. Combine the beans, catsup, ground beef, bacon, chili powder, garlic powder, onion powder, and hot pepper sauce in a large saucepan. Stir in the onions and mix well. Cover and simmer over low heat until the meat is cooked, about 30 to 35 minutes. Refrigerate overnight to blend flavors. Reheat to serve.

MAKES 8 SERVINGS

1 small onion, diced

2 tablespoons butter or margarine

½ cup brown sugar, packed

2 (1-pound, 13-ounce) cans pinto beans

1 cup catsup

¼ cup ground beef

¼ pound bacon, chopped

1½ teaspoons chili powder

1½ teaspoons garlic powder

1½ teaspoons onion powder

1 teaspoon hot pepper sauce

LAYERED BEER BEAN POT

Serve this bean pot with hot grilled sausages or hamburgers for an easy outdoor barbecue meal.

Combine the onion, garlic, dry mustard, brown sugar, and beer in a bowl or measuring cup. Mix well and season to taste with salt and pepper. Layer the butter beans, red kidney beans, pinto beans, green lima beans, and Great Northern beans in a casserole or bean pot, adding some of the beer mixture between each layer. Pour any remaining mixture over the beans. Cover and bake at 325 degrees for 1 hour, or place over low heat and simmer 40 minutes.

MAKES 6 SERVINGS

1 cup minced onion

1 clove garlic, minced

1 tablespoon dry mustard

¼ cup brown sugar, packed

2 cups beer

Salt, pepper

1 (15-ounce) can butter beans

1 (15¼-ounce) can red kidney beans

1 (15-ounce) can pinto beans

1 (1-pound, 1-ounce) can green lima beans

1 (15-ounce) can Great Northern beans

CALIFORNIA CASSOULET

This California version of the classic French bean, duck, and sausage casserole has drawn hundreds of repeat requests over the years. This is one of those casseroles that requires a crowd to do it justice as it simply doesn't reduce well.

Soak the beans overnight in a generous covering of water. Add salt, pepper, ham hock, whole onion studded with cloves, carrots, and thyme, stirring to blend. Bring to a boil, reduce heat and simmer, covered, 1½ hours. Add more water during cooking if needed.

Place the salt pork in a small pan, cover with boiling water, and cook 10 minutes. Remove from the pan, dice, and add to the beans.

Sauté the chicken in a large skillet in the oil until well browned on all sides. Remove from the pan and set aside. Add the chopped onions and garlic to the pan drippings and cook until tender.

Remove the ham hock from the beans and cut the meat into 1-inch chunks; discard the skin and bones. Cut the sausage into 1-inch pieces. Stir the onion and garlic mixture into the beans.

Layer the beans, meats, and chicken in a 6-quart casserole. Cover and bake at 350 degrees for 3 hours, adding water if necessary during cooking. Mix the bread crumbs with the butter and sprinkle over the beans. Bake 30 minutes longer.

MAKES 10 TO 12 SERVINGS

1 pound large dried white beans
1 tablespoon salt
1 teaspoon black pepper
1 smoked ham hock
1 large onion
6 whole cloves
2 carrots, sliced
¼ teaspoon dried thyme
½ pound salt pork
8 to 10 chicken thighs
2 tablespoons oil
1 cup chopped onions
2 cloves garlic, minced
1 pound garlic sausage
1 cup dried bread crumbs
3 tablespoons butter or margarine, melted

WILD RICE CASSEROLE

With so much wild rice being grown in California these days, it is no longer priced out of the average budget. The nutty flavor of this grass seed, which isn't a true rice, complements cold ham or any fowl.

Cook the bacon until crisp. Drain and set aside; reserve 2 tablespoons bacon fat. Add the onions to the fat and cook until tender. Add the mushrooms and cook until warmed through. In a 2-quart casserole, combine the bacon, onions, and mushrooms with the rice, celery, seasoned salt, and broth. Season to taste with salt and pepper. Cover and bake at 325 degrees for 2 hours, or until rice is cooked.

MAKES 8 TO 10 SERVINGS

4 strips bacon, cut into 1-inch pieces
1 cup chopped onions
1 cup sliced mushrooms
1 cup wild rice, rinsed
3 stalks celery, chopped
1 teaspoon seasoned salt, optional
4½ cups chicken broth
Salt, pepper

MINTED APRICOT DOUBLE RICE SALAD

Rice salads are good additions for any portable feast. This one is festive enough to bring on a Fourth of July picnic supper.

Combine the apricots, triple sec, orange peel and juice in a small saucepan. Bring to a boil. Remove from the heat, set aside, and let cool completely. Place the pecans on a baking sheet and bake at 350 degrees until lightly browned. Cool completely.

Combine the apricots and any remaining liquid, wild and white rices, pecans, and mint leaves, tossing lightly. Chill thoroughly.

At serving time, toss again with the olive oil and season to taste with salt and pepper.

MAKES 6 TO 8 SERVINGS

1 cup finely chopped dried apricots
2 tablespoons triple sec
Grated peel and juice of 1 orange
1 cup pecan halves
1½ cups cooked and chilled wild rice
1½ cups cooked and chilled white rice, preferably cooked in chicken broth
¾ cup chopped mint leaves
2 tablespoons light olive oil
Salt, pepper

MEAT-FILLED RICE BALLS

The secret to these delicious snacks lies in the rice. The recipe came from chef Celestino Drago of Celestino Ristorante in Beverly Hills, who uses arborio rice to make them. If you can't find the rice in your supermarket, try any Italian or Mediterranean grocery.

Cook the rice in chicken broth to cover, adding more liquid as it is absorbed until all chicken broth is used and rice is tender. Let the rice stand 10 minutes to absorb excess moisture. Add the egg yolks, Parmesan cheese, and season to taste with salt. Mix well. Set aside.

Sauté the shallots with the veal in butter until the veal is crumbly and browned. Add wine and simmer until wine is absorbed. Add nutmeg, peas, and tomato sauce, and season to taste with salt and pepper. Simmer a few minutes until the liquid is absorbed. Set aside.

Combine the mozzarella and hard-cooked egg in a small bowl. Make a rice ball, using 2 tablespoons cooked rice. Make a cavity in the ball and place a scant tablespoon of the veal mixture, then a small amount of the mozzarella and egg mixture. Cover with another tablespoon rice and seal the cavity to make a ball or pyramid shape.

Dip the rice balls in the beaten egg and roll in bread crumbs. Heat 1½ inches olive oil in a skillet to 400 degrees or until very hot. Add the rice balls a few at a time to avoid overcrowding the pan. Fry until golden brown on all sides, about 3 minutes, turning often to brown evenly.

MAKES 8 RICE BALLS

5 ounces arborio rice

2 cups chicken broth

2 egg yolks

2 tablespoons grated Parmesan cheese

Salt

1½ teaspoons chopped shallots

2 ounces ground veal or beef

1½ teaspoons butter

½ cup dry white wine

Pinch nutmeg

1 tablespoon canned tiny peas

2 tablespoons canned tomato sauce or purée

Pepper

1 tablespoon diced mozzarella cheese

1 hard-cooked egg, chopped

1 egg, beaten

Fine dried bread crumbs

Olive oil for frying

CHICKEN COUSCOUS

Joaquim Splichal, who has been busy opening a new restaurant in Los Angeles, has always had a light touch with his food. This chicken and cilantro couscous is low both in calories and in fat. It's listed on the special gourmet diet menu for one of our hospitals.

Place the chicken in a steamer basket. Place the chicken stock, carrot, celery, onion, leek, turnip, and lemon halves in the bottom of the steamer and bring to a boil. Steam the chicken until tender, about 35 to 40 minutes. Remove and cool chicken.

Meanwhile, return the chicken broth to a boil in the steamer pot. Add the cilantro and red onion. Place the couscous in the rinsed steamer basket and cook the couscous until done, according to package directions.

Skin and bone the chicken. Slice the meat and the steamed vegetables. Discard the lemon. Arrange the chicken and vegetables over the couscous. Serve with cold tomato sauce.

MAKES 4 SERVINGS

1 (2- to 3-pound) chicken, cut up and skinned
3 cups defatted chicken stock
1 carrot, peeled
½ stalk celery, peeled
1 small onion, chopped
1 leek, rinsed well
1 turnip, peeled
1 lemon, halved
½ bunch cilantro, chopped
1 red onion
1½ cups couscous
Cold Tomato Sauce (recipe follows)

COLD TOMATO SAUCE

Dice the tomatoes and combine with the cilantro. Add the tomato juice and green onions.

8 plum tomatoes
1 bunch cilantro, chopped
1 (8-ounce) can tomato juice
1 bunch green onions, finely julienned

MEXICAN RICE

One of the reasons this sturdy rice dish tastes so good is that chef Michel Grobon from the Acapulco-Los Arcos restaurant in Los Angeles, who sent us this recipe, followed the Mexican tradition of using lard to sauté the onion and rice. Those watching their cholesterol intake can substitute any other fat at the expense of losing a little flavor.

Sauté the onion and rice in lard until lightly browned, about 6 to 10 minutes, stirring constantly. In a large saucepan combine the chicken broth, tomato juice, tomatoes, parsley, garlic, cumin, and salt and pepper. Bring to a boil. Add the broth to the rice. Cover and bake at 350 degrees for 20 to 30 minutes, or until rice is fluffy. Use a fork to mix the rice. Let stand 15 minutes before serving.

MAKES 6 TO 8 SERVINGS

1 large onion, chopped
2 cups long-grain rice
2 ounces lard or chicken fat
2 cups chicken broth
1 cup tomato juice
1 cup diced tomatoes
1 tablespoon chopped parsley
1 teaspoon minced garlic
Pinch ground cumin
1 teaspoon salt
Pinch white pepper

CARBONARA AL FRANCO

In this interesting version of carbonara from Little Joe's on Broadway in San Francisco, the ingredients may not be the traditional ones for this classic Italian favorite. But the result is definitely pleasing.

Heat the oil in a large skillet. Add the prosciutto, mushrooms, garlic, and olives. Sauté until the mushrooms are tender. Add the wine and broth and bring to a boil. Simmer over high heat until the liquid is reduced by half. Add parsley and season to taste with pepper. (Do not add salt.) Break the egg into the mushroom mixture and stir until egg is cooked. Add Parmesan cheese and mix well. Pour over cooked spaghetti and toss until mixed.

MAKES 2 TO 4 SERVINGS

2 tablespoons olive oil
1/2 cup ground or finely diced prosciutto
1 cup sliced mushrooms
1 teaspoon minced garlic
1/4 cup chopped pitted black olives
1/3 cup dry white wine
1/3 cup chicken broth
1 tablespoon chopped parsley
Pepper
1 egg
6 tablespoons grated Parmesan cheese
1/2 pound spaghetti, cooked

FETTUCCINE TATYANA

When Tony Bartholomew sent us this recipe, named for his Russian wife, she had not, at the time, been allowed to join him in this country. The recipe was a takeoff on his mother's fettuccine Alfredo using ingredients available in Moscow. The adaptation was a success as were his efforts in getting his wife the exit visas she needed to join him in California.

Heat 3 tablespoons of the butter and the olive oil in a skillet. Sauté the onion and garlic until tender. Add the clam juice, lemon juice, parsley, lemon peel, pepper, and bay leaves. Simmer until the liquid is reduced to about 1 cup. Remove bay leaves. Add the oysters and heat thoroughly. Cook the fettuccine according to package directions. Drain and keep in a warmed bowl.

Lightly beat the egg yolks and add to the sour cream. Add the remaining butter to oysters and melt through. Pour the sour cream mixture and oyster sauce over the fettuccine. Add half of the Parmesan cheese. Toss gently, adding the remaining cheese a small amount at a time until well blended. Season to taste with salt.

MAKES 6 SERVINGS

8 tablespoons butter
3 tablespoons olive oil
⅓ cup chopped onion
2 cloves garlic, minced
6 tablespoons clam juice
3 tablespoons lemon juice
1 tablespoon minced parsley
2 teaspoons grated lemon peel
¼ teaspoon black pepper
3 bay leaves
2 (3¾-ounce) cans smoked oysters, drained
1 pound green fettuccine
2 egg yolks
1⅓ cups sour cream
1 cup grated Parmesan cheese
Salt

LASAGNA ALLA PINA

Pina De Gaspardis, chef-owner of the Al Fogher restaurant in Rome, shared this trendy lasagna recipe when he visited Los Angeles during Cucina Italiana Week in 1987. He made his own pasta, cutting it in sheets large enough to fit a 13 × 9-inch pan. The recipe is easy, but if you aren't up to tackling this type of project, substitute cooked dried lasagna noodles.

Sauté the leeks in 2 tablespoons of the butter over medium-low heat until tender, about 5 minutes. Season lightly with pepper. Add 2 tablespoons of the red wine and cook until wine evaporates. Set aside.

Sauté the radicchio in the remaining 2 tablespoons butter until tender, about 3 minutes. Season lightly with pepper. Add the remaining 2 tablespoons red wine and cook until wine evaporates. Set aside.

Add ½ to ¾ cup béchamel sauce to the leeks and mix lightly. Separately add ½ to ¾ cup béchamel sauce to radicchio and mix lightly.

Place 1 sheet of the lasagna noodle dough—rolled wide enough to fit pan (or 4 packaged lasagna noodles)—in the bottom of a well-buttered 13 × 9-inch baking pan. Spread half the leek mixture over the noodles. Sprinkle with some Parmesan cheese. Top with one-third of the remaining béchamel sauce. Add half the radicchio mixture, spreading evenly. Dust with more cheese and cover with another layer of noodles.

Repeat layering. Cover with dough and spread with the remaining one-third béchamel sauce. Sprinkle with remaining cheese. Garnish with tomato slices and parsley. Bake at 350 degrees for 45 minutes, or until lasagna is golden in color. Let stand 10 minutes before cutting into squares.

MAKES 6 SERVINGS

Melt the butter in a saucepan. Add the flour, stirring until smooth. Gradually add 1½ quarts milk, stirring constantly until well blended. Bring to a boil, then reduce heat and continue to simmer, stirring, until creamy and smooth. Stir in salt to taste and ½ cup cheese and cook, stirring, until sauce is smooth and slightly thickened. If too thick, add more milk. If too thin, stir in more cheese.

Lightly beat the eggs and water. Place the flour on a board and make a well in the center. Add the egg-water mixture and incorporate it into the flour until a soft, pliable dough is formed. Roll out the dough with a pasta machine or by hand until it becomes too large to handle. Cut in half and roll each half ¼-inch thick. Cut into 4 (13 × 9-inch) rectangles.

3 leeks, sliced ¼-inch thick
4 tablespoons butter
Pepper
¼ cup red wine
2 radicchio, sliced ¼-inch thick
Béchamel Sauce (recipe follows)
4 (13 × 9-inch) sheets fresh Lasagna Noodle Dough (recipe follows), or 12 packaged lasagna noodles, cooked
1 to 1½ cups grated Parmesan cheese, preferably Reggiano
4 small or 3 medium tomatoes, sliced
Parsley

BÉCHAMEL SAUCE
½ cup butter
¾ cup flour
1½ quarts milk, approximately
Salt
½ to ¾ cup grated Parmesan cheese

LASAGNA NOODLE DOUGH
2 eggs
¼ cup water
½ pound semolina flour (about 2 cups)

HOT SHELLS STUFFED WITH SHRIMP

The tart, lemony flavor of fresh sorrel adds a delightful tang to the bay shrimp used to stuff large pasta shells in this easy luncheon or supper dish. Many markets now supply fresh sorrel in their fresh herb sections. If you can't find it, try substituting spinach leaves and adding some lemon juice to the shrimp filling.

Cook the pasta shells according to package directions. Drain well and keep warm.

Sauté the garlic and onion in olive oil just until tender. Add the shrimp and sauté 2 to 3 minutes longer, or until shrimp turn pink.

Stir in the sorrel. Fill the shells with the shrimp and sorrel mixture. Serve with lemon wedges.

MAKES 4 SERVINGS

12 large pasta shells
1 clove garlic, minced
1/4 cup finely chopped onion
2 tablespoons olive oil
1 pound small or bay shrimp, cleaned
1/2 cup finely chopped fresh sorrel
Lemon wedges

PEANUT NOODLES AND PORK

In 1987 reader Karen Nichols sent this Oriental-style pork and noodle recipe to our "My Best Recipe" column.

Cook the noodles in boiling water, then drain. Keep warm. Cut pork tenderloin into 1/8-inch-thick slices. In a medium bowl, mix the pork with 1/4 cup soy sauce and 1 tablespoon oil. Set aside.

Combine the peanut butter, sugar, hot pepper sauce, remaining 1/4 cup soy sauce, and 2/3 cup hot tap water in a small bowl until blended. Set aside.

Heat 3 tablespoons oil in a wok or 12-inch skillet over medium heat. Cook the green onions until tender. Turn the heat to high and cook the pork in its marinade until it loses its pink color, 2 to 3 minutes, stirring constantly. Remove the pan from the heat.

Add the noodles, peanut sauce, and spinach to mixture, tossing gently to mix well. Briefly heat until hot, if desired.

MAKES 4 TO 6 SERVINGS

1 (8-ounce) package wide egg noodles
1 (1 1/4-pound) pork tenderloin
1/2 cup soy sauce
Oil
2/3 cup chunky peanut butter
1 tablespoon sugar
1/2 to 1 teaspoon hot pepper sauce
3 green onions, sliced
1 small bunch spinach, coarsely sliced

ANGEL HAIR PASTA WITH RED AND GREEN PEPPERS

When Elka Gilmore, a chef whose fans are devoted to her, was at Camelions in West Los Angeles, she prepared this garlicky, sun-dried tomato and red and green pepper-laden pasta to the delight of all who sampled it. It's a recipe we are frequently asked to repeat.

Cook the pasta in boiling salted water just until tender. Drain. Meanwhile, melt the butter in a saucepan. Add olive oil and heat. Add the tomatoes, basil, parsley, garlic, and peppers, and sauté until heated through. Season to taste with salt and pepper.

Add to the drained pasta and toss to mix well. Top with Parmesan cheese.

MAKES 6 TO 8 SERVINGS

1 pound angel hair pasta
2 tablespoons unsalted butter
2 tablespoons olive oil
8 sun-dried tomatoes, packed in oil, finely chopped
¼ cup chopped fresh basil
¼ cup chopped parsley, leaves only
4 cloves garlic, minced
2 sweet red peppers, roasted, peeled, and cut julienne
2 green peppers, roasted, peeled, and cut julienne
Salt, pepper
¼ cup grated Parmesan cheese

PESTO CHICKEN PASTA

Cutting down on calories is rarely fun for anyone who likes to eat. That's why we were so pleased with this recipe, which was developed in our test kitchen for a story on quick, easy, and light entrées.

Poach, skin, and bone the chicken breast. Cut the meat into ½-inch cubes. Heat the pesto sauce, chicken, and dried tomatoes together in a small saucepan.

Cook the pasta according to package directions and drain. Toss the pasta with the pesto mixture and serve hot or chilled.

MAKES 6 SERVINGS

1 whole chicken breast, about 1 pound
½ cup Pesto Sauce (recipe follows)
¼ cup diced dry-pack dried tomatoes
8-ounces bowtie pasta

PESTO SAUCE
¼ cup olive oil
¼ cup fresh basil leaves, packed
2 tablespoons toasted pine nuts
1 clove garlic

Combine the oil, basil, pine nuts, and garlic in blender container and blend until creamy.

MAKES ABOUT ½ CUP SAUCE

SPINACH LINGUINE WITH TOMATOES, PINE NUTS, AND OLIVES

Greens, a vegetarian restaurant run by the Zen Center in San Francisco, has as wide a following among non-vegetarians as vegetarians. Chef Annie Somerville gave us this recipe.

Marinate the vine-ripened tomatoes, pear and cherry tomatoes in ½ cup olive oil and half of the basil. Add the garlic, balsamic vinegar, and salt and pepper to taste. Set aside.

Cook the linguine in boiling salted water about 2 minutes, or until barely tender. Drain. Toss with the tomato mixture. Add the pine nuts, olives, and remaining olive oil and basil. Correct seasoning with salt and pepper and a few splashes of vinegar to taste. Serve in warm pasta bowls. Sprinkle with Parmesan cheese.

MAKES 8 SERVINGS

2 medium vine-ripened tomatoes, blanched, peeled, seeded, and diced into ½-inch pieces

12 yellow pear tomatoes, cut into halves

12 cherry tomatoes, cut into halves

1 cup fruity olive oil

1 bunch basil leaves, thinly sliced

4 medium cloves garlic, minced

1 teaspoon balsamic vinegar

Salt, pepper

1 pound fresh spinach linguine

¼ cup toasted pine nuts

¼ cup pitted small black Niçoise olives

1 cup grated Parmesan cheese, preferably Reggiano

FISH AND SHELLFISH

By and large, shellfish, salmon, trout, sole, and a few other fish were found on most restaurant menus as we entered the eighties, but that was about it. The home cook fared no better. Shellfish such as shrimp, crabs, and scallops were readily available at markets, but the array of either fresh water or ocean fish was limited. The fact was, we simply didn't eat much fish.

Shellfish had always been popular. Cioppinos, the California version of bouillabaise, were favorite choices for winter meals. We liked Chinese sweet-and-sour shrimp and shrimp and crab salads. But we really weren't very imaginative in the ways we prepared either shellfish or fish.

Then came news of that bugaboo, cholesterol, and it did as much for fish as it did to eggs. As our eating habits changed, and we moved toward lighter meals and smaller portions in the mid-eighties, we wanted more fish and shellfish on our menus. And we wanted more variety.

Swordfish, catfish, imported seafood such as orange roughy, and other fish about which we knew little began to appear in our markets and on restaurant menus. Green-tipped mussels from New Zealand and giant prawns from Indonesia joined other shellfish at the fish counter.

It followed that as we ate more fish, we began to search out new methods of preparation. We grilled fish over mesquite. We smoked it over grapevines. And we wanted to know how other cultures prepared it. Seviches and other Mexican-style methods of preparing fish were familiar to us. So when new Southern Californians from the Philippines, Thailand, China, and Japan introduced us to their methods of cooking fish and shellfish, we were instant fans. Seafood soon became a regular several times a week on home menus.

By the end of the decade, it had become obvious that fish was going to be in demand for some years to come.

POACHED SALMON CELESTE

Odette Berry, chef-owner of Another Season, a seafood restaurant in Boston, shared this recipe for a delicious poached salmon when she spoke at the Los Angeles Sea Fare in 1985. The basic recipe is simple, and our tasters liked it even better when the salmon steaks were stuffed with some shiitake mushrooms.

Using an enamel or stainless steel pan, reduce the fish stock to about half. Set aside.

Bone, skin, and trim the salmon steaks. Form medallions by shaping the fish into circles. Secure each steak with oiled wood picks. Combine the lemon juice to taste, Madeira, and fish stock in a pan with the butter and heat until warm. Add the salmon and gently poach for 7 to 10 minutes, or until just cooked. (Do not overcook as fish continues to cook upon standing.) Remove fish from liquid and keep warm.

Turn up the heat and add the orange peel. Reduce the liquid to ¼ cup. Add the crème fraîche and continue to reduce until sauce has a light syrupy consistency. Season to taste with salt, if desired.

Arrange the salmon medallions on a platter and spoon over the sauce. Garnish with orange and lemon slices and watercress.

MAKES 4 SERVINGS

Variations: Stuff the salmon steaks with a vegetable mousse or purée, or with some sautéed shiitake, shrimp, or crawfish. Surround or cover the salmon with finely julienned leeks and carrots, steamed or sautéed. Or, wrap the medallions in lettuce leaves and steam in Chinese steamer.

1 cup **Fish Stock** *(recipe follows)*

4 (8-ounce) salmon steaks

1 to 2 tablespoons lemon juice

3 tablespoons Madeira

2 tablespoons butter, softened

2 teaspoons grated orange peel

½ cup crème fraîche (or use 1 cup whipping cream reduced to ½ cup)

Salt, optional

Orange and lemon slices and watercress, for garnish

For a clear stock, remove the bloody parts from the fish bones. Melt the butter in a large stainless steel or enamel pot over medium heat. Add the onion and celery, gently sautéing until tender. Do not brown. Add the bones, parsley, peppercorns, bay leaf, mace, and enough cold water to cover. Bring to a boil and boil 5 minutes. Skim off residue at top and lower heat. Cover and simmer gently for 40 minutes. Remove bones and strain stock through a clean cheesecloth.

MAKES ABOUT 4 QUARTS

FISH STOCK

3 pounds fish bones, without heads

2 tablespoons butter

1 onion, peeled and thinly sliced

3 stalks celery, sliced

Few sprigs parsley

3 whole peppercorns

½ bay leaf

Pinch mace

GRAVAD LAX (SCANDINAVIAN SALMON)

We have run Scandia restaurant's recipe for gravad lax many times in the past. But it has only been in recent years that we have told readers how to crisp the skin to serve with this long-lived Hollywood Danish restaurant's specialty.

Thaw the salmon, if frozen. Cut salmon in halves lengthwise. Remove bones. Combine the salt, sugar, and peppercorns. Rub half the spice mixture over one salmon half and place the fish, skin side down, in a baking dish. Spread dill over. Rub other half of salmon with remaining spice mixture and place, skin side up, on first salmon half. Cover with foil. Place a plate on top of the fish and a weight on top of the plate. Refrigerate 48 hours. Turn fish over every 12 hours, separating fillets slightly to baste with pan liquid. When ready to serve, scrape away the dill and seasonings. Place fillets, skin side down, on a cutting board. Cut salmon diagonally in thin slices away from skin. Serve cold with mustard dill sauce and sprinkle with crisp skin.

MAKES 12 TO 16 APPETIZER SERVINGS

1 (2-pound) piece salmon
3 tablespoons salt
3 tablespoons sugar
1 tablespoon crushed peppercorns
1/2 bunch dill
Mustard Dill Sauce *(recipe follows)*
Crisp Skin *(recipe follows)*

Combine mustard, sugar, vinegar, and dry mustard. Slowly beat in oil until thick. Stir in dill. Chill.

MAKES 3/4 CUP

MUSTARD DILL SAUCE
1/4 cup Dijon-style mustard
3 tablespoons sugar
2 tablespoons vinegar
1 teaspoon dry mustard
1/3 cup oil
3 tablespoons chopped dill

After slicing salmon flesh, reserve skin. Cut into narrow strips and cook in very hot deep oil until crisp.

CRISP SKIN
Salmon skin
Oil for deep frying

SWORDFISH WITH MUSTARD SAUCE

Swordfish is a firm enough fish to stand up to the spiciness of the mustard sauce. This recipe came from chef Christian Chemin at the Surf & Sand Hotel in Laguna Beach.

Combine the shallots and wine in a saucepan. Bring to a boil, then simmer over medium-high heat until the wine is reduced by one-third. Blend in the whipping cream, mustards, and season to taste with salt and pepper.

Broil the swordfish 4 inches from the heat source until browned on both sides and the flesh flakes easily with a fork. To serve, arrange the fish on a platter, and spoon over it some of the mustard sauce.

MAKES 4 SERVINGS

½ teaspoon finely chopped shallots

3 tablespoons dry white wine

1 cup whipping cream

½ teaspoon Dijon mustard

1 tablespoon Pommery or Meaux mustard

Salt, pepper

4 (6-ounce) swordfish fillets

ORANGE ROUGHY IN ORANGE-MINT-YOGURT SAUCE

Orange roughy, a firm fish imported from New Zealand, has won a place on many Southern California dinner tables. The orange-mint-yogurt sauce that accompanies it in this recipe provides just the right amount of tart sweetness to complement the fish perfectly.

Brush the fish fillets with olive oil and sprinkle lightly with ginger and garlic. Broil 3 to 4 inches from the heat source for about 5 minutes, or until fish flakes when tested with a fork.

Meanwhile stir together the yogurt, orange peel, and mint leaves. Season to taste with white pepper. To serve, spoon the yogurt sauce over fish or serve separately.

MAKES 6 SERVINGS

1½ pounds orange roughy fillets

1 teaspoon olive oil

½ teaspoon minced ginger root

½ teaspoon minced garlic

1 (8-ounce) container plain nonfat yogurt

1 teaspoon grated orange peel

1 teaspoon minced fresh mint leaves

White pepper

FISH MACADAMIA WITH CHIVE BEURRE BLANC

With more and more macadamia nut orchards being planted in the Temecula area where the Callaway Vineyard and Winery is located, no one was surprised when the winery came up with this excellent fish recipe in which diced macadamias were added to the breading. The chardonnay used in the sauce also makes a most companionable beverage.

Rinse the fish and pat dry. Combine the milk, salt, and pepper in a shallow dish. In another shallow dish, combine the macadamia nuts, bread crumbs, parsley, and paprika. Dip the fish in the milk mixture, then coat both sides with the macadamia mixture. Place in a single layer in a well-greased baking pan.

Melt the butter and combine with the lemon juice and chardonnay. Drizzle over the fish. Bake at 350 degrees until fish flakes easily with fork, 10 to 15 minutes. Serve with the beurre blanc.

MAKES 4 TO 6 SERVINGS

6 (6-ounce) fresh fish steaks or fillets
1/3 cup milk
1/2 teaspoon salt
Pinch freshly ground black pepper
1/2 cup diced macadamia nuts
2/3 cup fine dried bread crumbs
2 tablespoons finely chopped parsley
1/2 teaspoon paprika
1/4 cup unsalted butter
1 tablespoon lemon juice
1 tablespoon chardonnay
Chive Beurre Blanc (recipe follows)

CHIVE BEURRE BLANC

1 cup unsalted butter
1/4 cup finely chopped shallots
1/4 cup chardonnay
1/4 cup whipping cream
1/4 teaspoon white pepper
1 cup finely snipped fresh chives

Melt 1 tablespoon butter in a skillet over medium heat. Add the shallots and sauté until limp and transparent. Stir in the chardonnay. Very gradually add the cream, whisking constantly. Continue to cook over low heat, stirring occasionally. Add the remaining butter, a little at a time. Add the pepper. Blend well and heat through, but do not boil. Stir in the chives at the last moment to retain the color.

MAKES ABOUT 1½ CUPS

BROILED SCALLOPS WITH GINGER SAUCE

*Nick Dockmonish, executive chef at the New Otani Hotel and Gardens in the center
of Los Angeles Little Tokyo, came up with this simple sea scallop dish for a summertime
fish feature. The sauce can be made in advance and reheated briefly while the
scallops are broiling.*

Combine the mirin, sake, soy sauce, water, ginger, and brown sugar in a saucepan. Boil until reduced to ⅔ cup. Dip each scallop lightly in sesame oil and place on a rack in a broiler pan. Broil 1½ minutes on each side. Line 4 plates with the sauce. Place 3 scallops on each plate and garnish with chopped chives.

MAKES 4 SERVINGS

½ cup mirin
½ cup sake
½ cup soy sauce
½ cup water
2 teaspoons grated ginger root
2 tablespoons brown sugar, packed
12 sea scallops
Sesame oil
Chopped chives, for garnish

SHRIMP IN LIME SAUCE

The old Stratton's Grill in Westwood used lime juice and vermouth to enhance sautéed shrimp.

◻

Heat the oil until hot. Add the shrimp, and sauté until they turn pink and are almost cooked. Drain off excess oil. Add the shallots, garlic, vermouth, and lime juice, and bring to a boil. Boil vigorously about 30 seconds to reduce the liquid.

Remove the saucepan from the heat and stir in the butter until the sauce is smooth. (Care must be taken so that the pan is hot enough to warm butter immediately, but not so hot as to cause the sauce to curdle.) Sprinkle with salt and pepper to taste. Garnish with parsley and chives.

MAKES 6 TO 8 SERVINGS

2 tablespoons oil

12 to 16 shrimp (36 size), peeled and deveined

2 medium shallots, minced

2 cloves garlic, minced

1 cup dry vermouth

Juice of 3 limes

¼ to ⅓ cup whipped butter or margarine, at room temperature

Salt, pepper

Chopped parsley, for garnish

Chopped chives, for garnish

SHRIMP DE JONGHE

Always a popular party dish, shrimp de jonghe can be prepared ahead to the point where it's ready for the oven and then refrigerated.

◻

Melt ½ cup butter in a skillet. Add ¾ cup of the bread crumbs, green onions, garlic, parsley, chervil, thyme, nutmeg, mace, vinegar, and sherry. Spread alternate layers of the bread crumb mixture and shrimp into a well-greased, 1-quart baking dish or into individual baking dishes.

Melt the remaining 2 tablespoons butter in a skillet, add the remaining ½ cup bread crumbs, and toss well. Sprinkle over the casserole or baking dishes and bake at 375 degrees for 20 minutes.

MAKES 6 SERVINGS

½ cup plus 2 tablespoons butter or margarine

1¼ cups fine dried bread crumbs

¼ cup minced green onions

2 cloves garlic, minced

2 tablespoons minced parsley

1 teaspoon dried chervil, optional

1 teaspoon crushed dried thyme leaves

¼ teaspoon ground nutmeg

Pinch ground mace

1 teaspoon tarragon vinegar

½ cup sherry

1 pound cooked, peeled shrimp

SHRIMP WITH GREEN PEPPERCORN SAUCE

Joe Allen's in Hollywood supplied us with this spicy treatment for shrimp.

Peel shrimp, leaving tails intact. Heat the oil and butter in large pan. Add the shrimp and sauté 4 to 5 minutes, or until shrimp turn pink. Remove shrimp and keep warm.

Deglaze the pan with brandy and add the shallot, garlic, and green peppercorns. Reduce the liquid by half or until slightly thickened. Add whipping cream. Bring to a boil and boil until reduced by half. Remove from the heat. Whisk in the sour cream. Season to taste with salt and white pepper.

Return the shrimp to the pan and toss to coat well with the sauce. Fold in the dill.

MAKES 6 SERVINGS

24 large shrimp
1½ tablespoons olive oil
1½ tablespoons butter
¼ cup brandy
1 shallot, minced
¼ teaspoon minced garlic
2½ tablespoons green peppercorns
1 cup whipping cream
¼ cup sour cream
Salt
White pepper
1 bunch dill, chopped

SHRIMP ONO NUI

This Hawaiian-style shrimp dish came from the Safari Steakhouse restaurant in the Sheraton Waikiki Hotel in Honolulu. The shrimp are heavily coated with shredded coconut before being deep-fried and served with a pineapple-flavored cocktail sauce. Ono nui means "very good" in Hawaiian and this dish definitely lives up to its name.

Roll the shrimp in flour seasoned with salt, then dip in the beaten egg. Roll the shrimp in the coconut, covering thoroughly. Deep-fry the shrimp in oil heated to about 350 degrees until browned and cooked through, about 3 to 4 minutes. Drain on paper towels. Mix the cocktail sauce with the crushed pineapple. Serve the shrimp with the sauce on the side.

MAKES 8 SERVINGS

24 raw jumbo shrimp, peeled
¼ to ½ cup flour
Salt
1 to 2 eggs, beaten
1½ cups shredded coconut
Oil for deep frying
1 cup bottled cocktail sauce
¼ cup crushed pineapple

CRACKERJACK SHRIMP

At Genghis Cohen's in Hollywood is one of the best oriental-style shrimp dishes. The ginger-flavored cocktail sauce gives a burst of flavor.

Shell and devein the shrimp. Rinse in cold water and pat dry. Place the shrimp in the marinade for 30 minutes.

Put the cornstarch in a bowl. Coat the shrimp well with the cornstarch, using a colander to remove any excess.

Heat the wok until very hot, then add 2 cups oil. Heat to 375 degrees. Add half the shrimp to the hot oil and cook 2 minutes. Remove with a strainer; drain. Add remaining shrimp and cook until golden. Drain.

Drain the oil from the wok (reserving for future use). Add the ginger sauce to the hot wok and bring to a boil. Add the shrimp and toss to coat evenly with the sauce. Pour the shrimp mixture over the lettuce.

MAKES 6 SERVINGS

1 pound shrimp (41 to 50)
Marinade (recipe follows)
1 cup cornstarch
2 cups cottonseed or peanut oil
Ginger Sauce (recipe follows)
2 cups shredded lettuce

Combine the wine, oil, salt, beaten egg white, and cornstarch.

MARINADE

1 tablespoon Shaoshing wine or sherry
1/2 tablespoon oil
1/2 teaspoon salt
1 small egg white, beaten
1 tablespoon cornstarch

Combine the catsup, chili sauce, chicken broth, sugar, garlic, and ginger.

GINGER SAUCE

1 tablespoon catsup
1/2 teaspoon chili sauce
1 tablespoon chicken broth
2 tablespoons sugar
3 cloves garlic, thinly sliced
1/2 teaspoon chopped ginger

CHINESE POPCORN (SWEET AND PUNGENT SHRIMP)

A reader who requested the recipe for a sweet and pungent shrimp from the Panda Inn in Pasadena won the everlasting thanks of our tasting panel. Because it's as impossible to eat just one of these as it is to eat a single kernel of popcorn, the recipe is often called Chinese popcorn.

Peel and devein the shrimp. Slice in halves lengthwise. Rinse well and pat dry. Add the egg white to the shrimp and mix well. Mix 1½ tablespoons cornstarch with salt and add to the shrimp. Stir to coat well. Add 1½ tablespoons oil and mix well again. Place the shrimp in a bowl and refrigerate at least 2 hours.

Remove the shrimp and dust with the remaining cornstarch. Shrimp should be dry to the touch.

Heat the remaining oil in a large wok to 350 to 375 degrees. Fry the shrimp 1½ to 2 minutes until crisp, being careful to separate them with a long-handled wooden spoon or chopsticks to prevent sticking. It may be necessary to fry the shrimp in several batches. When done, remove the shrimp with a slotted spoon and drain well.

Combine the shrimp and the sweet and pungent sauce and toss quickly to coat. Immediately turn out onto a platter and sprinkle with finely chopped green onions.

MAKES 4 SERVINGS

1 pound (36 to 40) raw shrimp
½ egg white, beaten
1 cup cornstarch
½ teaspoon salt
3 to 4 cups oil for deep frying
Sweet and Pungent Sauce *(recipe follows)*
Green onions, for garnish

Combine the sugar, catsup, vinegar, and salt, and set aside. Mix the sherry and cornstarch and set aside.

Heat the oil in a wok. Add the garlic, ginger, green onion, red pepper, and zests of lemon and orange; cook 30 seconds. Stir in the sugar-catsup mixture. Immediately add the sherry mixture and cook until slightly thickened.

SWEET AND PUNGENT SAUCE

4½ tablespoons sugar
4½ tablespoons catsup
¼ cup vinegar
½ teaspoon salt
1 tablespoon sherry
½ teaspoon cornstarch
1 teaspoon oil
2 large cloves garlic, minced
¾ teaspoon minced fresh ginger root
1 tablespoon chopped green onion
1 teaspoon crushed red pepper
1 teaspoon lemon zest
1 teaspoon orange zest

SCAMPI SPUMANTI

The Magia Caffe Italiano on Melrose in Los Angeles provided us with this interesting treatment for butterflied shrimp. The recipe is designed to serve one, but can easily be increased.

Cook the fettuccine in a large pot of boiling salted water until barely tender. Remove the fettuccine to a colander, but retain the pasta water in the pan and keep hot. Heat a skillet and add olive oil, garlic, thyme, oregano, and crushed chiles. When the mixture sizzles add the shrimp and sauté until the shrimp turn pink. Remove the shrimp and set aside. Add sherry to the skillet, ignite, and boil until reduced by half. Add the butter and tomatoes, and cook, tossing tomatoes in the pan until heated through. Return the shrimp to the skillet. Add the arugula and basil, and season to taste with salt and pepper.

Meanwhile, return the pasta water to a boil. Add the fettuccine to the water and boil 10 seconds to reheat. Drain and place on a heated plate. Arrange the scampi mixture on top of the fettuccine, with the tails upward.

MAKES 1 SERVING

2 ounces fettuccine

3 tablespoons virgin olive oil

1½ teaspoons minced garlic

1 teaspoon fresh thyme leaves

1 teaspoon fresh oregano leaves

Pinch crushed dried red chiles

6 large shrimp, peeled, deveined, and butterflied

3 ounces dry sherry (6 tablespoons)

3 tablespoons unsalted butter

3 medium Roma tomatoes, cut into ¼ inch cubes

1 (½-ounce) package arugula

3 large fresh basil leaves

Salt, pepper

STUFFED SCAMPI

This impressive shrimp recipe was given to us back in 1982 by Boccaccio Ristorante in Westlake Village. It's a great party dish, but don't save it just for company. Give the family a break and let them sample it on occasion.

Peel and clean the shrimp. Butterfly by cutting in half lengthwise, but not all the way through. Sauté the onion and celery in butter until golden. Add the shrimp and sauté 5 to 7 minutes, just until the shrimp are cooked. Remove from the heat. Add the garlic, thyme, parsley, tomato sauce, wine, and Parmesan cheese. Mix to blend, then add the bread crumbs. Sauté 3 minutes. Cool.

Arrange the shrimp, butterfly fashion, cut side up, in a baking pan. Pile stuffing on each shrimp to cover completely. Brush with melted butter. Bake at 400 degrees for 10 to 15 minutes, or until shrimp are cooked through. Serve 2 or 3 shrimp per person.

MAKES 4 TO 6 SERVINGS

12 large shrimp

1 onion, chopped

2 cups chopped celery

½ cup butter or margarine

¾ pound tiny shrimp

¼ teaspoon minced garlic

¼ teaspoon dried thyme

1 tablespoon chopped parsley

2 tablespoons tomato sauce

3 tablespoons white wine

1 cup grated Parmesan cheese

1 cup dried bread crumbs

2 tablespoons melted butter or margarine

SALT-BAKED PRAWNS

This four-ingredient shrimp dish couldn't be simpler to make. Fung Lum restaurant's chef, W. K. So, showed us how to twice-cook the shrimp to make the shells crisp and crunchy. And, yes, you eat the shells and all in this easy shrimp dish.

Trim the legs from the shrimp but do not remove the shells. Wash well and place in a colander to drain for 15 minutes. Turn the shrimp into a bowl, add cornstarch, and mix. Heat the oil in a wok until very hot. Add the shrimp and fry 50 seconds or until 80 percent cooked. Drain the shrimp and the oil, leaving only a light coating of oil.

Quickly reheat the wok to a high temperature. Add the shrimp and the salt. Cook, stirring, 40 seconds. Turn out onto a heated platter.

MAKES 6 SERVINGS

1 pound unshelled medium shrimp

2 tablespoons cornstarch

5 cups oil for deep frying

1 teaspoon salt

PRATAAD LOM (PRAWN ROLLS)

When Times *writer Barbara Hansen attended a Thai cooking class in Bangkok, it was hardly surprising she found the food there quite different from the Thai food available in the Los Angeles area. We were able to duplicate this typical shellfish dish with ease by looking for the needed ingredients in our local Asian markets.*

◻

Sprinkle or brush the bean curd sheets with water and allow to soften. Shell and clean the shrimp, retaining the tails. Make slits along the inner curves so the shrimp will lie flat. Combine the coriander root, garlic, and pepper in a mortar and pound to make a paste. Stir in the fish sauce. Combine the mixture with the shrimp and marinate 5 minutes.

Cut the bean curd sheet into 3-inch squares. Place 1 shrimp on each square near the top, allowing the tail to extend over the edge. Fold the top of the square over the shrimp, and roll up tightly. Brush the lower edge of the bean curd sheet with egg yolk to seal. Set the rolls on a rack until ready to fry. Deep-fry in hot oil until golden brown. Drain on paper towels. Serve with bowls of plum sauce or *Sriracha* sauce for dipping.

MAKES ABOUT 2 DOZEN

Note: Sriracha, which is Thai hot sauce, and bean curd sheets are available in Asian markets.

Combine the water, sugar, rice vinegar, salt, and whole plums in a small saucepan. Bring to a boil and boil until liquid is reduced to ¾ cup. Remove the plums and cool sauce to room temperature.

Dried bean curd sheets

1 pound shrimp, with heads attached

1 teaspoon coriander root

1 teaspoon minced garlic

1 teaspoon white pepper

1 tablespoon fish sauce or soy sauce

2 egg yolks, beaten

Oil for deep frying

Plum Sauce *(recipe follows) or bottled* **Sriracha** *chile sauce*

PLUM SAUCE

1 cup water

1 cup sugar

1½ tablespoons rice vinegar

¼ teaspoon salt

6 Chinese dried preserved plums

CALIFORNIA PAELLA

Juan Jose, the original chef-owner of La Masia in Beverly Hills, served this Americanized version of paella to restaurant customers. So that a crisp crust forms, be sure not to stir the paella after the rice has been added. Paella does need to be watched carefully, however, as it can burn easily if not removed from the heat at the proper time.

Heat the olive oil in paellera or 12- to 14-inch skillet or flat, flameproof casserole. Add the chicken and sauté until browned, turning often. Remove the chicken and keep warm. Add the lobster to the pan and sauté 3 to 4 minutes, or until golden brown. Remove from pan and keep warm. Add the pork to pan and sauté 4 minutes, or until browned. Remove pork from pan and keep warm. Add the sausage and sauté until browned. Remove and keep warm.

For the paella tomato base (*sofrito*), add the onion and red pepper to the remaining oil in the pan. Sauté 3 minutes, or until tender. Add the tomatoes, garlic, and parsley. Sauté until slightly thickened. Add rice. Sauté until the grains are translucent. Add the boiling broth, saffron, and pepper, and season with salt, stirring well.

Place the chicken, lobster, pork, chorizo, clams, shrimps, scallops, and crab over the rice. Reduce the heat and simmer, covered, 30 minutes, or until the rice is tender but firm. Do not stir paella after it begins to cook.

Remove the pan from the heat and add the peas and pimientos, but do not stir. Cover loosely with foil. Let stand 8 to 10 minutes. Garnish with lemon wedges and parsley sprigs.

MAKES 12 SERVINGS

Note: If necessary, Polish or any other smoked pork sausage (but not Mexican chorizo) may be substituted for Spanish chorizo.

½ cup olive oil

1 (2-pound) chicken, cut in 12 pieces

1 (1½- to 2-pound) lobster or small lobster tails

¼ pound lean boneless pork, cut in ½-inch cubes

½ pound Spanish chorizo

1 large onion, cut julienne

1 large sweet red or green pepper, cut in thin strips

2 medium tomatoes, chopped

1 tablespoon finely chopped garlic

½ cup chopped parsley

3 cups medium- or short-grain rice

6 cups boiling chicken broth

¼ teaspoon ground saffron

½ teaspoon black pepper

Salt

12 clams or cherrystone clams

12 small or medium shrimp

½ pound scallops

½ pound crab legs with shell, cut in 1-inch pieces

½ cup cooked peas

½ cup chopped roasted fresh or canned pimiento

12 lemon wedges, for garnish

Parsley sprigs, for garnish

MARINATED GREEN MUSSELS

The opalescent green mussels now being imported from New Zealand have developed quite a following among those who have tried them. As that island nation's aquiculture industry grows, these large shellfish are becoming more sought after in this country. We found that a touch of ginger root added a piquant flavor to this tangy appetizer.

Scrub the mussels under cold running water with a brush, scraping off the beards. Discard any opened mussel shells that don't close when touched. Place the mussels on a rack over boiling water in a large pan or steamer. Cover and steam about 5 minutes, or until mussel shells open. Discard any unopened shells.

Drain and shell the mussels, retaining the deepest shell half of each. Set aside reserved shells; place the mussels in a small deep bowl. Add the lemon juice and olive oil, stirring to coat well. Add the ginger root, red pepper, and onions, tossing lightly. Season to taste with pepper. Cover and refrigerate several hours, stirring occasionally.

To serve, toss mussels to coat well and place one mussel on each shell half. Top with several sprigs of vegetables and ginger root. Sprinkle with a small amount of marinade.

MAKES ABOUT 6 APPETIZER SERVINGS

18 green mussels

2 tablespoons lemon juice

5 tablespoons olive oil

1 tablespoon peeled and slivered ginger root

1/4 sweet red pepper, cut in very thin strips

4 green onions, white part only, cut in very thin strips

Pepper

MUSSELS WITH ARTICHOKES, CORN, AND MÂCHE IN HERB SAUCE

When Roy Yamaguchi was chef at the old 385 North restaurant, he took advantage of mussel season to serve this elegant herb-flavored shellfish dish. It's a real winner with mussels, but don't hesitate to substitute other shellfish such as shrimp, oysters, crabs, or clams when mussels aren't available.

Cook the onion, carrots, celery, and garlic in oil until the onion is translucent. Add the wine and water; bring to a boil. Add the mussels and cook until the shells barely open. Shell the mussels. Set aside in a covered bowl.

Strain the pan liquids and reduce to about ⅓ cup. Add whipping cream and simmer until reduced to about 1½ cups. Reserve.

Slice the artichoke bottoms and place in a bowl with the basil, parsley, tarragon, and chives. Cut the kernels from the corn and add to the artichoke mixture. Stir into the cream sauce and bring to a boil. Add the mussels, and cook until tender, making sure not to overcook mussels.

Arrange the mâche on a large platter. Pour over the mussels and sauce. Serve at once.

MAKES 4 SERVINGS

½ cup chopped onion

½ cup chopped carrots

½ cup chopped celery

3 whole cloves garlic

¼ cup oil

1 cup wine

3 cups water

30 mussels

2 cups whipping cream

3 artichoke bottoms, cooked

½ teaspoon chopped fresh basil

½ teaspoon chopped fresh parsley

½ teaspoon chopped fresh tarragon

½ teaspoon chopped fresh chives

1 ear corn

3 cups mâche

SAN PEDRO CIOPPINO

Grant Savage, executive chef at Cigo's, an old-time restaurant in San Pedro, won a Fisherman's Fiesta cioppino contest with this recipe in 1982. The recipe was created by the restaurant's original owner, a Yugoslav named Cigo, who first served the rich fish stew to customers over thirty years ago.

Sauté the onions, parsley, and garlic in oil in a large Dutch oven or saucepan until the onions are tender. Add oregano and basil, and season to taste with salt and white pepper. Cook, stirring, a few minutes to blend flavors. Stir in the vinegar and wine. Simmer 5 minutes.

Drain and chop the tomatoes, reserving liquid. Stir the tomatoes into the onion mixture and simmer 5 minutes. Add the reserved tomato liquid and simmer 15 minutes longer. Add the fish, crab meat, squid, scallops, shrimp, and clams. Simmer 10 to 15 minutes until the clams open and the fish and shellfish are tender but not dry.

MAKES 6 TO 8 SERVINGS

2 onions, chopped

1 bunch parsley, cleaned and chopped, stems discarded

6 cloves garlic, minced

¼ cup oil

1 tablespoon dried oregano

1 tablespoon dried basil

Salt, white pepper

½ cup red wine vinegar

1 cup chablis

2 (1-pound) cans tomatoes

1 pound fresh fish of any type, cut into pieces

1 pound crab meat

2 cleaned squid, cut into strips

1 pound scallops

1 pound large shrimp

1 dozen clams

CIOPPINO

Scoma's, an Italian restaurant on San Francisco's Fisherman's Wharf, makes a smashing cioppino. This rich fish stew has long been popular along the California coast.

Heat the oil in a saucepan. Add the garlic and sauté just until browned. Add the onion, ¼ cup wine, bay leaves, and oregano. Cook 10 minutes over low heat. Add the crushed tomatoes and sugar. Season to taste with salt. Simmer 20 minutes, adding more wine if necessary. Add the crab, clams, prawns, shrimp, and crab meat. Cook until the clams open, about 10 to 15 minutes.

MAKES 6 TO 8 SERVINGS

¼ cup olive oil

1 tablespoon chopped garlic

1 onion, chopped

¼ cup sauterne, approximately

6 bay leaves

1 tablespoon dried oregano

4 (1-pound) cans whole peeled
   tomatoes, crushed

2 tablespoons sugar

Salt

1 large crab, cracked

8 clams

8 prawns

½ pound bay shrimp

¼ pound crab meat

POULTRY

We've eaten a lot of chicken in the past ten years, thanks partially to the impact of our concern over cholesterol in the diet, and also to the fact that chicken cooks quickly.

We also ate more turkey and duck than we used to, although we saved duck for special occasions.

Home-fried chicken almost disappeared from the scene; it was too easy to buy at take-outs. When we cooked at home, grilled chicken and simple sautés fitted in with our desire to cut calories and reduce our fat intake. We discovered how much difference using fresh tarragon or sweet basil or oregano could make in the flavor of chicken and how lemon juice could help eliminate the need for salt.

Fresh salsas or reduced vegetable sauces were our choices for simply grilled chicken rather than cream sauces. We also liked chicken and turkey in fajitas or in an exotic, but fast, stir-fry and in pasta dishes. And we ate so many chicken wing appetizers, supermarket butchers finally began cutting them apart for us.

By the mid-eighties, turkey parts, mainly the breast, were frequent choices for dinner and brown-bag lunches. And because we ate out so much, we soon learned how good duck could taste other than simply roasted.

We converted family recipes that called for beef and pork to chicken or turkey. We removed the skin from chicken and used a nonstick pan to help reduce the calories. We also learned that steaming a chicken breast cooked it to perfection.

As the eighties wound down, some of the wonderful old chicken casseroles our mothers used to make enjoyed a resurgence in popularity. Chicken and biscuits, chicken and dumplings, and chicken hash all began to reappear on dinner tables. Home cooking was back with a vengeance, and poultry of all kinds seemed destined to remain as major contributors to our menus for many years.

CHICKEN CHARLESTON

The delicate herbed lemon-butter flavor of this simple chicken entrée from the Ritz Grill in Pasadena fits nicely into the lighter menus that have become a norm. The speed with which this dish can be prepared is also a plus for a busy cook.

Brush the chicken breasts with olive oil and sprinkle with rosemary. Season with salt and pepper. Place under a hot broiler or on a hot grill and cook 3 to 4 minutes, or until just cooked.

Combine the white wine and shallots in a saucepan and cook over high heat until liquid is reduced by half. Add the butter, lemon juice, parsley, and salt and pepper to taste. When butter is partially melted, remove from the heat and beat to thicken slightly. Pour some of the sauce over the chicken breasts and serve the remainder with the chicken.

MAKES 6 SERVINGS

12 chicken breast halves, skinned
½ cup extra-virgin olive oil
¼ cup chopped fresh rosemary
Salt, pepper
6 tablespoons dry white wine
2 shallots, minced
½ cup butter
Juice of 2 medium lemons
¼ cup chopped Italian parsley

CHICKEN WITH GARLIC

Garlic lovers, arise! Here's your chance to emulate the skills of one of the West's finest young chefs and indulge your hankering for the "stinkin' rose" at the same time. In 1984 Spago's Wolfgang Puck gave us this recipe for garlicky chicken that is as aromatic as it is tasty.

If using whole chickens, halve chickens and bone completely except for wing joint. If only using breasts, bone completely. Place the heads of garlic in water to cover in a small saucepan and bring to a boil. Drain. Peel the garlic and cut each clove into paper-thin slices. Toss in a bowl with the parsley, and season to taste with salt and pepper.

Loosen the chicken skin and stuff about 2 teaspoons garlic mixture between the skin and the meat. Reserve remaining garlic mixture. Set chicken aside.

Prepare hot coals in a grill. When the coals are ready, grill the chicken 5 to 7 minutes on each side, or until the flesh is no longer pink. Do not overcook the chicken or it will become dry.

Heat the butter in a skillet, add the reserved garlic mixture, and sauté a few seconds. Add the lemon juice and adjust seasonings. Heat through. Place the chicken on a large heated platter and spoon the garlic sauce over it.

MAKES 4 SERVINGS

2 (2-pound) chickens or chicken breasts
2 small heads garlic
Water
¼ cup chopped Italian parsley
Salt, pepper
2 tablespoons unsalted butter
Juice of 1 large lemon

MELLOW CHICKEN SAUTÉ

Reader Suzanne Carr developed this recipe when she became concerned about her husband's diet. It fits nicely into a menu whether or not one is watching calories and fat intake.

Remove the skin from the chicken. Melt the butter in a large skillet. Sauté the garlic, leeks, onion, tomatoes, and mushrooms until tender. Push the vegetables to the side of the skillet and add the chicken. Brown on 1 side, then brown other side. (Or, remove the vegetables and brown the chicken in a small amount of butter in the skillet.)

Spoon the vegetables over the chicken and add the wine. Season with basil, parsley, salt, and pepper. Simmer over low heat, uncovered, basting frequently with the vegetables until the chicken is tender and the sauce is of desired consistency. Adjust salt and pepper to taste.

MAKES 8 SERVINGS

4 *whole chicken breasts, halved and boned*

1 *tablespoon butter or low-calorie margarine*

3 *cloves garlic, crushed*

2 *large leeks, sliced in thin rings*

1 *small onion, sliced in thin rings*

4 *large tomatoes, thickly sliced*

1 *pound mushrooms, quartered*

5 *tablespoons white zinfandel*

Crushed dried basil

Minced parsley

Salt substitute or salt

Freshly ground pepper

JAPANESE TEPPAN CHICKEN

Half the fun of dining on Japanese teppan foods lies in being seated around a 6-foot-long grill watching a master teppan chef wield his knives with showy ease. You may not be able to match the skills of the professional chefs, but with a large heavy griddle and a fair amount of practice, you can successfully prepare this quickly cooked chicken dinner at home.

Remove the skin from the chicken breasts. Heat the griddle and grease with oil or chicken fat taken from the skin, if available. Cook the breasts on the hottest part of the griddle until browned, basting or sprinkling with ginger sauce to keep moist.

Move the breasts to the edge of the grill. Cut into large bite-size pieces and turn cut side down. Cook and turn until done as desired, sprinkling with more ginger sauce. Push to the edge of the griddle to keep warm.

Meanwhile, cook the mushrooms, zucchini, and bean sprouts in the remaining fat on the griddle and cook, tossing, until lightly browned and tender-crisp. Sprinkle with ginger sauce and sesame seeds.

Arrange the meat and vegetables on a serving platter. Top the chicken with garlic slices. Serve with ginger sauce or dipping sauce.

MAKES 1 TO 2 SERVINGS

2 boneless chicken breast halves
Oil
Ginger Sauce *(recipe follows)*
5 or 6 large mushrooms, thinly sliced
1 or 2 zucchini, quartered lengthwise and thinly sliced
½ cup bean sprouts, appoximately
Sesame seeds, optional
Garlic slices
Dipping Sauce *(recipe follows)*

Combine and heat together the soy sauce, sugar, oil, ginger, and garlic. Use as a basting and dipping sauce.

GINGER SAUCE
1 cup soy sauce
½ cup sugar
¼ cup oil
2 teaspoons grated ginger root
1 clove garlic, minced or mashed

Combine the broth, soy sauce, and onion. Mix well.

DIPPING SAUCE
½ cup chicken broth
½ cup soy sauce
1 green onion top, minced

CHICKEN DIJON

We receive so many requests for recipes for Chicken Dijon, our card file is filled with them. This one, from the Century Plaza Hotel in Century City, is definitely one of the best of the group.

Season the chicken breasts with salt and pepper. Dust with flour. Heat the clarified butter in a skillet. Sauté the chicken breasts until golden brown on both sides, about 15 minutes.

Add the wine and cook, scraping brown bits from pan until the liquid is reduced by one-third. Add the chicken stock, tarragon, and bay leaf, and simmer 10 minutes until chicken is tender. Transfer the chicken breasts to a heated platter and keep warm.

Reduce the liquid by one-third and discard the bay leaf. Blend the egg yolks with sour cream and mustard. Add the red pepper. Stir the sour cream mixture into the pan liquids, using a whisk and cook, stirring constantly, until thickened. Do not let boil. Spoon the sauce over the chicken and sprinkle with chives.

MAKES 6 SERVINGS

Note: To clarify butter, heat until milky residue rises to the surface. Skim off the residue, or continue to cook without burning, until the residue evaporates and butter is clear.

6 chicken breast halves
½ teaspoon salt
⅛ teaspoon black pepper
¼ cup flour
¼ cup butter, clarified
1 cup dry white wine
½ cup chicken stock
½ teaspoon chopped fresh tarragon
1 small bay leaf
2 egg yolks
3 tablespoons sour cream
2 tablespoons Dijon mustard
Pinch cayenne pepper
1 tablespoon minced chives

CHICKEN CALCUTTA

When the Hungry Tiger chain had a restaurant in Los Angeles's downtown Music Center in 1984, we asked for their recipe for a simple, well-flavored chicken curry. It could be dressed up for a party with the addition of small bowls of condiments such as chutney, raisins, peanuts, and crumbled bacon among others.

Dust the chicken strips with flour. Melt the butter in a large saucepan. Add the chicken strips and sauté until golden. Add the curry powder, mushrooms, and green onions, and sauté until the mushrooms are tender, about 2 to 3 minutes. Add the cream, bring to a boil, reduce the heat, and simmer until the mixture is slightly thickened. Season to taste with salt and pepper. Spoon into a small casserole or 4 ramekins. Sprinkle with toasted coconut.

MAKES 4 SERVINGS

1 pound chicken breast, cut in strips
½ cup flour
¼ cup butter or margarine
1 tablespoon curry powder
1 cup sliced mushrooms
1 cup sliced green onions
1 cup whipping cream
Salt, pepper
Toasted shredded coconut

CHICKEN OF THE GODS

This recipe for chicken topped with a light cream sauce came from the Bali Hai restaurant on Shelter Island in San Diego many years ago and still has a devoted following among our readers. The water chestnut powder needed as a coating can be found in most Oriental markets or specialty stores.

Combine the egg, sherry, soy sauce, ¼ teaspoon salt, and dash of pepper. Marinate the chicken in the sauce for 15 to 20 minutes. Coat each piece of chicken with water chestnut powder. Heat about 1 inch oil in a skillet. Add the chicken and cook until tender and brown on both sides.

Melt the butter over medium heat and blend in the flour and cornstarch. Bring the chicken stock to a boil and stir rapidly while adding butter mixture. Reduce heat and add the whipping cream, and salt and pepper to taste. Slice the chicken pieces and arrange on a hot platter. Cover with the cream sauce. Sprinkle with sesame seeds.

MAKES 4 SERVINGS

1 egg, beaten
1 tablespoon sherry
1 teaspoon soy sauce
Salt, pepper
1 (2½- to 3-pound) chicken, cut up and boned
½ cup water chestnut powder
Oil
¼ cup butter or margarine, softened
¼ cup flour
1 tablespoon cornstarch
2 cups seasoned chicken stock
½ cup whipping cream or half and half
2 teaspoons toasted sesame seeds

CHICKEN CURRY

It may take a visit to an Asian or Oriental market to unearth some of the ingredients needed to make the Chan Dara Siamese Kitchen's chicken and vegetable curry. One taste, however, will prove such an effort is well worth the bother.

Heat the oil in a large skillet. Add the red curry paste and curry powder. Stir-fry over high heat for 1 minute. Add the fish sauce, chicken, potatoes, and carrots. Stir-fry until chicken is golden brown.

Add the coconut milk and bring to a boil. Reduce heat, cover, and simmer for 30 minutes.

MAKES 4 SERVINGS

¼ cup oil
¼ cup red curry paste (kang pet dang)
2 teaspoons curry powder
6 tablespoons fish sauce
1 chicken breast, boned and sliced
2 potatoes, peeled and cut into 16 to 20 slices
2 carrots, cut into 16 to 20 slices
4 cups coconut milk

LEMON CHICKEN

Maybe it's the addition of white wine vinegar. Or maybe it's the tad of sugar. Whatever it is, something seems to set the Lemon Chicken from Fung Lum's in Universal City apart from all others.

Combine the chicken, egg, 2 drops sesame oil, 1 tablespoon cornstarch, 2 teaspoons salt, and pepper until the chicken pieces are coated and the ingredients are blended. Deep-fry in peanut oil at 400 degrees until browned. Drain the chicken on paper towels. Cut into smaller pieces. Keep warm while preparing the lemon sauce.

Blend ½ cup water, the vinegar, lemon juice, sugar, lemon extract, remaining 1 drop sesame oil, and some salt in a wok or small saucepan. Bring to a boil.

Blend 1 tablespoon water and remaining 1 tablespoon cornstarch until smooth. Stir into the lemon mixture. Heat, stirring, until smooth and clear. Pour the sauce over the chicken.

MAKES 2 TO 4 SERVINGS

1 pound boneless chicken, cut into thin strips

1 egg, lightly beaten

3 drops sesame oil

2 tablespoons cornstarch

Salt

Pinch black pepper

Peanut oil for deep frying

2 tablespoons white wine vinegar

2 tablespoons lemon juice

⅓ cup sugar

2 drops lemon extract

CHICKEN NAMASU

Whenever one of our readers, Florence Rosales, pays a visit to her hometown of Kohala on the Big Island of Hawaii, she returns to Southern California with yet another special recipe. She sent this one to our "My Best Recipe" column.

Cover the chicken with water in a large saucepan. Season with garlic salt. Bring to a boil, reduce heat, and simmer for 30 minutes. Remove from pan and set aside to cool.

Remove the chicken from the bones and cut into strips. Place in a large bowl. Peel the cucumbers, halve lengthwise, and remove the seeds. Cut into ¼-inch slices and add to the chicken.

Toast the sesame seeds in a small skillet, shaking over medium heat until light brown. Add to the chicken and cucumbers.

Combine the sesame oil, sugar, soy sauce, vinegar, green onions, garlic, chile, and hon-dashi. Pour over the chicken mixture. Mix well and marinate for 1 to 2 hours, stirring often.

MAKES 4 TO 6 SERVINGS

Note: The Japanese soup stock seasoning hon-dashi can be found at Japanese markets or in the Oriental section of supermarkets.

2 or 3 whole chicken breasts

Garlic salt

4 cucumbers

3 tablespoons sesame seeds

½ cup sesame oil

½ cup sugar

½ cup soy sauce

½ cup vinegar

4 green onions, finely sliced

4 cloves garlic, finely chopped

1 chile, seeded and chopped

1 tablespoon hon-dashi

HERB CHICKEN BREASTS STUFFED WITH CILANTRO AND MUSHROOM RICE

Josie Wiley was named one of our "My Best" weekly winners with this flavorful chicken dish.

Bone the chicken breasts. Wash, pat dry, and season to taste with salt, pepper, cumin, garlic, cayenne, and some chopped cilantro. Set aside.

Melt ¼ cup butter in a skillet over medium heat. Sauté the onion and mushrooms until tender, about 15 minutes. Add the beer and simmer 15 minutes longer. Combine with the cilantro, basmati and wild rice. Season to taste with salt and pepper, cumin, garlic, and cayenne.

Stuff the chicken breasts with the rice mixture. Place any leftover rice in a small ovenproof dish, which can be baked with the chicken. Place the stuffed breasts in a large ovenproof glass baking dish. Dot with slices of butter, if desired. Bake at 350 degrees for 45 minutes, or until chicken is tender. Remove from the oven and serve with the cilantro and mushroom herb sauce and remaining rice mixture.

MAKES 6 SERVINGS

6 whole chicken breasts

Salt, pepper

Ground cumin

Minced garlic

Cayenne pepper

½ to 1 bunch cilantro, coarsely chopped

½ cup butter or to taste

1 medium onion, chopped

½ pound mushrooms, sliced

1 cup beer

2 cups cooked basmati rice

1 cup cooked wild rice

Cilantro and Mushroom Herb Sauce (recipe follows)

CILANTRO AND MUSHROOM HERB SAUCE

Melt the butter over low heat. Sauté the mushrooms until tender, about 15 minutes. Season to taste with cumin, garlic, and cayenne. Stir in the whipping cream and continue cooking over low heat for 30 minutes, stirring frequently. Season to taste with salt and pepper. Stir in the lemon juice and cook just until slightly thickened. Remove from heat. Stir in the green onions and cilantro.

¼ to ½ cup butter or margarine

½ to 1 pound mushrooms, sliced

Ground cumin

Minced garlic

Cayenne pepper

2 cups whipping cream

Salt, pepper

Juice of 1 lemon

1 bunch green onions, sliced

1 bunch cilantro, chopped

CHICKEN ROULADE

Patrick Terrail, whose Ma Maison restaurant was a favorite hangout for hundreds of Hollywood celebrities until it closed several years ago, later opened the Hollywood Diner in West Hollywood. That, too, has since changed, but before Terrail went on to bigger and better culinary challenges, he gave us this recipe for a spectacular chicken roulade.

Flatten each whole chicken breast between two sheets of wax paper into a large, thin cutlet. Brush with melted butter. Grill over coals, on a griddle, or under a broiler. Cook about 5 minutes under a broiler or 10 to 15 minutes on a griddle, turning once.

Place one whole chicken breast on each sheet of seaweed to cover the entire sheet. Arrange 2 sticks each of carrots and cucumbers on the lower one-third of the chicken. Sprinkle with cilantro and season with salt and pepper to taste. Drizzle with olive oil.

Roll in a tight roll as for a jellyroll, aligning stuffing evenly. Place the seaweed roll on a flour tortilla. Trim the ends to match the length of the roll. Roll tightly in the tortilla.

Secure each roulade by rolling in plastic wrap and tying a knot on each end. Place the roulades on steamer rack over, but not touching, hot water. Cover and steam for 15 minutes, or until heated through.

To serve, remove plastic wrap. Slice the roulades into ½-inch slices. Arrange the slices in overlapping fashion and serve with salsa and boiled new potatoes.

MAKES 8 SERVINGS

Combine the tomato, jalapeño chile, onion, avocado, cilantro, wine vinegar, olive oil, and tomato juice in a blender container. Blend until smooth. Season to taste with salt and pepper. Chill before serving.

MAKES 1½ CUPS

Note: Salsa ingredients may be chopped by hand for a coarser texture.

4 whole chicken breasts, skin removed
3 tablespoons melted butter
4 sheets dried seaweed (8 × 8-inch square)
2 carrots, peeled and cut into ¼-inch sticks
1 cucumber, peeled and cut into ¼-inch sticks
1 bunch cilantro, trimmed, washed, and chopped
Salt, pepper
4 teaspoons olive oil
4 (10-inch) flour tortillas
4 sheets plastic wrap
Salsa (recipe follows)
Boiled new potatoes

SALSA
1 large tomato, peeled, seeded, and squeezed
½ jalapeño chile, minced
¼ onion, diced
¼ avocado, diced
1 tablespoon minced cilantro
2 tablespoons white wine vinegar
2 tablespoons virgin olive oil
¼ cup tomato juice
Salt, pepper

CHEESE-STUFFED CHICKEN BREASTS

When Production Caterers of North Hollywood set up their portable kitchens in the driveway of staff writer Barbara Hansen's home to feed a television production crew, everyone was happy—and Barbara obtained some great recipes. This one, from Rose Rever, who, with husband David and son Rick, runs the catering firm, was so good it took top spot on our list of 1988s twelve best recipes.

Thaw the spinach and drain thoroughly. Combine the spinach, ricotta, Parmesan, cottage cheese, and eggs. Gently stuff the mixture under the skin of each chicken breast. Brush generously with butter topping. Bake at 350 degrees for 20 to 25 minutes. Let cool and cut in half. The chicken may also be served hot. Accompany with a bowl of the yogurt sauce.

MAKES 8 SERVINGS

½ cup frozen chopped spinach, loosely packed
½ cup ricotta cheese
¼ cup grated Parmesan cheese
¼ cup cottage cheese
3 eggs, beaten
4 whole chicken breasts, boned
Butter Topping (recipe follows)
Yogurt Sauce (recipe follows)

BUTTER TOPPING

Combine the butter, paprika, garlic powder, salt, and pepper.

MAKES ½ CUP

½ cup butter, melted
1 teaspoon paprika
¼ teaspoon garlic powder
¼ teaspoon salt
¼ teaspoon white pepper

YOGURT SAUCE

Combine the tomatoes, yogurt, and basil, and season with vinegar, salt, and pepper.

MAKES 2½ CUPS

6 tomatoes, chopped
¼ cup yogurt
½ (½-ounce) package fresh basil leaves, finely chopped
4 drops red wine vinegar
Pinch salt
White pepper

BAKED STUFFED PAPAYA

The Willow's, a landmark restaurant in Honolulu, has for years offered a wonderful chicken curry served in half a papaya.

Combine the chicken, wine, and oil in a bowl and let stand 15 minutes. In a large skillet stir the curry powder over medium heat for 2 minutes. Add the chicken mixture and toss over medium-high heat for about 5 minutes, or until chicken is cooked through. Stir in the hot curry sauce.

To serve, mound the chicken mixture in papaya halves. Sprinkle each with 2 tablespoons coconut. Place on a baking sheet and bake at 350 degrees for about 10 minutes, or until heated through and coconut is lightly browned. Garnish with lime slices.

MAKES 4 SERVINGS

1 pound boned and skinned
   chicken breast, cut in 1-inch
   cubes (about 2 cups)
¼ cup white wine or dry vermouth
2 tablespoons oil
1 teaspoon curry powder
Curry Sauce (recipe follows)
2 papayas, halved and seeded
½ cup flaked coconut
Lime slices for garnish, optional

CURRY SAUCE

Melt the butter in 1-quart saucepan over medium heat. Add the onion, ginger, and garlic, and sauté about 5 minutes. Add the flour and curry powder and cook 2 minutes longer. Gradually stir in the chicken broth and milk. Season to taste with salt and cook, stirring frequently, about 5 minutes or until thickened.

MAKES ABOUT 1½ CUPS SAUCE

2 tablespoons butter or margarine
½ cup chopped onion
1½ teaspoons finely chopped
   ginger root
1 clove garlic, minced
1½ tablespoons flour
2 teaspoons curry powder
½ cup chicken broth
½ cup milk
Salt

CHICKEN RELLENO

The recipe calls for the Spanish chorizo de Bilbao, which we found in Philippine and Spanish markets. Pepperoni will make a good substitute if necessary.

Bone the chicken for stuffing, splitting along the backbone, leaving the wing and drumstick bones intact. Season with salt and pepper and rub with soy sauce and lemon juice. Let stand at least 30 minutes. (Refrigerate if marinating longer.)

Combine the ground pork, bacon, cheese, raisins, pickle relish, and egg. Mix well. Place chicken on board, skin side down. Place half the stuffing in the cavity of the chicken. Arrange the carrot and ham strips, sausage, and egg halves in rows on top of the pork mixture. Cover with the remaining pork mixture, also stuffing the thighs.

Bring together the 2 cut sides of the chicken. Secure the edges at 1-inch intervals with wood picks or skewers, then lace with string. Turn the bird over and mold back to resemble its original shape. Tie the legs with string and tuck the wings akimbo. Place on a rack in a roasting pan and cover with foil. Bake at 350 degrees for 30 minutes, then remove foil. Continue baking for 1 hour or more until golden brown, basting with melted butter. Collect drippings, if desired, and make flour gravy.

Remove the skewers and string. Place on a serving platter. Carve into ½-inch-thick diagonal or crosswise slices, starting from the wing sides.

MAKES 10 TO 12 SERVINGS

1 (3-pound) chicken

Salt, pepper

1 to 2 tablespoons soy sauce

2 tablespoons lemon juice

¾ pound ground pork

¼ pound lean bacon, chopped or coarsely ground

6 ounces Cheddar cheese, shredded

½ cup raisins

3 tablespoons sweet pickle relish

1 egg

1 carrot, cooked and cut julienne, or ½ cup green peas, cooked

3 ounces cooked ham, cut julienne

2 Spanish chorizo de Bilbao or pepperoni, about 5 ounces

2 hard-cooked eggs, cut in halves

1 to 2 tablespoons butter, melted

CHICKEN HASH

*Hash is one of those foods that some people will do anything to avoid. What a pity!
Particularly since hash recipes, such as this one, which we acquired in 1985 from the old 21
Club in New York, can be works of culinary art. One would be hard put to refuse this
elegant, creamy chicken mixture on toast or a waffle.*

Melt the butter in a heavy medium saucepan with an oven-proof handle. Blend in the flour until smooth. Gradually stir in the milk until smooth and thickened. Stir in the hot pepper sauce, Worcestershire, white pepper, and season to taste with salt. Cover and bake at 300 degrees for 1½ hours.

Strain the sauce. Stir in the half and half, sherry, and chicken. Heat over low heat until heated through. Adjust seasonings. Add a small amount of hot sauce to the egg yolks. Return the yolks to the saucepan. Heat, stirring, until slightly thickened. Do not boil. Serve hot over toast, waffle, baked potato shell, or wild rice.

MAKES 4 SERVINGS

2 tablespoons butter
2 tablespoons flour
2 cups hot milk
Dash hot pepper sauce
Dash Worcestershire sauce
¼ teaspoon white pepper
Salt
½ cup half and half
¼ cup dry sherry
2 cups diced cooked chicken
2 egg yolks, beaten
*Hot toast, waffles, baked potato
    shells, or wild rice*

Poached Salmon Celeste (page 152)

Orange Roughy in Orange-Mint-Yogurt Sauce (page 154)

Marinated Green Mussels (page 166)

Scaloppine alla Fiorentina (page 225)

CHICKEN MOLE

Southern Californians truly have a love affair going with Mexican cuisine, especially with this excellent mole from Antonio's restaurant in Los Angeles. You may have to search out a Mexican market to get some ingredients, particularly the chocolate, which is very different from most chocolate used in cooking.

Simmer the chicken in salted water to cover until tender. Drain, reserving broth.

Meanwhile, soak pasila negro, and the Anaheim, New Mexican, and California chiles for 30 minutes in warm water. Drain; remove stems and seeds. Grind the chiles in a food processor or blender until puréed, adding a small amount of chicken broth or hot water to facilitate blending. Sieve the chiles to remove bits of peel.

Combine the chile pulp, peanuts, pecans, walnuts, chocolate, banana, large tomato, onion, 2 cloves garlic, oregano, cumin, sugar, 1 teaspoon salt, and 2 cups broth in a large pot. Cook 15 minutes, stirring occasionally.

Turn the mixture into blender and process until puréed. Heat 2 teaspoons oil in a large pot. Return the sauce to the pot, add the remaining 2 cups chicken broth and simmer slowly for 30 minutes. Heat 1 tablespoon oil in a medium skillet. Add the onions and remaining clove garlic and cook until the onion is tender. Add the medium tomato and cook until tender. Add the mole sauce and chicken, and stir to mix. Heat through and season to taste with salt.

MAKES 4 TO 6 SERVINGS

1 (2½- to 3-pound) chicken, cut up

2 pasila negro chiles (black pasila)

2 Anaheim chiles

2 New Mexican chiles

2 California chiles

½ cup peanuts

½ cup pecans

¼ cup walnuts

1 (3.1-ounce) tablet Mexican chocolate

1 banana, cut up

1 large tomato, peeled and chopped, and 1 medium tomato, peeled and chopped

½ onion, chopped

3 cloves garlic, minced

Pinch dried oregano

Pinch ground cumin

1 teaspoon sugar

Salt

4 cups chicken broth

2 tablespoons oil

½ small onion, chopped

CHICKEN AND SCALLOPS

The Jarlsberg cheese topping on this delicate combination of chicken and seafood is that perfect added touch so many simple recipes lack. When Joey of Joey D's in Woodland Hills shared the recipe with us in 1985, he said it was one of their most popular menu items.

Season the chicken and scallops with salt and pepper. Dredge in flour, shaking off excess. Heat the clarified butter in a 8- to 10-inch skillet. Add the scallops and chicken and sauté until pale golden. Remove from skillet.

Add the shallots and mushrooms to the pan drippings and sauté until tender. Add the white wine and simmer over high heat until wine is reduced and forms a glaze. Add the cream and tarragon, stir to combine, and simmer over high heat just until the cream coats a metal spoon. Return the chicken and scallops, and season with salt and pepper to taste. Toss lightly to coat the chicken and scallops.

Spoon into 4 ramekins or a 1-quart baking dish. Top with cheese. Bake at 375 degrees for 4 to 5 minutes until cheese melts and sauce is bubbly.

MAKES 4 SERVINGS

1 (½-pound) chicken breast, diced
½ pound scallops
Salt, pepper
¼ cup flour
¼ cup clarified butter
2 shallots, minced
6 mushrooms
¼ cup dry white wine
½ cup whipping cream
½ teaspoon minced fresh tarragon leaves
¼ cup shredded Jarlsberg cheese

ROSEMARY-GRILLED TURKEY BREAST WITH MUSHROOMS

*When talented young chef Dale Payne was at Bistango on La Cienega, he gave us
this recipe for turkey breast served with a wonderful sauce made with enoki and
shiitake mushrooms.*

Combine the olive oil and rosemary in a shallow pan. Add the turkey breast and turn to coat well. Cover and marinate several hours. When ready to grill, place the turkey on the grill over high heat and sear on both sides. Cover and cook with open vents, basting with vinegar and honey until medium rare, or done as desired, from 20 to 30 minutes for a 1½- to 2-pound turkey breast. If broiling, set on a broiler rack 3 inches from the heat source and broil until desired doneness, turning once.

Remove from the heat and keep warm. Meanwhile, melt 3 tablespoons butter in a skillet. Add the shiitake and enoki mushrooms and sauté until mushrooms glisten. Add the stock, salt, pepper, and 2 teaspoons butter. Cook 1 minute longer or until butter melts.

Slice the turkey breast on the bias and overlap or fan out slices on a platter over the parsnip-carrot cakes. Spoon the mushroom ragout over the turkey.

MAKES 6 SERVINGS

¼ cup olive oil

1 tablespoon fresh rosemary or 1 sprig rosemary

1½- to 2-pound turkey breast

¼ cup balsamic vinegar

2 tablespoons honey

3 tablespoons plus 2 teaspoons butter

¼ pound shiitake mushrooms

¼ pound enoki mushrooms

¼ cup reduced chicken or turkey stock

Salt, pepper

Parsnip-Carrot Cakes (recipe follows)

Combine the parsnips, carrots, and Chinese pea pods. Combine the onion, egg, half and half, flour, and salt and pepper to taste. Melt 1 tablespoon butter in a small nonstick skillet. Dredge the vegetables in the batter; spoon about 3 tablespoons into the pan. Cook, patting down with plastic spatula as soon as batter has bound together. (Should take about 45 seconds in hot pan). Flip, and cook 15 seconds on the other side. Place on moistened towels until ready to serve.

MAKES 12 TO 18 CAKES

PARSNIP-CARROT CAKES

1 parsnip, peeled and julienned

1 carrot, peeled and julienned

12 finely julienned Chinese pea pods

⅛ red onion, grated

1 egg, beaten

½ cup half and half

½ cup flour

Salt, pepper

Butter

STUFFED TURKEY BREAST

When slow cookers were the appliances of the hour in the early eighties, we cooked everything in them, including party fare like this unusual stuffed turkey breast. If, as trend watchers are saying, families will be spending more time at home in the nineties, it may be time to dust off your slow cooker and try this recipe on your next dinner guests.

Combine the butter, onion, celery, croutons, bacon, broth, parsley, and poultry seasoning. Cut the turkey breast in thick slices vertically from the breastbone to the rib cage, leaving the slices attached to the bone. Sprinkle lightly with salt and pepper. Soak a piece of cheesecloth large enough to wrap around the turkey breast in wine. Place the turkey on the wine-soaked cloth. Stuff the crouton mixture into slits of turkey. Fold the cheesecloth ends so as to completely enclose the turkey breast. (This will also hold the stuffing in place.) Set the turkey on the metal rack in a slow cooker.

Cover, and cook on low for 7 to 9 hours, or until turkey breast is tender. Pour additional wine over the turkey during cooking to keep it moist. Remove the turkey from the cooker and immediately discard the cheesecloth. To brown the turkey, place on a rack in a baking pan and bake at 400 degrees for 15 to 20 minutes, if desired. Let the turkey stand, loosely covered with foil, 10 minutes while preparing sauce.

While turkey is standing, turn the slow cooker to high. Dissolve the flour in a small amount of water and stir into the drippings in the cooker. Cover and cook on high for 10 to 15 minutes, stirring occasionally. Blend in the sour cream and heat through but do not boil. Serve the sauce on the side.

MAKES 8 TO 10 SERVINGS

¼ cup melted butter or margarine

1 small onion, chopped

½ cup finely chopped celery

1 (2½-ounce) package croutons or 2½ cups

1 slice bacon, cooked and crumbled

1 cup chicken broth

2 tablespoons minced parsley

½ teaspoon poultry seasoning

1 whole, uncooked turkey breast (about 5 pounds)

Salt, pepper

Dry white wine

¼ cup flour

1 cup sour cream

TURKEY ROLL

Adriana Pacifici cooks what she likes to call Northern Italian Judaic cuisine. When she gave
Home Magazine, *predecessor to the present* Sunday Los Angeles Times Magazine,
this recipe for a cooking column feature in 1985, she was running a catering business,
teaching cooking classes, and writing a cookbook.

◘

Have the butcher bone and butterfly the turkey. Spread the meat out on a flat sheet. Using a sharp knife, make 6 random incisions in the breast and place a garlic half in each. Sprinkle with salt and pepper to taste. Cover with a layer of prosciutto slices.

Beat the eggs with salt and pepper to taste. Stir in the parsley. Heat 1 to 2 tablespoons butter in a large nonstick skillet placed over medium heat. Pour in the eggs and cook to make a soft, whole round omelet or frittata (do not overcook). Cool slightly. Place omelet over prosciutto. Top with mortadella slices.

Roll breast as tightly as possible, jelly-roll fashion, and tie with string all around. If using fresh rosemary, insert the sprigs under the string; if using dried, rub the rosemary over the turkey roll. Season with salt and pepper.

Heat the olive oil in a large Dutch oven or roasting skillet placed over low heat. Add the turkey roll and cook to brown evenly, turning occasionally. Increase the heat and sprinkle with wine. After about 5 minutes or after wine has evaporated, add ⅓ cup butter, and the onion and shallot. Reduce heat to low and simmer for 1 hour, 15 minutes, basting top occasionally.

Let stand about 15 minutes before carving. Cut into thin slices and arrange on a serving platter. Heat the sauce, pour some over the slices, and pass the remainder.

MAKES 16 TO 20 SERVINGS

1 (6- to 8-pound) whole turkey breast

3 cloves garlic, cut in halves

Salt, pepper

6 slices prosciutto or cooked ham

4 eggs

2 tablespoons chopped parsley

Butter or margarine

6 slices mortadella

Fresh rosemary sprigs or dried rosemary leaves

½ cup olive oil

½ cup wine

1 onion, sliced

1 shallot, sliced

CRISPY THAI DUCK

In his West Hollywood restaurant, local chef Tommy Tang combines culinary cultures with ease. His recipe for crispy duck pleases Western palates while remaining essentially true to its Southeastern Asian origin.

Cut the ducks into serving pieces, removing excess fat. Rinse in cold water and pat dry.

Add the duck pieces to the marinade; turn and rub surface of duck pieces to coat well. Marinate 3 hours in the refrigerator.

Remove the duck from the marinade and wipe off any excess. Place the duck in a baking pan and strain the marinade over the duck. Bake at 300 degrees for 1 to 1½ hours, basting every 15 minutes with the marinade. Remove duck from oven and set aside.

Heat the oil to 375 to 400 degrees. Cook the duck in the hot oil, a few pieces at a time, 3 to 5 minutes, until the skin is crispy. Do not overcook. Remove with a slotted spoon and pat dry with paper towels to remove excess oil. Drizzle with the honey-ginger sauce.

Bone the duck and cut each piece into serving slices.

MAKES 4 TO 6 SERVINGS

2 (5- to 5½-pound) Long Island ducklings
Marinade *(recipe follows)*
3 cups oil
Honey-Ginger Sauce *(recipe follows)*

In a large bowl combine the ginger, onion, and soy sauce with water. Mix well.

MAKES 2 CUPS

MARINADE
¼ *cup grated ginger root*
½ *cup grated brown onion*
½ *cup thin soy sauce*
1 *cup water*

Combine the honey, plum sauce, soy sauce, water, and ginger root in a small saucepan. Bring to a boil over medium heat. Reduce the heat and simmer for 20 minutes. Sauce should be syrupy.

MAKES ABOUT 2 CUPS

HONEY-GINGER SAUCE
1 *cup honey*
¼ *cup plum sauce*
¼ *cup soy sauce*
½ *cup water*
¼ *pound sliced ginger root*

SAKE DUCK

The New Otani Hotel and Gardens in Little Tokyo in downtown Los Angeles has long been a favorite dining spot with local government officials and business people who work nearby. Their spectacular Sake Duck is one reason diners return to the hotel's restaurants time and again.

Place the duckling in a baking pan. Bake at 300 degrees for 2 hours, basting with honey every 15 minutes. Remove from the oven and cool to room temperature. Bone the duck and slice the meat. Grate the orange over the duck and sprinkle with green onions. Pour sake sauce over duck.

MAKES 2 TO 4 SERVINGS

1 (2- to 4-pound) duckling
Honey
1 orange or mandarin orange
½ bunch green onions or 1 leek, finely julienned
Sake Sauce *(recipe follows)*

SAKE SAUCE
1 cup mirin (sweet sake)
½ cup soy sauce
¼ cup orange juice
1 teaspoon grated ginger root
¼ cup brown sugar, packed
1 tablespoon arrowroot or cornstarch
1 leek, finely julienned

Combine the mirin, soy sauce, orange juice, and ginger in a small saucepan. Heat until hot, but do not boil. Remove from heat and stir in the brown sugar. Stir arrowroot or starch with some of the hot liquid until smooth and return to pan. Cook, stirring, until sauce thickens slightly. Strain the sauce through a fine strainer into another pot or sauce boat. Add the leek to sauce and mix gently. Let stand 10 minutes to blend flavors.

MAKES ABOUT 2 CUPS

MEAT

Red meats have not fared well during the past ten years. As our life-styles and dining habits changed, we moved toward fish and chicken as our preferred choices for entrées. Not that we completely moved away from eating meats—to the contrary, we continued to eat beef and pork and lamb, but in smaller quantities.

The result was unexpected. Both the beef and pork industries provided markets with leaner, lighter cuts of meat, which we accepted happily.

As we entered the eighties, we were still devoted to roasts, thick steaks and chops, and other large cuts of meat. But as the decade progressed, the focal point of the meal shifted away from these standard cuts. Our fascination with the everchanging variety of ethnic foods continued to grow, and no doubt that's where we learned to economize on the quantity of meat in our diet. We began cooking stir-fry meals, we found out all about fajitas. And with great enthusiasm we embraced a whole battery of fresh sausages made with everything from red meats to pork, chicken, fish, and vegetables.

With all this flux, some favorite foods stayed with us, although sometimes in new guises. Hamburger was, and is, still a favorite. Stews and other casseroles that combined meats and vegetables were popular, and continued to be served at home. Our devotion to chili remained, too, with changes in the types of seasonings used or the types of meats and vegetables added. And thanks in large part to the trendy American chefs who had the courage to recognize its merit, the humble meat loaf surfaced: we ate Cajun meat loaf, Italian-style meat loaf, and fortunately, a more traditional meat-and-potatoes meat loaf.

Considering all these changes, it seems we adapted meat as an ingredient rather than as the mainstay of an entrée. Time and health were the great shapers when it came to cooking with meat.

MONGOLIAN BEEF

This simple stir-fry dish from the Wang Kung restaurant in Los Angeles is typical of its genre. The brown pepper powder is available in most Oriental markets. If you can't find it, however, a few drops of hot pepper sauce will make an adequate replacement.

Slice the beef very thin. (Meat will slice easily if partially frozen.) Place in a bowl and add 1 tablespoon soy sauce, salt, rice wine, pepper powder, and 2 tablespoons vegetable oil. Toss to coat well.

Cut the onion lengthwise, then in diagonal strips. Set aside. Mix together 1 tablespoon soy sauce and sesame oil in small bowl.

Heat ½ cup vegetable oil in a large skillet or wok until very hot. Add the sliced garlic and cook 3 seconds. Add the beef and stir-fry over high heat for about 1 minute. Add onion and sesame oil mixture and stir-fry until thoroughly heated.

MAKES 6 TO 8 SERVINGS

1 pound lean beef

Soy sauce

½ teaspoon salt

1 tablespoon rice wine or other sweet white wine

½ teaspoon brown pepper powder

Vegetable oil

1 pound green onions

1 tablespoon sesame oil

3 tablespoons sliced garlic

CHINESE ORANGE BEEF

Versions of this popular Chinese stir-fry dish abound. This is one that has found favor over the years with our readers.

Trim the fat from the steak and slice into thin strips. Combine the soy sauce, cornstarch, and ginger. Pour over the steak and toss to mix well.

Heat 2 teaspoons oil in a nonstick skillet until hot. Add the orange peel and chile peppers and cook over high heat for 1 minute. Add the beef and stir-fry until browned, about 3 minutes. Remove the beef to a plate.

Add the remaining 1 teaspoon oil to the wok and heat. Add the carrot, peppers, pea pods, and water chestnuts, and stir-fry 3 to 4 minutes. Return the beef to the skillet and stir-fry until beef is heated through.

Discard the chiles and orange peel. Garnish a serving platter with the lettuce and mound with the beef.

MAKES 4 SERVINGS

1 pound top sirloin or round steak

¼ cup soy sauce

1½ teaspoons cornstarch

1 tablespoon grated ginger root

1 tablespoon oil

3 pieces dried orange peel

1 or 2 dried red chile peppers

1 carrot, sliced

1 green pepper, sliced

1 sweet red pepper, sliced

¼ pound Chinese pea pods, trimmed

1 (8-ounce) can sliced water chestnuts

1 head iceberg lettuce, shredded, for garnish

TATAKI OF BEEF (MARINATED BEEF)

When 385 North was in its glory days as one of L.A.'s trendiest restaurants, Roy Yamaguchi came up with this interesting marinated cold beef entrée. It makes a super light supper for a hot summer day. Look for chiso leaves in an Oriental market; otherwise substitute sorrel leaves or lemon grass.

Combine the ginger, garlic, soy sauce, chiso, and lime juice in a flat glass dish just large enough to hold the steak. Set aside. Trim the steak of excess fat and season with pepper on top and bottom. Quickly sear the beef in hot peanut oil on all sides over high heat. Cook to rare stage only.

Add to the marinade and turn to coat the beef well. Refrigerate, turning occasionally, at least 1 hour. Steak should be very cold and firm before slicing.

To serve, thinly slice meat on the diagonal. Sprinkle the steak slices with thinly sliced green onions cut on the bias and spoon a small amount of marinade over them.

MAKES 4 SERVINGS

Note: If desired, the steak may be served on a bed of julienned carrots, Chinese pea pods, or other thinly sliced vegetables.

1½ teaspoons grated ginger root
¾ teaspoon grated garlic
½ cup dark soy sauce
1 bunch chiso (ooba leaf), julienned
¼ cup lime juice
14 ounces culotte or New York steak
Pepper
2 tablespoons peanut oil
Green onions

BEEF PAPRIKASH FOR TWO

Sweet Hungarian paprika is a must when fixing this simple dish.

Chill the beef until very firm but not frozen. Thinly slice into 3-inch-long strips. Brown in 1 tablespoon oil in a heavy skillet. Remove beef from skillet and set aside.

Pour off the excess fat. Add remaining 1 tablespoon oil and the butter. Sauté the onion and garlic until tender, but not browned. Return the beef to the pan and add the beef stock, paprika, and mushrooms. Season to taste with salt and pepper. Bring to a boil, reduce heat, cover, and simmer until the meat is tender, 45 minutes to 1 hour.

When the beef is tender, stir the flour into the sour cream and add to the beef. Bring to a boil and cook, stirring, until thickened. Stir in lemon juice. Serve over hot noodles.

MAKES 2 SERVINGS

¾ pound beef sirloin
2 tablespoons oil
1½ teaspoons butter or margarine
½ cup chopped onion
1 clove garlic, minced
2 cups beef stock
2 tablespoons sweet Hungarian paprika
½ cup sliced mushrooms
Salt, pepper
1 tablespoon flour
½ cup sour cream
1½ teaspoons lemon juice
Hot cooked noodles

KOREAN BARBECUED BEEF

With an ever-growing Korean population, it isn't surprising that Korean food has developed a following in Los Angeles. This recipe for Korean barbecued beef was sent to us in 1983 by Yunsoo Chang, who had moved to Southern California from Seoul.

Slice the steak very thin. (Partially freeze meat for ease in slicing.) Combine the soy sauce, sesame oil, sherry, sugar, green onions, onion, mushrooms, garlic, salt to taste, and pepper. Marinate the meat for several hours. Grill the meat and mushrooms for 5 to 8 minutes, or until cooked to desired degree of doneness, turning occasionally.

MAKES ABOUT 6 SERVINGS

Note: Short ribs or flank steak may be substituted for sirloin, if desired.

2 pounds sirloin steak
5 tablespoons soy sauce
2 tablespoons sesame oil
1 to 2 tablespoons dry sherry
¼ cup sugar
3 green onions, chopped
1 small onion, chopped
¼ cup sliced mushrooms
3 cloves garlic, crushed
Salt
⅛ teaspoon black pepper

SIZZLING BEEF FAJITAS

The seasonings and some of the ingredients differ a bit, yet there is a strong resemblance between Mexican fajitas and Oriental stir-fry dishes. But while most stir-fries are served over rice, the sautéed fajita filling is piled in warm corn or flour tortillas, as at the El Torito restaurant chain in Southern California.

Place the meat in a shallow pan. Pour the marinade over it and let marinate in the refrigerator for 3 hours.

Remove meat from marinade and cut into ½ × 3-inch strips. Melt the margarine in a large skillet. Add the onions, green peppers, and seasoned salt and sauté until vegetables are tender.

Sear the meat in a large cast-iron skillet over medium heat. Remove from skillet when browned. Place another iron skillet upside down over a high flame. Heat almost to the point of smoking, about 90 seconds.

Remove hot serving skillet from burner and pile with the meat strips and vegetables. Place tomato wedges over the meat and vegetables. Garnish with lemon wedges.

MAKES 6 SERVINGS

Combine the soy sauce, water, vinegar, garlic, and pepper in a large container. Whip with a wire whisk until well mixed.

Variation: For Chicken Fajitas, use 3 pounds chicken breasts. Marinate and cut according to recipe for beef fajitas. Prepare as for beef, but baste chicken with achiote sauce while sautéing.

Blend the achiote powder, orange juice, garlic, and oregano in a blender container until smooth.

Note: Achiote powder can be found in Mexican grocery stores or in the Mexican products section of supermarkets.

3 pounds tri-tip or bottom sirloin of beef

Marinade *(recipe follows)*

⅓ cup margarine

2 medium Spanish onions, cut julienne

4 medium green peppers, cut julienne

1 teaspoon seasoned salt

1 pound tomatoes, cut into wedges

Lemon wedges, for garnish

MARINADE

2½ cups soy sauce

1¼ cups water

1¼ cups white vinegar

1 teaspoon minced garlic

1 teaspoon white pepper

ACHIOTE SAUCE

4 ounces achiote powder

1¼ cups orange juice

1 teaspoon granulated garlic or 1 tablespoon minced garlic

Pinch oregano

BEEF SHORT RIBS

One of Los Angeles's most famous hotels, the legendary old Ambassador, finally closed its doors in 1989. Not, however, before we fortunately acquired the recipe for their beef short ribs, which graced many a Rotary luncheon among others.

◻

Sprinkle each rib with salt, pepper, and rosemary to taste. Place in a baking pan with the celery and carrots. Bake at 350 degrees for 1 hour. Add the red wine and brown gravy. Cover with foil and bake 1½ hours, or until meat is tender when fork is inserted.

MAKES 6 SERVINGS

Melt the butter and stir in the flour until smooth and pale gold. Stir in the chicken broth, beef broth, and beef concentrate until blended. Bring to a boil and simmer for 10 minutes. Season to taste with salt and pepper if needed.

6 (12-ounce) beef short ribs

Salt, pepper, and rosemary

1 cup diced celery

1 cup diced carrots

½ cup red wine

Brown Gravy (recipe follows)

BROWN GRAVY

6 tablespoons butter

6 tablespoons flour

1 (14½-ounce) can clear chicken broth

1 (14½-ounce) can clear beef broth

1 tablespoon beef concentrate powder

Salt, pepper

DEVILED BEEF RIBS WITH MUSTARD SAUCE

The crisp, crunchy texture of the deviled ribs from the Waldorf-Astoria Hotel in New York has great appeal for Westerners. We liked them so much they made the list of twelve best recipes of the year for 1987.

Lightly season the bones with salt and pepper. Place the bones on a baking sheet and roast at 325 degrees for 1½ hours. After the bones have cooked, allow to cool until easy to handle, about 15 minutes.

Combine 3 tablespoons olive oil and all but 3 tablespoons mustard, blending well. Separate the bones into rib sections and lightly coat with the mustard and oil mixture. Dredge each piece in bread crumbs and place on a baking sheet. Lightly sprinkle with more olive oil. Bake at 375 degrees about 15 to 20 minutes, or until golden brown.

Combine the stock and Madeira in a saucepan. Reduce by half. Combine the cornstarch with ½ teaspoon water until smooth. Stir into the sauce and cook until the sauce coats the back of a spoon. Continue to simmer for several minutes over low heat to blend flavors. Add the butter and the remaining 3 tablespoons mustard. Stir until smooth.

MAKES 6 TO 8 SERVINGS

8 pounds beef ribs (from prime rib of beef), about 2 racks

Salt, pepper

¼ cup virgin olive oil, approximately

1 cup Dijon mustard

2½ cups plain bread crumbs

10 ounces veal or beef stock

½ cup Madeira

½ teaspoon cornstarch

2 tablespoons butter

Pinwheel Pork Rib Roast (page 227)

World Championship Chili (page 220)

Opposite: *Cajun Meat Loaf (page 218)*

214

Right: *Prosciutto Waffles (page 249)*

Below: *Rosemary Brioche (page 237)*

Opposite: *Angel Biscuits (page 238)*

Afternoon Tea Scones (page 243)

MEAT LOAF 72 MARKET STREET

When meat loaf enjoyed a resurgence in popularity in the mid- to late 1980s, requests for the one served at 72 Market Street, a restaurant in Venice (California, not Italy), poured in. Happily, the restaurant shared its recipe with us.

Sauté the onion, green onion, celery, carrot, green pepper, red pepper, and garlic in the butter until the vegetables are soft. Remove from skillet to a large bowl. Add the salt, cayenne, black and white pepper, cumin, and nutmeg to the vegetable mixture. Stir in the half and half, catsup, beef, pork, eggs, and bread crumbs. Mix well. Form into a loaf and place in a greased baking dish. Bake at 350 degrees for 45 to 50 minutes. Let stand 10 minutes before slicing. Pour off excess fat. Slice and serve with gravy.

MAKES 6 TO 8 SERVINGS

¾ *cup minced onion*
¾ *cup minced green onion*
½ *cup minced celery*
½ *cup minced carrot*
¼ *cup minced green pepper*
¼ *cup minced red pepper*
2 *teaspoons minced garlic*
3 *tablespoons butter*
1 *teaspoon salt*
¼ *teaspoon cayenne pepper*
1 *teaspoon black pepper*
½ *teaspoon white pepper*
½ *teaspoon ground cumin*
½ *teaspoon nutmeg*
½ *cup half and half*
½ *cup catsup*
1½ *pounds lean ground beef*
½ *pound lean ground pork*
3 *eggs, beaten*
¾ *cup dried bread crumbs*
Gravy *(recipe follows)*

GRAVY

4 *shallots, minced*
2 *tablespoons butter*
1 *sprig thyme*
1 *bay leaf*
Pinch *crushed black pepper*
1 *cup dry white wine*
1 *cup veal or beef stock*
1 *cup chicken stock*
Salt, *pepper*

Sauté the shallots in 1 tablespoon butter with the thyme, bay leaf, and black pepper. Add white wine and simmer over high heat until reduced to a glaze. Add the veal stock and the chicken stock, and simmer over high heat until sauce is reduced by one-third to one-half. Stir in remaining 1 tablespoon butter, and salt and pepper to taste until butter melts. Discard thyme sprig and bay leaf. Serve with the meat loaf.

MAKES 1 CUP

CAJUN MEAT LOAF

A reader asked for this spicy meat loaf recipe from Yanks in Beverly Hills, and the restaurant graciously complied. They use their own spice blend, however, so this recipe may not quite match the original. Anyone who isn't into spicy food would be wise to reduce the amount of chiles. This meat loaf has authority!

Melt the butter in a large skillet. Sauté the green onions, pepper, onions, celery, and chiles until tender, about 10 minutes. Add the cayenne, hot pepper sauce, Worcestershire, bay leaves, and Cajun spices. Sauté 5 minutes longer.

Add the milk, steak sauce, and catsup. Simmer for 5 minutes. Remove from the heat, then add the beef, pork, eggs, and bread crumbs. Mix well.

Pack the mixture into a 9 × 5-inch glass loaf pan. Cover with foil. Bake in a pan of hot water at 350 degrees for 30 minutes. Remove cover and bake another 30 minutes. Remove from the oven and cool before slicing.

MAKES 6 TO 8 SERVINGS

¼ cup unsalted butter

½ cup chopped green onions

1 cup finely diced sweet red, green, or yellow pepper

1 cup diced onions

¼ cup diced celery

2 small jalapeño chiles

½ teaspoon cayenne pepper

1¼ tablespoons hot pepper sauce

1¼ tablespoons Worcestershire sauce

2 bay leaves

2 tablespoons to ¼ cup Cajun spices (bottled blend)

⅓ cup milk

⅓ cup steak sauce

⅓ cup catsup

1 pound very lean ground beef

¾ pound ground pork

2 eggs

¾ cup bread crumbs

MEAT-AND-POTATOES MEAT LOAF

We were intrigued by the fact that Louise's Pantry, a favorite dining spot of both residents and visitors in Palm Springs, adds potatoes to their meat loaf. The result is one of those wonderful homey meat dishes that everyone enjoys.

Combine the beef, potatoes, bread, onion, and garlic. Put through a grinder using fine grind. Toss lightly to mix. Do not knead. Add the flour, eggs, water, poultry seasoning, and season to taste with salt and pepper. Mix well.

Pack into a 9 × 5-inch loaf pan. Cover loosely with wax paper. Place the loaf pan in a large pan with ½-inch water in the bottom of the pan. Bake at 375 degrees for 1½ hours. Add more water to large pan if needed.

MAKES 8 TO 10 SERVINGS

2½ pounds lean beef, cut into chunks

2 medium potatoes, cooked and peeled

3 slices white bread, soaked in water and squeezed dry

½ onion

½ clove garlic, minced

2 tablespoons flour

2 eggs, lightly beaten

½ cup water

½ teaspoon poultry seasoning

Salt, pepper

WORLD CHAMPIONSHIP CHILI

Chili doesn't get any better than this. C. V. Wood, Jr., one of the instigators and guiding lights of the International Chili Society, won the annual International World Championship Chili cookoff several times with this painstaking recipe. It makes 6 quarts, but freezes well so it's worth the bother.

Cut the chicken in pieces and combine with the water or broth in a large saucepan. Simmer for 2 hours, then strain off the broth. (Reserve the chicken for another use.) Melt the suet to make 6 to 8 tablespoons drippings. In a 2-quart saucepan combine the celery, tomatoes, and sugar, and simmer for 1½ hours. Trim all the fat from the flank steak and cut in ¾-inch cubes.

Boil the peeled chiles for 15 minutes until tender, remove seeds, and cut in ¼-inch squares. Mix the oregano, cumin, pepper, salt, chili powder, cilantro, and thyme with the beer until all the lumps have dissolved. Add the tomato mixture, chilies, beer mixture, and garlic to a large pot filled with the chicken broth.

Pour one-third of the suet drippings into a large skillet, add half the pork chops and brown. Repeat for the remaining pork. Add the pork to the broth and cook slowly for 30 minutes.

Brown the flank steak in the remaining suet drippings, in about 3 batches. Add to the pork and return to a simmer. Cook slowly for about 1 hour. Add the onions and green peppers, and simmer 2 to 3 hours longer, stirring with a wooden spoon every 15 to 20 minutes. Cool for 1 hour, then refrigerate 24 hours.

Reheat the chili. About 5 minutes before serving, add the cheese. If reheating only part of the chili, use ⅙ pound cheese per quart. Just before serving, add lime juice and stir with a wooden spoon.

MAKES 6 QUARTS

1 (3-pound) chicken
1½ quarts water or 4 (10¾-ounce) cans chicken broth
½ pound beef suet or ½ cup oil
¼ cup finely chopped celery
7 cups peeled, chopped tomatoes
2 teaspoons sugar
4 pounds flank steak
6 long green chiles, peeled
1 tablespoon dried oregano
1 tablespoon ground cumin
1 tablespoon black pepper
4 teaspoons salt
5 tablespoons chili powder
1 teaspoon chopped cilantro
1 teaspoon dried thyme
1 cup beer
2 cloves garlic, minced
5 pounds boneless thin center-cut pork chops
3 medium onions, cut in ½-inch pieces
2 green peppers, cut in ¼-inch pieces
1 pound Jack cheese, shredded
Juice of 1 lime

SANTA ANITA RACETRACK BEEF STEW

The beef stew served at Santa Anita Racetrack is outstanding. Tony Pope has been the culinary force at the track for a number of years.

Melt the shortening in a large saucepan. Add the onions and shallots. Sauté 5 minutes or until tender.

Dredge the meat in flour, shaking off the excess. Sauté the meat until lightly browned, about 10 minutes. Add the beef broth. Cook until meat is almost done, about 30 minutes. Then add the carrots, celery, leeks, and tomatoes. Cover and simmer over medium heat about 20 minutes. Add the potatoes and cook 20 to 25 minutes, or until the potatoes and vegetables are done. Add more beef broth, if necessary. Season to taste with salt and pepper.

MAKES 6 TO 8 SERVINGS

3 tablespoons shortening

½ pound onions, minced

¼ pound shallots, minced

2 pounds top sirloin or chuck beef, cut into 1-inch cubes

½ cup seasoned flour

1 quart beef broth, approximately

1 pound carrots, peeled and cut into chunks

1 pound celery, cut into chunks

½ pound leeks, white part only, cut into chunks

1 pound tomatoes, peeled and quartered

1 pound potatoes, peeled and sliced

Salt, pepper

AL'S GOULASH

When a reader requested a recipe for a rich, rib-sticking Hungarian-style goulash, staff writer Rose Dosti had just the thing. She provided one she knew well—a recipe her father, a professional chef, served at his restaurants.

Combine the beef, bay leaf, onions, garlic, paprika, and salt in a large saucepan. Add the tomatoes. Cover and simmer over very low heat for 2 to 2½ hours, or until the meat falls apart when tested with a fork. Add a small amount of broth, if needed, to keep the sauce from scorching. Serve over noodles.

MAKES 6 TO 8 SERVINGS

Note: As the onions and tomatoes produce the liquid for the thick sauce, they must be cooked over very low heat to prevent rapid evaporation. If necessary, additional liquid may be added to keep the mixture the consistency of a thick sauce.

2½ pounds boneless chuck beef, cut into 1½-inch pieces

1 bay leaf, crumbled

5 onions, sliced

2 cloves garlic, minced

2 tablespoons Hungarian sweet paprika

1 teaspoon salt

4 tomatoes, coarsely chopped

Broth or water, optional

Hot cooked egg noodles, optional

CALIFORNIA TAMALE PIE

When we couldn't find the right recipe for a typical tamale pie, which is a familiar casserole dish for most Southern Californians, a reader sent us this one.

Mix the cornmeal, milk, and egg in a 2½-quart casserole. Brown the meat in a skillet, stirring to keep crumbly.

Add the chili seasoning mix, salt, tomatoes, corn, and olives, mixing well. Stir into the cornmeal mixture. Bake at 350 degrees for 1 hour, 15 minutes. Sprinkle with cheese and bake until cheese melts, about 5 minutes longer.

MAKES 6 TO 8 SERVINGS

¾ cup yellow cornmeal

1½ cups milk

1 egg, beaten

1 pound lean ground beef

1 package chili seasoning mix

2 teaspoons seasoned salt

1 (1-pound) can whole tomatoes

1 (17-ounce) can whole kernel corn, drained

1 (7½-ounce) can pitted black olives, drained

1 cup shredded Cheddar cheese

DONNA'S BEEF POT PIES

When homey foods like meat loaf and meat pies regained popularity in the late eighties, this beef pot pie created by our test kitchen chef Donna Deane was an instant success. It was so good, in fact, it won a spot on the list of 1987 best recipes of the year.

Heat the oil in a large saucepan. Sauté the onion, garlic, celery, and carrot until tender. Combine the beef and chicken broths. Add enough water to measure 4 cups. Add to the vegetables. Cover and simmer about 10 minutes.

Combine the flour and ⅔ cup water, stirring until smooth. Stir into the simmering broth. Heat, stirring, until boiling and thickened. Stir in the meat, horseradish, peas, and corn. Add the beef drippings, if any, to the broth. Simmer about 5 minutes, stirring occasionally, to blend flavors. Season to taste with salt and pepper. Spoon the mixture into a 2½-quart ovenproof casserole or individual 4- to 5-inch ovenproof casseroles. Set aside while making the pastry.

Roll the pastry to ¼-inch thickness. Depending on cookware used, cut rounds of dough ½ inch larger than the tops of the casseroles. Press the pastry against the edges to seal. Cut vent holes on top. Sprinkle cheese over the pastry. Place the casseroles on a baking sheet. Bake at 400 degrees for about 30 minutes, or until pastry is golden.

MAKES 6 TO 8 SERVINGS

Combine the flour and salt. Cut in the shortening until the dough is the size of peas. Stir in the cheese. Add enough water so that dough clings together. Gather into a ball.

2 tablespoons oil
½ cup chopped onion
1 clove garlic, minced
½ cup chopped celery
½ cup chopped peeled carrot
1 (14½-ounce) can clear beef broth
1 (14½-ounce) can clear chicken broth
½ cup flour
4 cups diced cooked beef, drippings reserved
2 tablespoons prepared horseradish
1 cup frozen peas, thawed and drained
1 cup frozen corn, thawed and drained
Salt, pepper
Pastry (recipe follows)
½ cup shredded Swiss cheese

PASTRY
1½ cups flour
¾ teaspoon salt
10 tablespoons shortening
½ cup shredded Swiss cheese
4 to 5 tablespoons ice water

INDONESIAN RACK OF LAMB

Trader Vic's in Beverly Hills is famous for its ingenious use of Oriental flavorings. When it closed briefly for a face-lift in 1986, we were lucky enough to acquire a number of recipes that could be prepared at home, including this marinated lamb rack. It's a wonderful dish for company.

Sauté the celery, onion, and garlic in oil. Add the vinegar, steak sauce, curry powder, hot pepper sauce, honey, oregano, bay leaves, mustard, and lemon juice and peel. Bring to a boil, reduce heat, and simmer for 2 minutes. Chill.

Add the lamb chops or rack to the mixture. Marinate about 4 hours in the refrigerator. Drain. Wrap the bones with foil, leaving only the meat exposed. Arrange in a shallow baking pan. Brush the meat with the marinade and bake at 400 degrees for about 20 minutes or longer, depending on thickness of meat and desired doneness. Turn meat once and baste frequently with marinade. Place under broiler to brown top of roast, if necessary.

MAKES 6 SERVINGS

⅓ cup finely chopped celery
⅓ cup finely chopped onion
1 clove garlic, minced
¾ cup oil
¼ cup vinegar
2 teaspoons steak sauce
3 tablespoons curry powder
2 dashes hot pepper sauce
3 tablespoons honey
1 teaspoon dried oregano
2 bay leaves
½ cup prepared mustard
Juice and peel of 1 large lemon
6 lamb chops or rack of lamb with 6 chops, trimmed of fat

LAMB SHANKS WITH ONIONS, GREEK STYLE

When Helen Gilmore submitted this recipe to our "My Best Recipe" column, our tasters decreed it a winner. The pickling spices give the meat a delicious tang.

Heat the olive oil in a large skillet over medium heat. Brown the lamb shanks and garlic. Dilute the tomato purée with wine and water and pour over the shanks. Add the bag of pickling spices and bay leaves. Season to taste with salt and pepper. Simmer for 2½ hours. Add more water if sauce thickens too much.

Add the onions during the last 40 minutes. (Lamb will fall off the bone when done.) Remove the bay leaves and pickling spice bag.

MAKES 2 SERVINGS

Note: Serve with French bread and green salad.

3 tablespoons olive oil
2 lamb shanks
5 cloves garlic
1 (8-ounce) can tomato purée
1 cup red wine
2 cups water or enough to cover shanks
1 heaping teaspoon mixed pickling spices tied in cheesecloth
2 bay leaves
Salt, pepper
6 small white boiling onions

SCALOPPINE ALLA FIORENTINA

Silvio De Mori grew up in Paris, but went back to his Italian roots when he opened Tuttobene in West Hollywood. The fresh tomato-basil sauce served with thick slices of veal scaloppine makes the dish a real delight for those who have sampled it at his restaurant.

Rinse and pat veal scaloppine dry. Mix the bread crumbs with the rosemary leaves and use this to bread the scaloppine on both sides.

Heat 2 tablespoons olive oil in a large nonstick skillet. Add the scaloppine and cook for 1 minute on each side. Set aside and keep warm.

Heat the remaining 1 tablespoon olive oil in a separate skillet. Add the onion, garlic, celery, and carrot. Cook for 20 minutes until mushy and sauce-like. If too dry, add chicken broth as needed to keep moist.

Add the peeled tomatoes with 1 tablespoon basil. Simmer over low heat, whisking until the sauce is reduced to a smooth purée, about 10 minutes. Season to taste with salt and pepper.

Place the breaded scaloppine in the hot sauce. Transfer the scaloppine to a serving platter. Top with some of the sauce and sprinkle with fresh basil. Place the diced tomato around for garnish.

MAKES 4 SERVINGS

4 (½-inch thick) veal scaloppine (about 1 pound)
¼ cup fine, dried bread crumbs
1 tablespoon minced fresh rosemary leaves
3 tablespoons extra-virgin olive oil
1 onion, minced
1 clove garlic, minced
1 stalk celery, diced
1 carrot, diced
Chicken broth
1 pound tomatoes, peeled
2 tablespoons chopped fresh basil leaves
Salt, black pepper
1 tomato, diced, for garnish

PORK DIJONNAISE

This recipe from Sonoma's Au Relais is a true rarity. It earned a unanimous vote from the food staff as one of the year's twelve best recipes back in 1983. And it's just as popular today.

Sauté the pork chops in 1½ tablespoons butter until browned and almost done. Place in a baking dish and bake, covered, at 350 degrees for 15 minutes, or until well done. Keep warm. Drain off excess fat.

Melt the remaining ½ tablespoon butter in a skillet. Add the shallots and garlic and sauté briefly. Add the cornichons and wine. Simmer over medium-high heat until a glaze forms. Stir in the cream and mustard. Cook, stirring, until the sauce is smooth and heated through.

Place the chops on a serving platter and pour the sauce over the meat. Sprinkle with chopped parsley.

MAKES 6 SERVINGS

6 medium pork chops
2 tablespoons butter or margarine
2 shallots, chopped
2 cloves garlic, chopped
12 cornichons, julienned
½ cup dry white wine
½ cup whipping cream
2 tablespoons Dijon mustard
Chopped parsley or cilantro

PORK TENDERLOIN WITH ROSEMARY

One of the major joys of having a test kitchen at your beck and call is that it makes it possible to work out new (or adapted) recipes easily. This excellent pork tenderloin recipe was developed for a feature on cooking with fresh rosemary.

Place the tenderloins in a roasting pan. Season to taste with salt and pepper, sprinkle with the minced garlic. Arrange the onions around the pork. Melt 1 tablespoon butter, combine with the rosemary and oil, and drizzle over the pork and onions. Roast at 325 degrees for 45 minutes to 1 hour, until tenderloins are tender and cooked through.

Remove tenderloins and onions from roasting pan. Deglaze the pan with water. Bring to a boil. Stir in the wine. Blend together the flour and remaining 3 tablespoons butter. Beat into the sauce. Return to a boil, stirring until thickened. Season to taste with salt and pepper. Slice the tenderloins, and serve with the onions and sauce.

MAKES 4 TO 8 SERVINGS

2 whole (½- to 1-pound) pork tenderloins

Salt, pepper

3 cloves garlic, minced

4 small onions, cut into quarters

¼ cup butter or margarine

1 tablespoon fresh rosemary

1 tablespoon oil

1½ cups water

½ cup Madeira

3 tablespoons flour

ARISTA

This simple pork roast recipe from Evan Kleiman and Viana La Place at Angeli restaurant on Melrose in Los Angeles is absolutely delicious. We chose it as one of the twelve best recipes of 1985.

Make a paste of minced garlic, fennel seeds, and salt and pepper to taste in a mortar and pestle, or mash with the side of a chef's knife. Unroll roast, if tied. Spread most of the paste over the meat, reserving 1 tablespoon or more. Roll and tie roast so that the white tenderloin is in the center and dark meat is on the outside. Make a few incisions with a sharp knife about ½-inch deep in roast and stuff with some of the paste. Rub olive oil over meat and place in roasting pan.

Roast, uncovered, at 350 degrees for 2½ to 3 hours or until thermometer inserted in center registers 170 degrees. Baste the roast 2 or 3 times with pan juices. Remove roast from oven and cool slightly. Slice into ½-inch slices and drizzle olive oil over meat, if desired.

MAKES 8 TO 10 SERVINGS

6 cloves garlic, minced

1 to 2 tablespoons fennel seeds

2 teaspoons coarse salt

Freshly ground pepper

1 (7-pound) boneless pork rib roast

Fruity olive oil

PINWHEEL PORK RIB ROAST

This is definitely a special occasion entrée. With a long knife, you can cut the bone-in pork roast pinwheel fashion yourself. But don't even think about trying that if your knives aren't truly sharp. It's easier to ask a butcher to do it for you.

Soak the apricots in the apricot brandy overnight.

Prepare the pork roast (or have a butcher do it for you) by first trimming any meat or fat from the tips of the bones to a depth of about 1 inch. Place roast on bony end so that trimmed rib ends are pointing up. Then, with a very sharp knife, cut through the meat about ½-inch from the trimmed ribs to ½-inch from the bottom. Press the meat away from the bones and turning the knife blade so that it is parallel with the cutting board, pinwheel fashion, until you have an unrolled ½-inch-thick flat rectangle of meat extending from the bone side. Reroll the roast and set aside.

Melt the butter in a skillet. Sauté 1 clove garlic until lightly golden. Then sauté the onion and celery until tender. Stir in the rosemary, sage, and thyme. Remove from the skillet to a mixing bowl.

Drain the apricot halves and set aside. Add the brandy to the garlic mixture. Reserve 8 apricot halves. Cut the remaining apricots into quarters and add to the brandy and garlic mixture. Stir in the bread. Add enough chicken broth to moisten the stuffing.

Unroll the roast and rub all over with salt and pepper and the remaining clove of minced garlic. Spread the stuffing evenly over the meat. Arrange the reserved apricot halves in a row along the short edge of the meat rectangle. Roll up tightly and firmly tie.

Place the roast, bone side down, on a rack in a heavy roasting pan. Place in a 425-degree oven. Reduce the temperature to 325 degrees and roast for 2½ to 3 hours, or until meat thermometer registers 165 degrees. Remove the roast and let rest 10 to 15 minutes before carving. Reserve about 2 tablespoons of the drippings to make the gravy. (Or skim the fat from the drippings and serve the pan juices with the roast.)

MAKES 6 TO 7 SERVINGS

1 (6-ounce) package apricot halves
½ cup apricot brandy
1 7-rib pork roast, about 4 pounds
½ cup butter or margarine
2 cloves garlic, minced
1 onion, chopped
2 stalks celery, chopped
1 tablespoon fresh rosemary
1 tablespoon fresh sage
1 tablespoon fresh thyme
1 (1-pound) loaf day-old white bread, cubed
1 to 1½ cups chicken broth
Salt, pepper
Gravy (recipe follows)

Heat the drippings in a saucepan over medium heat. Stir in the flour and cook for 1 minute. Add the chicken broth and continue to cook, stirring until the mixture thickens. Season to taste with salt and pepper. Serve hot with the roast.

GRAVY

2 tablespoons butter or pork drippings
3 tablespoons flour
2 cups chicken broth
Salt, pepper

BARBECUED CHICKEN AND RIBS

This recipe won honors for Lynn and Tonia Hopkins of Richmond, Utah, in a Dutch oven cookoff held in Logan, Utah, in 1987. It's great for a backyard barbecue or a potluck. The Dutch oven referred to here is the footed type of camping oven, not the ordinary black cast iron pot most of us eventually acquire for our kitchens. For those not into camping, this recipe adapts nicely to indoor cooking on a conventional range.

Trim any excess fat from the beef and pork ribs. Season the ribs and chicken to taste with salt and pepper. Heat the oil in a 12-inch Dutch oven placed on 9 to 10 evenly distributed hot coals. Add the onions and sauté until transparent but not browned. Stir in the water, vinegar, catsup, and brown sugar. Cook, stirring often, until the mixture thickens, about 1 hour.

Add the ribs to the sauce, stirring to coat well. Continue cooking, stirring often and replacing coals as needed, about 1 hour.

Add the chicken, stir to coat well, and continue cooking until ribs and chicken are very tender, about 1 hour longer. The oven may be covered or not, but the sauce will be thicker if the oven is left uncovered.

MAKES ABOUT 10 SERVINGS

Note: For conventional range cooking, use an 8-quart pot and cook on the stove, following the same directions.

1 to 2 pounds beef short ribs

1 to 2 pounds country-style pork ribs

2 whole chickens, skinned and cut up

Salt, pepper

2 tablespoons oil

2 onions, chopped

2 cups water

1 cup vinegar

4 cups catsup

1 cup brown sugar, packed

PEPPER-WRAPPED ITALIAN SAUSAGE

*A boutique deli, Tutto Italia, on Sunset Boulevard in Los Angeles, sent us this unusual recipe
for hot Italian sausages wrapped in roasted red peppers or pimientos.*

Place the sausages in a baking dish. Sprinkle with the crushed red pepper and half the lemon juice. Bake at 375 degrees for 1 hour, or until the sausages are browned and crispy. Drain on paper towels.

Wrap each sausage with roasted peppers and place seam-side-down on a serving platter. Combine the remaining lemon juice, red wine vinegar, and oregano in a small bowl. Season to taste with salt and pepper. Blend well and pour over sausages. Garnish with chopped green onions.

MAKES 8 SERVINGS

8 hot Italian sausages
¼ teaspoon crushed red pepper
Juice of 1 lemon
8 pieces roasted peeled sweet red
    peppers or canned whole
    pimientos
1 tablespoon red wine vinegar
¼ teaspoon dried oregano
Salt, pepper
Chopped green onions, for garnish

HONEY HAM

*Commercial baked hams sweetened with a honey glaze are big sellers in Southern
California. A few years back one of our readers, Laura Wang, sent us this recipe. It was an
instant winner and also one of our most requested recipes.*

Make diagonal slits, ½-inch apart, halfway through the ham to where the knife touches the bone. Place the ham in a deep bowl and barely cover with water. Stir in the sugar. Soak for at least 2 days in the refrigerator. Drain.

Set the ham in a roasting dish lined with enough foil to completely wrap the ham. Cover with the honey and orange juice. Insert the cloves randomly over the meat. Wrap the ham tightly in the foil. Bake at 200 degrees for 6 to 7 hours, unwrapping and basting occasionally with the honey glaze. When the ham is cooked, unwrap and bake at 450 degrees for about 15 minutes for slightly crisp skin.

MAKES ABOUT 10 TO 12 SERVINGS

1 medium (about 7-pound) smoked
    pork picnic shoulder
Water
2 cups sugar
1 cup honey or brown sugar
1 (6-ounce) can frozen orange
    juice concentrate, thawed
1 teaspoon whole cloves

BREADS

The homey, heavy multi-grained breads of the late seventies gave way to some subtle changes in the early eighties. We no longer had the time to bake breads that required long rising periods. We still liked the sturdy breads but preferred to buy rather than make them at home.

Instead we fell in love with such wonderful indulgences as "maxi" muffins, which we ate on the run as we headed for the office. And we flavored them with vegetables and herbs rather than with sugar and other sweet flavorings.

Quick breads came into their own during the eighties. Fruit breads made with chutney, nut breads, and breads flavored with spicy sausages and chiles found their way to our tables.

Biscuits returned to favor, sometimes plain and sometimes flavored. We still liked our morning sweet rolls and cinnamon-flavored coffee cakes, and we dusted off the waffle iron as we discovered that breakfast meetings at home were more time and cost efficient—and more productive—than were luncheon meetings.

But probably the best thing that happened about breads in the eighties is that we realized what an important role they play in our diets. We need them. We need their fiber and the vitamins and carbohydrates they provide. And if they just happen to taste good, too, so much the better.

SEED BREAD

This sturdy fruit and nut bread came from Katie Trefethen, one of the owners of the Trefethen Winery in Napa Valley and an inspired cook.

Place ½ cup very warm water in a large, warmed bowl. Swirl water around bowl. Add the yeast and sugar. When mixture is bubbly and light, stir in 1¾ cups warm water, white flour, and warm milk. Set mixture in warm place, covered, until light and doubled in size.

Add the walnut oil, salt, egg, honey, rye flour, cornmeal, bran, whole wheat flour, raisins, walnuts, sunflower seeds, poppy seeds, and caraway seeds. Knead by hand or use dough hook attachment on mixer or processor. Add more white flour as needed. When mixture is no longer sticky, place in a greased bowl, turning to coat. Cover, and allow to rise until doubled.

Punch down. Divide into 3 pieces, so as to have 2 large portions and 1 small portion. Shape into loaves and place the 2 larger loaves in two 9 × 4-inch loaf pans; place the small loaf in a 7½ × 4-inch loaf pan. Let rise to top of pan or slightly over.

Bake at 350 degrees for 50 minutes or until done. Remove from oven and place on racks to cool. Brush with glaze.

MAKES TWO 9 × 4-INCH LOAVES AND ONE 7½ × 4-INCH LOAF

Combine the egg white and water. Mix well.

Water
3 packages dry yeast
1½ tablespoons sugar
3 cups unbleached white flour
1 cup warm milk
2 tablespoons walnut oil
1 tablespoon salt
1 egg
½ cup honey
1½ cups rye flour
1 cup cornmeal
1 cup unprocessed bran
3 cups whole wheat flour
½ cup golden raisins
½ cup chopped walnuts
½ cup sunflower seeds
½ cup poppy seeds
¼ cup caraway seeds
Glaze (recipe follows)

GLAZE
1 egg white
1 teaspoon water

LEMON TEA BREAD

Naomi Schwartz, chef de cuisine at St. Orres in Gualala, California, shared this recipe at a reader's request. She pointed out that hers is a variation on a classic.

Cream together the butter and sugar until light. Add the eggs and beat well. Stir in the lemon peel. Sift together the flour and baking powder. Alternately add milk and flour to the batter. Turn into a well-greased 9 × 5-inch loaf pan. Bake at 375 degrees for 45 minutes, or until loaf springs back when lightly touched. Remove from the oven and pierce the top of the loaf with the tines of a fork. Pour the lemon syrup over the bread. Let stand 10 minutes before turning out of the pan. Chill.

MAKES 1 LOAF

Combine the lemon peel, juice, and sugar in a small bowl. Stir to blend until the sugar is dissolved.

½ cup unsalted butter or margarine
1 cup sugar
2 eggs, lightly beaten
Grated peel of 1 lemon
1½ cups flour
1 teaspoon baking powder
½ cup milk
Lemon syrup *(recipe follows)*

LEMON SYRUP
Grated peel and juice of 1 lemon
¼ cup sugar

ORANGE-NUT BREAD

We had to go all the way to Gilford, New Hampshire, for this excellent orange bread. The recipe was shared by the Mountain Air Resort after readers raved about it.

Combine the flour, baking powder, salt, baking soda, and sugar in a bowl. In a large bowl beat the eggs. Stir in the milk, orange juice, oil, and grated orange peel. Add the flour mixture, mixing well. Stir in the nuts. Pour into a greased 9 × 5-inch loaf pan and bake at 350 degrees for 60 minutes.

MAKES 1 LOAF

2½ cups flour
½ teaspoon baking powder
¼ teaspoon salt
¼ teaspoon baking soda
1 cup sugar
2 eggs
½ cup milk
½ cup orange juice
¾ cup oil
Grated peel of 1 orange
½ cup chopped walnuts

MANGO BREAD

When mango season hits, we brush off this superb fruit bread recipe, a classic from the Kaanapali Beach Hotel on Maui in Hawaii.

Combine the flour, cinnamon, soda, salt, and sugar. Beat the eggs with the oil and add to the flour mixture. Blend in the mangoes, lemon juice, and raisins. Turn into 2 greased 8 × 4-inch loaf pans and bake at 350 degrees for 1 hour, or until wood pick inserted in the center comes out clean.

MAKES 2 LOAVES

2 cups flour, sifted
2 teaspoons ground cinnamon
2 teaspoons soda
½ teaspoon salt
1¼ cups sugar
2 eggs
¾ cup oil
2½ cups chopped mangoes
1 teaspoon lemon juice
½ cup raisins

MACADAMIA NUT BREAD

This is a personal favorite that freezes beautifully. It's a wonderful choice when a hostess or kitchen gift is needed.

Place the nuts, pineapple, and coconut in a large bowl. Sift the flour, sugar, baking powder, and salt over the nut mixture. Mix until the nuts and fruit are completely coated with the flour.

Beat the eggs until foamy, then add the vanilla. Stir in the nut mixture. Spoon into a greased wax paper-lined 8 × 4-inch loaf pan. Bake at 300 degrees for 50 minutes, or until wood pick inserted in the center comes out clean. Remove from the pan and cool completely. When cool, wrap in foil and refrigerate.

MAKES 1 LOAF

3 cups whole macadamia nuts
1 (15¼-ounce) can pineapple chunks, very well drained
1 (3½-ounce) can flaked coconut
¾ cup sifted flour
¾ cup sugar
½ teaspoon baking powder
½ teaspoon salt
3 eggs
1 teaspoon vanilla

CHUTNEY BREAD

This is a marvellous tea bread that freezes well. Try it the next time you want to make kitchen gifts for the holidays. But whip the curried cream cheese at the last minute.

Combine the flour, sugars, baking powder, salt, oil, milk, egg, and orange peel in a mixing bowl. Beat 30 seconds. Add the chutney and nuts. Mix lightly, do not overmix.

Turn into a greased (bottom only) 9 × 5-inch loaf or 9-inch tube pan and bake at 350 degrees for 55 to 65 minutes, or until a cake tester inserted in the center comes out clean.

Cool slightly. Loosen the sides of the pan and remove the bread. Cool. Serve with the curried cheese spread.

MAKES 1 LOAF

2½ cups flour
½ cup granulated sugar
½ cup brown sugar, packed
3½ teaspoons baking powder
1 teaspoon salt
3 tablespoons oil
1¼ cups milk
1 egg
1 tablespoon grated orange peel
1 (10-ounce) jar mild chutney
1 cup chopped nuts
Curried Cheese Spread (recipe follows)

CURRIED CHEESE SPREAD

Beat the cream cheese with the sugar, curry powder, and salt just until blended.

MAKES ABOUT 1 CUP

1 (8-ounce) package cream cheese, softened
2 teaspoons sugar
2 teaspoons curry powder
Pinch salt

SANTACAFE JALAPEÑO BRIOCHE

The Santacafe in Santa Fe, New Mexico, has made a name for itself with this unusual jalapeño-flavored brioche. It's a fine companion for a brunch featuring huevos rancheros or some other Mexican-style breakfast egg dish.

Combine the flour, sugar, yeast, salt, and red and black peppers. Mix well. Stir in the milk and water. Beat the eggs and add slowly, stirring. Add the chiles. Gradually blend in the butter. Cover and let rise until doubled. Punch down. Refrigerate 6 hours or overnight.

Place the dough in 2 9-inch loaf pans sprayed with nonstick spray. Bake at 375 degrees for 40 to 50 minutes, or until golden. Remove from pans immediately and cool on a wire rack before cutting.

MAKES 2 LOAVES

3½ cups flour
2 tablespoons sugar
1 tablespoon yeast
2 teaspoons salt
1 tablespoon crushed red pepper
¾ teaspoon black pepper
1½ tablespoons milk
1 tablespoon water
6 eggs, beaten
¾ cup diced green chiles, drained
1 pound butter, cut into pieces

ROSEMARY BRIOCHE

One of the great charms of rosemary is that it goes so well with such a variety of foods. We added it to brioche dough and discovered the result was superb . . . as aromatic as it was tasty. Try this bread with a hot fresh tomato soup on a cold day.

Sprinkle the yeast over the water in a small bowl. Stir to dissolve. Heat together the milk, sugar, and salt until slightly warm. Beat 4 whole eggs with the egg yolks. Then beat in the yeast, milk mixture, and butter. Stir in the rosemary. Add enough flour to make a soft dough. Knead lightly and place in a lightly greased bowl in a warm place. Cover and let rise in a warm, draft-free spot until the dough doubles in size.

Punch down and turn out onto a lightly floured surface. Shape into 2 braided loaves or 12 individual brioche, adding flour as necessary.

For braided loaves, divide the dough into 4 parts. Roll each part into a strand about 16 inches long. Braid 2 strands together to make 1 loaf, pinching the ends together. Repeat for the second braid. Place on a greased baking sheet. Let rise until doubled. Beat the remaining whole egg and brush the braids. Bake at 400 degrees for 12 to 18 minutes, or until golden brown.

For individual brioche, grease 12 small brioche molds. Divide the dough into 12 parts. Pinch off ⅓ of each piece of dough and roll both large and small pieces into balls. Place the large portion in the mold. Make a slight indentation on top and place in it the small ball of dough. Repeat with the remaining dough. Let rise in a warm, draft-free place until doubled. Brush with beaten egg. Bake at 400 degrees for 10 to 15 minutes, or until golden brown. Remove to a wire rack to cool.

MAKES 2 BRAIDS OR 12 INDIVIDUAL BRIOCHE

1 package dry yeast
¼ cup warm water
½ cup milk
⅓ cup sugar
½ teaspoon salt
5 eggs
2 egg yolks
1 cup softened butter or margarine
2 tablespoons fresh rosemary
3½ to 4 cups flour

ANGEL BISCUITS

The recipe for these cloud-like baking powder biscuits obviously came West with a transplanted Southerner.

Combine 1½ cups flour, the sugar, salt, baking powder, soda, and yeast in the large bowl of an electric mixer. Combine the buttermilk, water, and shortening in a saucepan. Heat over low heat until the liquid is very warm, about 120 to 130 degrees (the shortening does not need to melt).

Gradually add the liquid to the dry ingredients and beat for 2 minutes at medium speed, scraping the bowl occasionally. Add ¾ cup flour or enough to make a thick batter. Beat at high speed for 2 minutes, scraping the bowl occasionally. Stir in enough additional flour to make a soft dough.

Turn out onto a lightly floured board. Knead about 20 to 25 times to form a ball. Roll the dough out on a floured board to ½-inch thickness. Using a 2-inch biscuit cutter, cut out the dough and place on ungreased baking sheets.

Cover and let rise in a warm place, free from drafts, about 1 hour. Bake at 400 degrees for about 20 minutes, or until golden. Remove from baking sheets to wire racks. Serve hot.

MAKES ABOUT 2½ DOZEN BISCUITS

5 cups flour, approximately
¼ cup sugar
1 teaspoon salt
1 tablespoon baking powder
1 teaspoon soda
1 package dry yeast
2 cups buttermilk
¼ cup water
¾ cup shortening

FRESH STRAWBERRY MUFFINS WITH STRAWBERRY-CREAM CHEESE SPREAD

Every year the strawberry growers in the Oxnard area have a contest to see who can come up with the best strawberry recipe. Catherine Camp was a winner one year with these excellent muffins served with a strawberry-flavored cream cheese spread.

Sprinkle the chopped strawberries with 1 tablespoon sugar and set aside. Sift together the flour, remaining ¾ cup sugar, baking powder, and salt in a large bowl.

Beat the eggs until light in a small bowl. Add the oil, milk, and orange peel, and blend well. Add the egg mixture to the flour mixture. Stir until mixed, 10 to 15 strokes.

Drain the chopped berries and fold into the batter. Fill paper-lined cups ⅔ full. Bake in a convection oven at 325 degrees for 20 minutes or in a regular oven at 400 degrees for 15 minutes, or until a wood pick inserted in center comes out clean.

Serve warm or cooled with the strawberry-cream cheese spread. Garnish each muffin with a fan-shaped berry.

MAKES ABOUT 1 DOZEN

1 cup chopped strawberries

¾ cup plus 1 tablespoon sugar

2 cups flour

2 teaspoons baking powder

1 teaspoon salt

3 eggs

¼ cup oil

½ cup milk

1 teaspoon grated orange peel

Strawberry-Cream Cheese Spread *(recipe follows)*

12 whole strawberries, approximately, cut fan-shape

STRAWBERRY-CREAM CHEESE SPREAD

1 (8-ounce) package cream cheese, softened

¼ cup crushed or chopped strawberries

Mix cream cheese and strawberries until blended.

ZUCCHINI MUFFINS

When zucchini floods the market each summer, readers flood us with requests for this recipe for zucchini muffins from the May Company department store's tearoom. They're wonderful fresh and they reheat well in the microwave.

Combine the eggs, zucchini, flour, sugar, baking powder, soda, salt, nutmeg, cinnamon, cloves, vanilla, water, and oil in a large bowl, blending well. (Batter can be refrigerated at this point until ready to use.)

Pour into 12 well-greased or paper-lined muffin cups and bake at 375 degrees for 15 minutes, or until a wood pick inserted in the center comes out clean.

MAKES 12 MUFFINS

2 eggs
½ cup grated zucchini
1 cup flour
½ cup sugar
½ teaspoon baking powder
½ teaspoon baking soda
½ teaspoon salt
½ teaspoon ground nutmeg
½ teaspoon ground cinnamon
⅛ teaspoon ground cloves
½ teaspoon vanilla
⅓ cup water
⅓ cup oil

HOT PUMPKIN BISCUITS

Debra Burton of Seal Beach won the "My Best Recipe" award one week in 1985 with her grandmother's recipe for hot pumpkin biscuits. They are super with a bowl of hot soup on a chilly evening.

Sift together the flour, sugar, baking powder, salt, and cinnamon into a bowl. Cut in the butter until the mixture looks like coarse crumbs. Stir in the pecans. Combine the half and half and canned pumpkin. Add to the flour mixture. (Dough should be quite stiff.)

Turn the dough out onto a lightly floured board and knead gently a few times. Roll out the dough to ½-inch thickness. Cut biscuits with a 2-inch-round cutter.

Set the biscuits 1 inch apart on a lightly greased baking sheet. Bake at 450 degrees until golden, about 20 minutes.

MAKES ABOUT 20 BISCUITS

2 cups sifted flour
3 tablespoons sugar
4 teaspoons baking powder
½ teaspoon salt
½ teaspoon ground cinnamon
½ cup butter, cut up
⅓ cup chopped pecans
½ cup half and half
⅔ cup canned or mashed cooked pumpkin

BULLOCK'S POPOVERS

Memorable popovers are served in bullock's department Store tea rooms. Just ask us, we can tell you how popular they are from the number of times we've been asked to repeat the recipe.

Beat the eggs in a bowl. Beat in the milk until blended. Combine the flour and salt, then work the butter into the flour. Gradually add the flour mixture to the milk and eggs and blend well. Fill 8 well-greased custard cups. Place on a baking sheet and bake at 400 degrees for about 1 hour or until golden.

MAKES 8 POPOVERS

Note: If using new custard cups, season to prevent sticking. Cups should be greased and placed in a hot oven for 30 minutes. Clean, and re-grease cups before using.

6 eggs
2 cups milk
2 cups flour
¾ teaspoon salt
6 tablespoons butter or margarine

PECAN STICKY BUNS

We've run the recipe for Pecan Sticky Buns so many times it's worn to a frazzle. Just shows how good these wonderful breakfast treats are.

Scald the milk and stir in the granulated sugar, salt, and ½ cup butter. Cool to lukewarm. Measure the warm water into a large warm bowl, sprinkle or crumble in the yeast and stir to dissolve. Stir in the lukewarm milk mixture, the egg, and half of the flour. Beat until smooth.

Stir in the remaining flour to make a stiff batter. Cover and refrigerate dough for at least 2 hours. Melt the remaining ½ cup butter and stir in the honey, 1 cup brown sugar, and 1 cup chopped nuts. Spoon this into well-greased muffin pans. Combine the remaining 1 cup brown sugar and remaining ½ cup nuts.

Remove the dough from the refrigerator and divide in half. Roll out each portion to form a 12-inch square. Sprinkle each with the brown sugar-nut filling and roll up jelly-roll fashion. Cut into 1-inch slices and place, cut side down, in the prepared pans. Cover and let rise in a warm place until doubled, about 1 hour. Bake at 350 degrees for about 25 minutes.

MAKES 24 BUNS

1 cup milk
½ cup granulated sugar
1 teaspoon salt
1 cup butter or margarine
¼ cup warm water
1 package cake yeast
1 egg
4 cups flour
½ cup honey
2 cups brown sugar, packed
1½ cups chopped pecans

AFTERNOON TEA SCONES

Mamie Meechan, a canny Scotch woman who escapes the worst of Edinburgh winters each year by visiting her daughter, Margaret Dennis, of Long Beach, has a deft hand at producing cloud-like Scottish scones. Her secret? Probably the self-rising flour she uses.

Place the flour in a large bowl. Cut in 3 tablespoons butter with a fork or pastry cutter until the mixture resembles coarse meal. Stir in the sugar. Whisk the egg and milk. Gradually, and stirring lightly, add all but 1 tablespoon of the liquid to obtain a soft dough. Turn out onto a floured board and lightly pat the dough into a round, handling as little as possible.

Roll the dough to about ¾-inch thickness with a floured rolling pin. Cut into 2-inch rounds with a biscuit cutter. (If the pastry sticks to the cutter, dip the cutter in flour.) Place the rounds 1 inch apart on a lightly greased baking sheet. Press trimmings together lightly and reroll to cut more rounds.

Brush the tops of the scones with the remaining 1 tablespoon egg and milk mixture. Bake at 450 degrees for 10 to 12 minutes, or until lightly browned. Serve at once with butter and raspberry jam or cool on a wire rack. Though best if eaten the day they are baked, scones can be frozen, and any leftovers can be toasted.

MAKES ABOUT 12 SCONES

2 cups self-rising flour
Butter or margarine
1 tablespoon sugar
1 egg
¾ cup milk
Raspberry jam

Variations:
SULTANA SCONES
Add 3 tablespoons golden raisins along with the sugar to basic recipe.

CHEESE SCONES
Omit the sugar from the basic recipe. Add ½ teaspoon salt, ¼ teaspoon dry mustard, ¼ teaspoon white pepper, and ¾ cup grated sharp Cheddar cheese. Reserve 2 tablespoons cheese to sprinkle over the scones after glazing with egg and milk mixture.

SWEET ROLLS

It may be popular to gripe about school food, but Angelenos seem more inclined to praise it, especially the city school sweet rolls. They crumbled leftover cake to make the filling.

❑

Dissolve the yeast in lukewarm milk. Combine the sugar, salt, shortening, and egg in a mixing bowl and mix for 1 minute at low speed.

Add the milk mixture and mix for 1 minute. Add the flours and nutmeg and mix only enough to just blend, not more than 5 minutes.

Roll out to a rectangle shape. Brush with butter and sprinkle with the crumb filling. Roll up jelly-roll fashion. Slice into 1½-inch slices. Place on greased baking sheets, cut side down, and pat out fairly flat. Let rise until doubled. Bake at 400 degrees for 15 minutes. When partially cool, brush with powdered sugar glaze.

MAKES 17 TO 18 ROLLS

4 cakes yeast
2 cups lukewarm milk
½ cup sugar
2 teaspoons salt
½ cup shortening
1 large egg
1 cup cake flour
5 cups bread flour
¾ to 1½ teaspoons ground nutmeg
¼ cup melted butter or margarine
Cake Crumb Filling *(recipe follows)*
Powdered Sugar Glaze *(recipe follows)*

CAKE CRUMB FILLING

1 cup plain cake crumbs
½ cup brown sugar, packed
1 teaspoon ground cinnamon

Combine the cake crumbs, brown sugar, and cinnamon, and mix well.

POWDERED SUGAR GLAZE

2 cups powdered sugar
¼ cup hot water
1 teaspoon vanilla

Mix the powdered sugar with the hot water until smooth. Stir in the vanilla.

CINNAMON ROLLS

We have lots of requests for baked goods from Longhi's on Maui in Hawaii. After tasting their cinnamon rolls, we understood why.

Combine the water and yeast, stirring until dissolved. Stir in 1 tablespoon granulated sugar. Let stand 15 to 20 minutes, or until the yeast begins to bubble.

Combine the yeast mixture, milk, ¼ cup melted butter, 2 tablespoons granulated sugar, eggs, and salt in a large bowl and mix well. Add the whole wheat flour and mix well. Add enough bread flour to make a semisoft dough (stiff enough to knead). Knead on a floured board until smooth and elastic, adding flour as needed to prevent sticking.

Place the dough in a greased bowl, turning to grease the top. Cover and let rise until doubled, about 1 to 1½ hours. Punch down dough. Knead briefly, then let rest about 10 minutes. Roll out on a floured board into a large, thin rectangle, about 23 × 14 inches.

Brush with about ¼ cup melted butter. Combine ½ cup granulated sugar, brown sugar, cinnamon, and walnuts. Sprinkle over the dough. Sprinkle the raisins evenly on top. Roll the dough into a cylinder shape as for a jelly roll, starting with the long edge. Seal the edges. Slice into 10 rolls.

Place, cut side down, on a greased baking sheet. Cover and let rise in a warm place until doubled, 45 minutes to 1 hour. Bake at 350 degrees for 20 to 25 minutes, or until browned. Brush with butter. Cool slightly. Drizzle with icing.

MAKES 10 ROLLS

½ cup warm water
1 package dry yeast
Granulated sugar
⅔ cup milk, scalded and cooled
Melted butter
2 eggs
½ teaspoon salt
2 cups whole wheat flour
2½ cups white bread flour, approximately
½ cup light brown sugar, packed
1 tablespoon ground cinnamon
1 cup chopped walnuts, optional
½ cup raisins, plumped in water and drained
Icing (recipe follows)

Combine the powdered sugar, corn syrup, and lemon juice. Blend until smooth.

ICING

2 cups powdered sugar
2 tablespoons corn syrup
Juice of 1 lemon or orange

FLUFFY ORANGE ROLLS

I was fascinated to see talented camp cooks bake meringues and other unusual foods over hot coals in footed, cast-iron Dutch ovens when I judged a cookoff in Logan, Utah, in 1987. Teammates Kathy Hogan of Logan and Marcia Moss of Elko, Nevada, won top honors for these unbelievably light orange rolls. The rolls are equally good when baked in a conventional oven.

Combine the yeast with 1 tablespoon granulated sugar and warm water. Set aside for 15 minutes until foamy. Beat together the eggs, milk, melted butter, ¼ cup granulated sugar, and salt.

Stir in the yeast mixture. Stir in the flour until no longer sticky, and a soft dough forms. Knead lightly 5 minutes. Place in a greased bowl, turn to grease top, cover the bowl with a cloth and place in a warm spot to rise until doubled, about 1 hour.

Reserve ¼ teaspoon grated peel for glaze. To make the filling, combine the rest of the orange peel with softened butter and remaining ¼ cup granulated sugar in a small bowl. Blend well. Set aside.

Combine the powdered sugar, orange juice, and reserved ¼ teaspoon grated peel. Blend well and set aside.

When the dough has doubled, punch down and let rest 10 minutes. Light 33 charcoal briquettes. Roll the dough out on a floured board to a 13 × 9-inch rectangle. Spread with the filling, covering completely except for ½ inch along one long side. Beginning at the opposite long side, roll the dough jelly-roll fashion, sealing well along the unfilled edge. With a very sharp floured knife, cut the roll into 12 to 15 pieces. Place the rolls cut sides up and touching in a 12-inch Dutch oven. (Place the ends in the center to avoid burning.)

Let rise in a warm place until the coals are moderately hot, about 20 to 30 minutes. Then place the oven on 8 evenly distributed coals and arrange 25 coals over the lid of the oven. Turn oven ¼ turn after 5 minutes and turn the lid in the opposite direction ¼ turn. After 8 minutes, remove the bottom coals. Continue to turn the lid ¼ turn every 5 minutes. After about 10 to 12 minutes, check to see if the rolls are browning evenly. If not, adjust the position of the top coals. Total cooking time should be 15 to 20 minutes. The rolls will pull away from the sides of the pan and be golden brown when done.

Spread with glaze while still warm.

MAKES 12 TO 15 ROLLS

Note: To bake rolls in a conventional oven, arrange the rolls in a 13 × 9-inch glass baking dish, allow to rise 20 to 30 minutes, then bake at 375 degrees for 20 to 25 minutes.

1 package dry yeast
½ cup plus 1 tablespoon granulated sugar
½ cup warm water
2 eggs
½ cup evaporated milk
¼ cup butter, melted
¼ teaspoon salt
3½ to 4½ cups flour
Grated peel of 1 orange
¼ cup butter, softened
1 cup powdered sugar
3 tablespoons orange juice

BUTTERMILK-CINNAMON COFFEE CAKE

Margaret Fox, chef-owner of Cafe Beaujolais in Mendocino's wine country, makes an outstanding coffee cake.

Combine the flour, brown sugar, granulated sugar, salt, 1 teaspoon cinnamon, and ginger. Blend in the oil until smooth. Remove ¾ cup of the mixture and combine with the almonds and the remaining 1 teaspoon cinnamon. Mix and set aside.

To the remaining flour mixture, add the baking powder, baking soda, egg, and buttermilk. Blend until smooth. Pour into a buttered 13 × 9-inch baking pan. Sprinkle reserved nut mixture evenly over the surface of the batter. Bake at 350 degrees for 35 to 40 minutes. Place the pan on a wire rack to cool. Cut into squares to serve.

MAKES 8 TO 12 SERVINGS

2¼ cups flour
1 cup brown sugar, packed
¾ cup granulated sugar
½ teaspoon salt
2 teaspoons ground cinnamon
¼ teaspoon ground ginger
¾ cup corn oil
1 cup sliced almonds
1 teaspoon baking powder
1 teaspoon baking soda
1 egg
1 cup buttermilk

WALNUT BREAD

At a dinner honoring sponsors of a fund-raising event in San Diego several years ago, Rancho Bernardo Inn served thin slices of this bread, crisply toasted, with pâté.

Cream the butter and sugar until fully blended. Slowly beat in the eggs. Sift the flour, salt, and baking soda, and add to the egg mixture. Blend in the nuts, vanilla, and sour cream. Pour batter into 2 greased and floured 9 × 5-inch loaf pans. Bake at 350 degrees for 45 minutes to 1 hour. Cool in pans for 10 minutes, then invert onto a wire rack.

MAKES 2 LOAVES

Note: This bread is excellent when thinly sliced and lightly toasted.

1 cup butter or margarine, at room temperature
2 cups sugar
4 eggs
4 cups flour
½ teaspoon salt
2 teaspoons baking soda
1½ cups chopped walnuts
2 teaspoons vanilla extract
2 cups sour cream

MAHONY'S BRUSCHETTA

This garlicky hot bread is a double winner. It won the annual garlic cookoff in Gilroy, California, in 1983, and it also was named one of The Times *food staff's twelve best recipes of the year. Be warned, however—you'd better like both the aroma and taste of garlic when you prepare it.*

Cut the bread diagonally in 1-inch slices, without cutting through the bottom crust. Chop the garlic fine in a blender or food processor fitted with the steel blade. With the machine running, slowly add the olive oil to make a thin paste. Slather the garlic paste on the cut surfaces, top, and sides of the bread. Place directly on an oven rack with a pan on the shelf below to catch drippings. Bake at 350 degrees for 10 to 12 minutes or until the top is crisp.

While the bread is in the oven, heat the whipping cream in a heavy saucepan. Do not boil. Slowly stir in the cheeses until the sauce is smooth. Stir in the butter and keep the sauce warm until the bread is ready. At serving time place the bread in a warmed, shallow serving dish with sides. Finish cutting through the bottom crust and pour the sauce over. Sprinkle with parsley and paprika.

MAKES 6 SERVINGS

Note: Locatelli is a hard Romano cheese usually available in Italian markets.

1 loaf French or Italian bread
10 large cloves garlic, peeled
¾ cup olive oil
1½ cups whipping cream
½ cup grated Locatelli cheese
½ cup grated Parmesan cheese
3 tablespoons butter or margarine
1 tablespoon chopped parsley
Paprika

LOS ANGELES SWEET CORN BREAD

Our test kitchen came up with this recipe after a reader gave us a hint about using commercial cake and corn bread mixes to match a very popular local restaurant chain's corn bread. It's one of those occasions when it's hard to improve on the ease and simplicity of store-bought mixes.

Mix the cake and corn bread batters according to package directions. Blend together and turn into 2 greased 9-inch square baking pans. Bake at 350 degrees for 30 to 35 minutes, or until the corn bread springs back when lightly touched.

MAKES ABOUT 32 SERVINGS

1 (18.5-ounce) package yellow cake mix

1 (15-ounce) package corn bread mix

PROSCIUTTO WAFFLES

This recipe was developed by Donna Deane in our test kitchen when we were working on a story on power breakfasts. It makes a great brunch or lunch dish, whether you're feeling powerful or not.

Beat the eggs until light and frothy. Stir the flour and baking powder together. Add to the eggs along with the milk and melted butter. Beat until blended. Stir in the prosciutto. Bake in a waffle iron according to manufacturer's direction.

To serve, top the waffles with a dollop of mascarpone and fresh fruit.

MAKES ABOUT 18 (4-INCH) WAFFLE SQUARES

Note: If desired, garnish with additional prosciutto cut in paper-thin strips.

2 eggs
2 cups flour
1 tablespoon baking powder
2 to 2½ cups milk
½ cup melted butter
¼ pound prosciutto, minced
¼ to ½ pound mascarpone cheese
Fresh fruit

DESSERTS

Forget the calories. Forget the cholesterol. Forget the sugar. Southern Californians simply don't want to be told anything bad about desserts. Where else will you find a weary looking jogger, who has just finished a five-mile stint, standing at the truffle counter of a mall candy shop?

We love desserts—the sweeter the better—and we don't want anyone laying a guilt trip on us while we enjoy them. Cheesecakes, cookies, tarts, tortes, and anything chocolate—they're all just what we want. And the health-conscious eighties with all the exercising and dieting we did in no way affected our love affair with sugar and butter and cream and, yes, chocolate.

We'd like to fool ourselves into thinking that we don't eat desserts, except maybe for a little fresh fruit or an absolutely, completely, unmistakably healthful oatmeal-raisin cookie. But the Times food staff knows better. Letters pour in daily asking for recipes for reams of luscious, sinfully rich desserts. The truth is, where desserts are concerned, most Southern Californians talk one thing and do another.

In the early eighties cheesecakes were the hot dessert item. Later, as the trend moved to lighter eating patterns in the mid-eighties, we found fruit tarts the perfect answer. By the end of the decade we were looking for anything that was sweet (but without sugar) and could be made with oats.

Through it all, however, we were devouring coconut and apple pies, rice puddings, crème brulées, caramel pecan cakes, and chocolate chestnut gâteaus and mousses. We loved them all and came back for more.

How about a piece of orange apple pie with almonds? No? Not even just a little piece . . . ?

DUTCH APPLE PIE

Ruth's Chris Steak House in Beverly Hills was the source for this exemplary apple pie. It's everything a Pennsylvania Dutch-style apple pie should be.

Combine 1½ cups water, both sugars, nutmeg, cinnamon, and liqueur in a large saucepan. Bring almost to a boil. Add the apple slices and cook 4 minutes. Add the raisins. Cook for 2 minutes or until apples are no longer crisp, but do not let them become mushy.

Mix cornstarch with ¼ cup water and add to the apples. Continue cooking, stirring, until slightly thickened and clear. Pour into a pie shell, making a slight mound. Crumble the topping over the apples, making a large mound and being sure to cover the filling completely. Bake at 350 degrees for 45 to 50 minutes, or until browned.

MAKES ABOUT 8 SERVINGS

Combine both sugars, the flour, nutmeg, and cinnamon, mixing thoroughly. In another bowl, combine the vanilla and butter, then add to the dry mixture. Be sure the butter is mixed in thoroughly. The consistency should be moist but not wet, and dry but not powdery.

MAKES 4 CUPS

1¾ cups water

6 tablespoons granulated sugar

2 tablespoons brown sugar, packed

Pinch ground nutmeg

¼ teaspoon ground cinnamon

¼ ounce orange liqueur

4 medium apples, peeled, cored, and sliced into wheels

3 tablespoons raisins

2½ tablespoons cornstarch

1 partially baked (9- or 10-inch) pie shell

Crumb Topping (recipe follows)

CRUMB TOPPING

½ cup brown sugar, packed

½ cup granulated sugar

1¾ cups self-rising flour, lightly packed

¾ teaspoon ground nutmeg

½ teaspoon ground cinnamon

¼ teaspoon vanilla

½ cup plus 2 tablespoons butter, softened

ORANGE APPLE PIE WITH ALMONDS

When 18-year-old Jeremy Kisner sent this recipe to our "My Best Recipe" column in 1988, he already knew it was a winner. He had just won second place in an apple pie contest with it.

Peel and slice the apples into thin wedges. Combine them with the cornstarch, sugar, raisins, orange liqueur, and zest. Turn into a pie plate lined with the orange crust. Cover with a top crust and brush with egg wash.

Seal and flute the edges, and sprinkle the top with almonds. Cut vents in the top and bake at 375 degrees for 1 hour or until golden brown. (If the crust browns too fast, cover with foil.)

MAKES ABOUT 8 SERVINGS

5 to 6 medium green pippin apples

3 tablespoons cornstarch

1¼ cups sugar

½ cup golden raisins

¼ cup orange liqueur

1 tablespoon freshly grated orange zest

Orange Crust *(recipe follows)*

1 egg yolk diluted with 2 tablespoons water

½ cup finely chopped almonds

ORANGE CRUST

2 cups flour

¼ teaspoon salt

2 tablespoons sugar

¾ cup shortening

3 to 4 tablespoons orange juice

Combine the flour, salt, and sugar in a small bowl. Cut in the shortening until crumbly. Slowly add the orange juice while mixing with the flour mixture. Add just enough juice until the dough adheres. Divide into 2 portions. Chill the dough while making the filling.

Roll out 1 portion of dough to line the bottom of a 9-inch pie plate. Roll out remaining portion for the top crust.

PEACH PIE

Trust a peach rancher to have the ultimate peach pie recipe. Chi Chi Wood of Atwater, California, uses both brown and white sugar to lightly sweeten the ripe fresh peaches that are the mainstay of this single-crust pie. An easy crumb topping finishes it off.

Mix both sugars, salt, and tapioca. Add the peaches and mix gently. Sprinkle with almond extract. Line a 9-inch pie pan with pastry. Pour in the peach mixture, and dot with butter.

Sprinkle with the crumb topping and bake at 450 degrees for 10 minutes. Reduce the heat to 375 degrees and continue baking for 20 to 25 minutes or until browned.

MAKES 6 TO 8 SERVINGS

½ cup brown sugar, packed
½ cup granulated sugar
Few grains salt
3 tablespoons instant tapioca
5 cups sliced freestone peaches
⅛ teaspoon almond extract
Pastry for single-crust (9-inch)
    pie shell
1 tablespoon butter
Crumb Topping *(recipe follows)*

Mix the butter, sugar, and flour together until crumbly.

CRUMB TOPPING
⅓ cup butter, softened
½ cup sugar
¾ cup flour

FAIRY PIE

A story on goat milk provided us with the recipe for this rich and airy pie. You may have to do a bit of searching to find goat milk in your area, but most health food stores carry it.

Cream together the butter and ½ cup sugar. Combine the flour, baking powder, and salt. Beat the egg yolks with the goat milk. Add the flour and egg mixtures alternately to creamed butter. Pour the batter into 2 greased 8-inch-round layer cake pans.

Spread evenly out to the edge, forming a thin layer. Beat the egg whites until stiff. Gradually beat in the remaining ¾ cup sugar. Fold in the vanilla and nuts.

Spread the meringue over the filling in the two layer pans to within 1 inch of the edge. Bake at 350 degrees for 25 minutes, or until a wood pick comes out clean. Remove from the oven. Cool on racks 10 minutes, then remove from the pans and cool completely. Drain the syrup from the raspberries into a saucepan. Blend in the cornstarch. Cook, stirring, until thickened. Add the berries, and gently combine.

To serve, cut each layer into 4 to 6 wedges. Top each wedge with a spoonful of whipped cream. Drizzle with some raspberry sauce.

MAKES 8 TO 12 SERVINGS

½ cup butter

1¼ cups sugar

½ cup plus 2 tablespoons flour

1 teaspoon baking powder

Pinch salt

4 eggs, separated

¼ cup goat milk

1 teaspoon vanilla

1 cup chopped walnuts, optional

1 (10-ounce) package frozen raspberries, packed in sugar syrup

1½ teaspoons cornstarch, or less

Whipped cream

OKLAHOMA OATMEAL PIE

While oatmeal pies are not widely sought after in the West, this recipe from Kat and Steph Rodosevich won our taste buds and one of the weekly "My Best Recipe" awards in 1988. The Rodoseviches credit a friend with introducing them to the pie, which apparently originated in the Midwest.

Beat the eggs lightly in large bowl. Add the sugar, corn syrup, milk, melted butter, coconut, oats, salt, and vanilla. Mix well. Pour into a pie shell. Bake at 350 degrees for 45 to 55 minutes, or until browned and set.

MAKES 8 TO 10 SERVINGS

3 eggs

1½ cups sugar

1⅛ cups light corn syrup

¾ cup milk or whipping cream

6 tablespoons butter, melted

1½ cups shredded coconut

1 cup plus 2 tablespoons oats

Pinch salt

1 ½ tablespoons vanilla

1 unbaked (10-inch) deep-dish pastry shell

COCONUT CREAM PIE

One might have expected this pie to be from Hawaii. It isn't. Instead, the recipe came from the Broadway department stores in Los Angeles where it is served in their restaurants.

Combine the cornstarch, sugar, and salt, and mix well. Gradually stir in the scalded milk. Bring to a boil, stirring constantly, and boil for 2 minutes until thickened and shiny. Add a small amount of the hot mixture to the eggs and beat until blended. Return to the pan and whip for 2 minutes over medium heat until slightly thickened, being careful not to curdle the mixture.

Remove from the heat and add the vanilla and margarine, mixing until smooth. Pour through a sieve into a bowl. Place plastic wrap directly over the cream and seal edges. Set aside to cool.

Add the coconut extract and ½ cup coconut to the cooled pie cream. Pour into a pie shell. Chill. Spread whipped topping over the pie, mounding in the center. Sprinkle with remaining ½ cup coconut.

MAKES 1 (10-INCH) PIE

¾ cup cornstarch

1½ cups sugar

½ teaspoon salt

1 quart milk, scalded

2 eggs

½ tablespoon vanilla

2 tablespoons margarine

½ teaspoon coconut extract

1 cup coarsely shredded fresh coconut

1 baked 10-inch pie shell

4 cups whipped topping or whipped cream

VOLCANO MACADAMIA PIE

Many years ago when I was food editor for a Hawaii newspaper, I acquired this recipe for macadamia nut pie from a now long gone restaurant in the volcano area on the Big Island of Hawaii.

Beat the eggs until well blended and foamy. Beat in the sugar and butter. Blend in the corn syrup and chopped nuts.

Pour into a prepared pie shell and bake at 350 degrees for 35 to 40 minutes, or until a wood pick inserted near the center comes out clean. Cool on a rack. Garnish with whole macadamia nuts and serve with rum sauce on the side.

MAKES 8 SERVINGS

3 eggs

⅔ cup sugar

⅓ cup butter or margarine, melted

1 cup dark corn syrup

1 cup finely chopped macadamia nuts

1 (9-inch) pie shell

Whole macadamia nuts

Rum Sauce, *optional (recipe follows)*

RUM SAUCE

½ cup butter or margarine

1 cup brown sugar, packed

½ cup light corn syrup

¼ cup light rum

2 teaspoons vanilla

Melt the butter in a saucepan over medium heat and stir in the brown sugar and corn syrup. Cook, stirring, until the sugar melts and the mixture becomes smooth. Stir in the rum and vanilla. Heat through.

FROZEN PEANUT BUTTER PIE

An instant hit with our readers, this super do-ahead dessert is a favorite with diners at Reese's Country Inn in Niagara Falls.

Combine the vanilla ice cream with the peanut butter and chocolate pieces. Spoon into the cocoa-graham cracker crust. Freeze immediately until solid, about 2 hours or overnight. Top with the chocolate sauce and whipped cream.

MAKES 8 SERVINGS

Note: Do not allow ice cream to become too soft before mixing with the peanut butter. If using an electric mixer, do not overwhip. Mix at slow speed.

Mix together the crumbs, butter, sugar, and cocoa until well incorporated. Press firmly into a 9-inch pie plate. Freeze until ready to use.

Combine the sugar, water, corn syrup, and chocolate in a saucepan. Bring to a boil. Remove immediately from the heat and stir until smooth. In a separate saucepan, bring the cream to a boil. Stir into the chocolate mixture until smooth.

MAKES 1½ CUPS

2¾ *pints vanilla ice cream*
½ *cup peanut butter*
2 *ounces semisweet chocolate pieces*
Cocoa-Graham Cracker Crust *(recipe follows)*
Chocolate Sauce *(recipe follows)*
Sweetened whipped cream

COCOA-GRAHAM CRACKER CRUST
2⅓ *cups graham cracker crumbs*
¾ *cup melted butter*
⅓ *cup superfine sugar*
⅔ *cup sifted cocoa powder*

CHOCOLATE SAUCE
½ *cup sugar*
⅓ *cup water*
1 *tablespoon corn syrup*
2¼ *ounces sweet chocolate, grated*
¼ *cup whipping cream*

EASY STREET APPLE TART

Easy Street, the bakery that supplies the Production Caterers of West Hollywood with their desserts, shared the recipe for this simple, totally scrumptious apple tart.

◻

Lightly sprinkle the apples with lemon juice. Add the sugar, flour, cinnamon, and nutmeg and mix well. Place the apples in a tart shell, mounding in the center. Cover evenly with the crumb topping and pack the apples securely into the shell. Bake at 350 degrees for 45 minutes. Remove to a rack to cool. Remove the outer rim of the tart pan to serve.

MAKES 1 (9-INCH) TART

Mix the flour and sugar in a bowl. Cut the butter into small pieces, add to the bowl, and mix until crumbly. Add the egg and vanilla. Form the dough into a ball, wrap securely, and refrigerate 4 hours or overnight. Roll out the dough and fit into a 9-inch tart pan with a removable bottom.

Combine the flour, sugar, and cinnamon in a bowl. Cut the butter into small pieces, add to the bowl, and mix until crumbly.

5 cups peeled and sliced apples (cut into eighths)

Lemon juice

¼ cup sugar

1½ tablespoons flour

1 teaspoon ground cinnamon

¼ teaspoon ground nutmeg

1 (9-inch) Tart Shell (recipe follows)

Crumb Topping *(recipe follows)*

TART SHELL

1 cup flour

3½ tablespoons sugar

3¼ ounces butter

½ lightly beaten egg

½ teaspoon vanilla

CRUMB TOPPING

¾ cup flour

¾ cup brown sugar, packed

1 teaspoon ground cinnamon

¼ pound butter

FRESH FIG TART

Fruit tarts are always popular, but this fresh fig one is truly special. It's a beautiful tart, almost too pretty to eat . . . until you taste it. One bite and you will be sold on this as a perfect way to use fresh figs.

Beat the cream cheese and sugar until light. Add as much milk as needed to make the mixture smooth and well blended. Spread on the bottom of the butter tart shell. Cut the figs into uniform wedges (quarters or thirds depending on size of figs) and arrange in a circular pattern over the surface of the tart. Combine the melted currant jelly with cassis and brush over the figs. Serve with whipped cream.

MAKES 1 (9-INCH) TART

6 ounces mascarpone or cream cheese
¼ cup powdered sugar or 2 tablespoons granulated sugar
¼ cup milk, approximately
Butter Tart Shell *(recipe follows)*
6 to 7 fresh figs
Currant jelly, melted
2 tablespoons cassis
Whipped cream

Sift together the flour, sugar, and salt. Work in the butter and egg with your fingertips to make a smooth dough. Roll out on a floured board. Fit into a greased and floured 9-inch fluted tart pan, pressing the dough against the sides and bottom of the pan. Run a rolling pin over the rim of the pan to remove excess dough. Pierce the bottom of the pastry with a fork. Cut a circle of foil to fit the shell, place on the bottom of the pan, and weight it with rice or beans to keep the pastry from puffing while baking. Bake at 425 degrees for 10 to 15 minutes, or until shell is lightly browned. Remove beans and foil and cool shell.

BUTTER TART SHELL
2 cups flour, sifted
½ cup sugar
Pinch salt
½ cup butter, softened
1 egg

PECAN TART

This is one of those deceptively simple desserts. Essentially, pecan halves are napped with a syrupy filling in a delicate individual tart shell and caramel sauce is spooned over at serving time. Unless you're an experienced baker, however, follow the instructions carefully. The recipe came from Spago's very experienced pastry chef and it's so good, we named it one of the year's best recipes for 1984.

Combine the corn syrup, granulated and brown sugars, eggs, and egg yolks in a medium bowl. Stir until blended. Heat the butter in a small skillet over medium heat until the butter is foamy and light brown in color. Remove from the heat and whisk into the corn syrup mixture. Set aside.

Set the pastry-lined tart pans on a large baking sheet. Arrange pecans in the tart pans and pour the filling over. Bake at 375 degrees for 35 to 40 minutes. Remove to a wire rack to cool. Serve the tarts at room temperature topped with caramel sauce.

MAKES 6 TO 8 SERVINGS

1½ cups light corn syrup
¾ cup granulated sugar
¾ cup light brown sugar, packed
4 eggs plus 2 egg yolks
3 tablespoons unsalted butter
Tart Shells *(recipe follows)*
1½ to 2 cups broken pecan halves (6 to 8 ounces)
Caramel Sauce *(recipe follows)*

TART SHELLS

3 cups pastry flour
1 cup very cold, unsalted butter, cut into ½-inch pieces
3 tablespoons sugar
Pinch salt
2 egg yolks
1 to 2 tablespoons very cold whipping cream

Place the flour, butter, sugar, and salt in a food processor container. Process, using quick on-off pulses, until the mixture resembles coarse meal. Combine the egg yolks and 1 tablespoon cream in a small bowl. With the motor running, add the egg mixture to the flour mixture in the processor bowl and process just until the dough begins to form. Add enough remaining cream to bind the dough. Scrape the dough onto a piece of foil, wrap airtight, and refrigerate until well chilled, at least 1 hour.

Divide the dough into 6 or 8 equal portions, depending on the diameter of the tart pans. Roll out each portion on a lightly floured pastry cloth. Carefully transfer the pastry to the tart pans. Press against the bottoms and sides of the pans, then trim any excess dough. If the pastry tears, patch with small bits of trimmings. Reserve any remaining pastry, wrapped airtight, for other use. Refrigerate tart pans until ready to use.

MAKES 6 TO 8 SHELLS

CARAMEL SAUCE

½ cup sugar, preferably vanilla sugar
⅔ cup whipping cream, at room temperature
2 tablespoons unsalted butter, at room temperature

Heat the sugar in a small heavy skillet or saucepan over medium heat until melted and medium-amber in color. Slowly pour in the cream all at once, being careful to avoid splatters. Stir in the butter. Cook, stirring constantly over medium heat, until the caramel dissolves and the sauce is smooth. Remove from the heat. Store at room temperature if not using immediately, as the sauce will harden if refrigerated.

MAKES ABOUT 1 CUP

RICE TART

When Wolfgang Puck opened Chinois on Main in Santa Monica in the early eighties, this rice tart quickly became a favorite.

Place the water in an ovenproof saucepan and bring to a boil. Add the rice and boil 1 to 2 minutes. Drain. Return the rice to the saucepan and add half and half, orange peel, vanilla bean and scrapings, and ½ cup sugar. Bring to a boil. Cover the pan and bake at 350 degrees for about 30 minutes, or until the rice is cooked and the liquid absorbed.

While the rice is cooking, whisk the softened butter with 1 egg yolk. When well mixed, add another egg yolk. Repeat process with remaining yolks. The mixture should look satiny. When the rice mixture is cooked, return to the top of the range. Remove the vanilla bean. Add the butter mixture and cook, stirring, until thickened. Let cool. Stir in the litchi wine and Grand Marnier. Fold in the whipped cream.

Line the tart shells with poached fruit. Spoon in the rice filling. Chill until set, about 30 minutes. Before serving, sprinkle the tops with additional sugar and place under the broiler for about 1 minute or until browned. To serve, spoon 3 or 4 tablespoons fruit sauce onto the bottom of each of 8 large individual serving plates. Place a tart in the center of each. Garnish the plates with additional poached fruit, if desired.

MAKES 8 SERVINGS

2 cups water
½ cup arborio rice
2 cups half and half
Grated peel of 2 oranges
1 vanilla bean, split and scraped
Sugar
½ cup butter or margarine, softened
4 egg yolks
¼ cup litchi wine
¼ cup Grand Marnier
1 cup lightly whipped cream
8 individual tart shells
Sliced poached pears, apricots, or peaches
Fruit Sauce (recipe follows)

Combine the wine, sugar, and lemon juice in a saucepan. Add the peaches and apricots and cook until the fruit is soft. Purée in a food processor or blender until smooth. If necessary, the purée may be thinned with a small amount of additional litchi wine. Sauce should be thin enough to flow easily onto serving plates.

MAKES ABOUT 3 CUPS

Note: Litchi wine is available in Chinese markets. Any sweet white wine could be substituted.

FRUIT SAUCE
2½ cups litchi wine, approximately
½ cup sugar
Juice of ½ lemon
2 peaches, peeled, seeded, and chopped
1 cup dried apricots, coarsely chopped

CARROT CAKE

In the late seventies carrot cakes were hot items. Everyone was making them. The recipe for the carrot cake served at the J. Paul Getty Museum in Pacific Palisades is popular with our readers.

Combine the oil, sugar, eggs, flour, baking soda, salt, cinnamon, vanilla, carrots, walnuts, and pineapple in a large bowl. Mix until blended. Pour into a greased 13 × 9-inch pan and bake at 350 degrees for 1 hour. Cool, then frost with the cream cheese frosting.

MAKES 12 SERVINGS

1½ cups corn oil

2 cups sugar

3 eggs

2 cups flour

2 teaspoons baking soda

2 teaspoons vanilla

1 teaspoon salt

2 teaspoons ground cinnamon

2 cups grated carrots

1 cup chopped walnuts

½ cup crushed pineapple, drained

Cream Cheese Frosting *(recipe follows)*

CREAM CHEESE FROSTING

1 (3-ounce) package cream cheese

1¼ cups powdered sugar

½ cup butter or margarine

⅛ cup crushed pineapple

¼ cup chopped walnuts

Mix the cream cheese, powdered sugar, and margarine until fluffy. Add the pineapple and walnuts, and mix well.

PUMPKIN CAKE

Over the years readers have asked us for many of the marvelous home-style recipes used at Clifton's Cafeterias, a popular small local restaurant chain. During the Thanksgiving and Christmas holidays each year, we receive numerous requests for their Pumpkin Cake recipe, which resembles an old-fashioned spice cake.

Blend together the sugar, flour, baking powder, soda, cinnamon, and salt with a mixer at medium speed until well mixed. Add the oil and continue to beat until the dry ingredients are moistened. Add the pumpkin and mix again until well blended. Add the eggs and blend 1 minute longer. Do not overmix.

Turn the batter into 3 lightly greased, paper-lined 9-inch cake pans. Smooth the batter with a spatula so that the cake will be level when baked. Bake at 325 degrees for 40 minutes or until done. Cool on racks thoroughly. Then turn out and fill and frost with cream cheese frosting.

MAKES 1 (3-LAYER) CAKE

3 cups sugar
3 cups flour
1 tablespoon baking powder
1 tablespoon baking soda
1 tablespoon ground cinnamon
3/4 teaspoon salt
1 1/2 cups oil
3 1/4 cups canned pumpkin
4 eggs, lightly beaten
Cream Cheese Frosting (recipe follows)

CREAM CHEESE FROSTING
1 pound powdered sugar
1 (8-ounce) package cream cheese
1/2 cup butter or margarine
2 teaspoons vanilla
1/2 cup chopped raisins

Combine the sugar, cream cheese, butter, and vanilla. Mix until blended. Add the raisins and stir to combine. Refrigerate until needed.

TUNNEL OF FUDGE CAKE

Sometimes success causes more problems than it helps. That was the case with the famous Pillsbury Bake-Off winner from some years ago, the Tunnel of Fudge Cake. After hundreds of thousands of these cakes were baked, the company stopped producing the cake and icing mixes needed to produce the fudgy center that graced the cake. Consumers protested to no avail until 1986. It was during that year that Pillsbury's home economists finally came up with a "from scratch" version of this popular dessert.

Beat the butter and granulated sugar in a large bowl until light and fluffy. Add the eggs, 1 at a time, beating well after each addition. Gradually add the powdered sugar, blending well. By hand, stir in the flour, cocoa, and walnuts until well blended.

Spoon the batter into a greased and floured 12-cup bundt pan or a 10-inch angel-food tube pan. Bake at 350 degrees for 58 to 62 minutes. Cool upright in the pan on a rack for 1 hour. Invert onto a serving plate. Cool completely. Spoon the glaze over the top of the cake, allowing some to run down the sides.

MAKES 16 SERVINGS

Note: Nuts are essential for the success of the recipe. Since the cake has a soft tunnel of fudge, ordinary testing for doneness cannot be used. Accurate oven temperature and baking time are critical. In altitudes above 3,500 feet, increase the flour to 2¼ cups plus 3 tablespoons.

Combine the sugar, cocoa, and milk in a small bowl until well blended. Store tightly covered.

1¾ cups butter or margarine, softened
1¾ cups granulated sugar
6 eggs
2 cups powdered sugar
2¼ cups flour
¾ cup cocoa powder
2 cups chopped walnuts
Glaze *(recipe follows)*

GLAZE
¾ cup powdered sugar
¼ cup cocoa powder
1½ to 2 tablespoons milk

DOUBLE CHOCOLATE CAKE

This rich chocolate creation is almost fudgy in consistency. It came to us from the Royal Sonesta Hotel in Cambridge, Massachusetts. Cut it in very small slices as it's unbelievably rich. A great cake for a tea party.

Cream together the butter and sugar until light and creamy. Stir in the cocoa and water. Beat for 7 minutes with an electric mixer. Add the flour, salt, baking powder, and soda. Beat 2 minutes longer. Add the eggs and mix 5 minutes longer.

Pour the batter into a greased and floured 9-inch layer cake pan. Bake at 350 degrees for 30 to 40 minutes, or until cake center springs back when lightly touched. Invert onto a wire rack to cool completely.

Split the cake horizontally into 3 layers. Drizzle some orange-flavored liqueur lightly over each layer. Frost the layers with the refrigerated ganache. Pour the remaining unrefrigerated ganache over the top layer to form a glaze.

MAKES 1 (3-LAYER) CAKE

½ cup plus 2 tablespoons unsalted butter
1 cup sugar
½ cup cocoa powder
½ cup water
½ cup plus 2 tablespoons flour
½ teaspoon salt
1½ teaspoons baking powder
¾ teaspoon baking soda
4 eggs
Orange-flavored liqueur
Ganache *(recipe follows)*

Melt the chocolate in the top of a double boiler over simmering water. Add the whipping cream. Remove from the heat. Remove 2 cups chocolate mixture and set aside. Refrigerate the remaining chocolate mixture until thick and creamy.

GANACHE
18 ounces semisweet chocolate (squares or pieces)
1½ cups whipping cream

WINTER CITRUS CHEESECAKE

The sweet-tart flavor of this California-style cheesecake comes both from lemons and limes. The crust is loaded with pecans and the cheesecake needs no garnishing. For a party, however, it's easy to drizzle a small amount of caramel in a lacy pattern over the top and add some pecan halves to dress it up.

Beat the cream cheese with 1½ cups sugar until smooth. Whisk in the whole eggs, egg yolks, flour, and whipping cream. Add the lime and lemon peels, and lime and lemon juices. Turn into a pan lined with the nut crust. Place the pan on a baking sheet. Bake at 425 degrees for 15 minutes. Reduce the oven temperature to 225 degrees and bake an additional 50 minutes or until set. The cake may be refrigerated, covered, up to 3 days.

Just before serving, caramelize the remaining ¼ cup sugar in a heavy skillet. Spoon over the cheesecake to form a lacy pattern. Garnish with pecan halves, if desired.

MAKES 10 TO 12 SERVINGS

Combine the flour, graham cracker crumbs, butter, pecans, and sugar in a bowl. Press evenly over the bottom of a 10-inch spring-form pan. Bake at 350 degrees for 15 minutes.

3 (8-ounce) packages cream cheese, softened
1¾ cups sugar
5 eggs
2 egg yolks
2 tablespoons flour
½ cup whipping cream
Grated peel of 1 lime
Grated peel of 1 lemon
2 tablespoons lime juice
¼ cup lemon juice
Nut Crust (recipe follows)
Pecan halves, for garnish, optional

NUT CRUST
½ cup flour
½ cup graham cracker crumbs
½ cup butter, softened
1 cup chopped pecans
2 tablespoons sugar

PUMPKIN CHEESECAKE

Most of us tend to think of using pumpkin only during the holidays. However, this recipe, from the Executive Inn in Tacoma, Washington, uses canned pumpkin, so there's no excuse for not making it often.

Blend the cream cheese with the sugar until smooth. Add the eggs, 1 at a time, beating until blended. Add the whipping cream, pumpkin, vanilla, and spice, blending thoroughly.

Pour into a springform pan with the graham cracker crust. Bake at 300 degrees for 1½ hours or until cake sets. Remove and let rest 10 minutes, then pour the sour cream topping over the cheesecake. Cool thoroughly before removing from the pan. Chill.

MAKES 1 (10-INCH) CHEESECAKE

2 pounds cream cheese
1½ cups sugar
3 eggs
1 cup whipping cream
2 (1-pound) cans pumpkin
2 teaspoons vanilla
1 tablespoon pumpkin pie spice
Graham Cracker Crust *(recipe follows)*
Sour Cream Topping *(recipe follows)*

GRAHAM CRACKER CRUST

Brush a 10-inch springform pan with the soft butter. Mix the graham cracker crumbs, cinnamon, sugar, and melted butter. Press onto the bottom of the pan.

1 teaspoon soft butter
1¼ cups graham cracker crumbs
1 teaspoon ground cinnamon
¼ cup sugar
¼ cup melted butter

SOUR CREAM TOPPING

Blend the sour cream, sugar, and vanilla until smooth.

1 pound sour cream
½ cup sugar
2 teaspoons vanilla

DALLAS CHEESECAKE

Baking this chocolate chip-laden cheesecake from the Hyatt Regency Hotel can be a bit tricky unless the springform pan you use has a good tight spring to keep the batter in and the water bath it is cooked in out. If you're uncertain about your pan, simply wrap some foil outside around the bottom and up the sides of the pan.

Beat the cream cheese until smooth. Add the sugar, cornstarch, and salt. Mix until smooth. Gradually add the whole eggs and egg yolks, a few at a time, scraping the bowl frequently. Stir in the sour cream, lemon peel and juice, and vanilla until smooth. Fold in the grated chocolate. Pour into the prepared pie pan. Place the pan in a larger pan containing 1 inch warm water on the middle shelf of the oven.

Bake at 425 degrees for 15 minutes. Remove both pans from the oven. Reduce the heat to 325 degrees. Fill the larger pan with 1 inch cold water and place on the lower shelf. Place the cheesecake pan on the middle shelf and continue baking for 1½ hours, or until a knife inserted near the center of the cheesecake comes out clean. Cool completely in the pan set on a cake rack, then remove the sides of the springform. Chill thoroughly.

MAKES 12 TO 14 SERVINGS

6 (8-ounce) packages cream cheese, at room temperature

2¾ cups sugar

3 tablespoons cornstarch

½ teaspoon salt

6 eggs

6 egg yolks

¾ cup sour cream

Grated peel and juice of 1 lemon

¼ teaspoon vanilla

¾ cup grated semisweet chocolate, optional

Graham Cracker Crust (recipe follows)

GRAHAM CRACKER CRUST

1½ cups graham cracker crumbs

2 tablespoons melted butter

2 tablespoons sugar

Combine the crumbs, butter, and sugar, mixing well. Press firmly against the bottom of a well-greased 10-inch springform pan with a tight-fitting spring. If the pan spring is not tight, wrap foil tightly over the bottom and around the outsides of the pan before preparing the crust.

CANDY BAR CHEESECAKE

Schaefer's Manawa Steak House in Manawa, Wisconsin, sent us this recipe for a cheesecake made with Hershey bars. Be warned, though. A sliver will be more than enough to start with, even though there undoubtedly will be considerable demand for seconds.

Melt the chocolate bar in the top of a double boiler over hot water. Meanwhile, beat the cream cheese until light and fluffy. Combine the sugar, cocoa, and salt and add to the cream cheese mixture. Beat in the eggs and vanilla. Stir in the melted chocolate bar. Beat just until blended, but do not overbeat.

Pour into the nut crust. Bake at 325 degrees for 40 minutes. Without opening the door, turn off the oven. Cool in the oven for 30 minutes, then remove. Chill at least 8 hours. Serve garnished with sour cream topping and chopped nuts.

MAKES 8 TO 10 SERVINGS

1 (8-ounce) bar milk chocolate

4 (3-ounce) packages cream cheese, softened

¾ cup sugar

2 tablespoons unsweetened cocoa powder

Pinch salt

2 eggs

½ teaspoon vanilla

Nut Crust *(recipe follows)*

Sour Cream Topping *(recipe follows)*

Chopped walnuts

NUT CRUST

¾ cup graham cracker crumbs

⅔ cup chopped walnuts

2 tablespoons sugar

¼ cup melted butter

Combine the crumbs, walnuts, and sugar. Add the melted butter and mix well. Press the crumb mixture into the bottom and up the sides of an 8-inch springform pan.

SOUR CREAM TOPPING

½ cup sour cream

2 tablespoons sugar

½ teaspoon vanilla

Combine the sour cream, sugar, and vanilla. Blend well.

CANDIED GINGER CHEESECAKE

A seminar on East-West culinary arts held at the Beringer Winery in Napa Valley in 1988 added this elegant cheesecake recipe to our files. The recipe came from Yoshi Katsumura of Yoshi's Cafe in Chicago.

With the food processor running, add the cream cheese bit by bit, occasionally scraping the sides and processing until completely smooth. Add the sugar and process until incorporated. Add the whipping cream, scrape down the sides of the bowl to remove any lumps and process until smooth.

Soften the gelatin in cold water. Heat the lemon juice until very hot and add the gelatin. Stir until dissolved. Remove from the heat and stir in the orange liqueur.

With the food processor running, add the lemon juice and process until incorporated. Turn into a large mixing bowl and add the lemon zest and candied ginger. Set the bowl over an ice bath and cool until quite thick. Turn into a 9 × 5-inch loaf pan. Smooth the top and sprinkle with pâte sucrée crumbs, pressing the crumbs to adhere. Refrigerate at least 4 hours or overnight. Unmold to serve. Slice the cheesecake and serve each slice ringed with crème anglaise.

MAKES 12 TO 15 SERVINGS

22 ounces cream cheese (2 (8-ounce) and 2 (3-ounce) packages), softened

1 cup superfine sugar

1⅔ cups whipping cream

2 envelopes unflavored gelatin

2 tablespoons cold water

½ cup lemon juice

Dash orange liqueur

Grated zest of 1 lemon

⅓ cup **Candied Ginger** *(recipe follows)*

½ to ¾ cup **Pâte Sucrée Crumbs** *(recipe follows)*

Crème Anglaise *(recipe follows)*

CANDIED GINGER

1 lemon, halved

4 ounces ginger root, peeled and diced

Water

1 cup sugar

Squeeze half of the lemon over the diced ginger. Cover with water, add the squeezed lemon half, and bring to a boil. Boil for 25 to 30 minutes. Drain, rinse, and repeat with the remaining lemon half. Drain again. Add 2 cups water and the sugar to the blanched ginger. Stir until the sugar is dissolved. Bring to a boil over medium-high heat until the mixture is reduced by two-thirds. Remove from the heat and cool.

PÂTE SUCRÉE CRUMBS

5 ounces unsalted butter (10 tablespoons), cut into pieces

1¾ cups flour, approximately

7 tablespoons sugar

½ cup ground almonds

1½ teaspoons vanilla

1 egg, well beaten

Let the butter stand in a warm place until very soft. In a mixing bowl combine 1¾ cups flour, sugar, almonds, and vanilla. With the machine at low speed, beat in the butter. Scrape down the bowl. Turn to medium speed, add the egg, and beat until combined. The dough should be pliable, not sticky. If sticky, add a small amount of flour. If too dry, add 1 tablespoon water. Roll or pat on a lightly buttered baking sheet into an 11 × 8-inch rectangle. Bake at 300 degrees for 30 minutes, or until golden. Cool completely. Remove from the baking sheet. Grind in a food processor until fine.

MAKES 3⅓ CUPS

Note: Remaining crumbs may be frozen and used in other recipes.

Place the milk in a saucepan and bring to a boil. Whisk together the egg yolks, sugar, and vanilla. Pour the boiled milk over the eggs, whisking until smooth. Return to the saucepan. Cook, stirring, over high heat until the mixture coats a spoon. Pour through a fine sieve into a metal pan. Set in an ice bath. Skim off the foam. Stir occasionally until cooled.

MAKES 2 CUPS

CRÈME ANGLAISE

1 1/2 cups milk

5 egg yolks

10 tablespoons sugar

1 tablespoon vanilla

RICH AND CREAMY FLAN

Professional chefs aren't the only ones who turn out award-winning flans. This remarkably easy version of the Latin dessert is thicker than most and somewhat like a cheesecake. It came from one of our readers, Mary Agabon.

Melt or caramelize the sugar in a heavy pan until golden brown. Pour into the bottom of a 2-quart dish. Stir together the egg yolks, condensed milk, evaporated milk, and lime peel. Mix until well blended. Strain into the prepared dish. Bake in a bain-marie at 350 degrees for 1 hour, or until the custard is set. Cool or chill to set. Cut in thin slices. Garnish with lime peel, if desired.

MAKES 12 TO 15 SERVINGS

1/2 cup sugar

12 egg yolks

2 (14-ounce) cans sweetened condensed milk

2 (13-ounce) cans evaporated milk

Grated peel of 1 lime

EL CHOLO'S FLAN

Los Angeles abounds in Mexican restaurants that serve flan. El Cholo restaurants, of which there are several in the Los Angeles area, serve one of the best.

Place the sweetened condensed milk, milk, cream of coconut, corn syrup, vanilla, and eggs in a blender container. Blend thoroughly, or beat vigorously with a wire whisk to blend well.

Melt the sugar in a heavy skillet over low heat, stirring occasionally to keep the caramel from scorching. Add a few drops of water a little at a time, stirring until the caramel is of spreading consistency.

Distribute the caramel evenly among 8 (4½- to 5-ounce) custard cups, tilting the cups to spread the caramel evenly. Or spread the caramel in a 13 × 9-inch rectangular baking pan. Pour the flan into the caramel-lined cups or the pan and place in a shallow baking pan with ¼-inch hot water.

Cover with foil. If using cups, bake at 350 degrees for 50 minutes; if using the baking pan, bake for 1 hour or until firm. When cool, place in a refrigerator for about 1 hour.

To serve, run a knife around the outer edges of the cups or pan and invert onto a serving platter.

MAKES 8 SERVINGS

2 (14-ounce) cans sweetened condensed milk
2 cups milk
½ cup cream of coconut
½ cup corn syrup
1 teaspoon vanilla
6 eggs
1 cup sugar

CRÈME BRÛLÉE

When trendy young chef Elka Gilmore was at Camelions restaurant, she made an extra-rich version of crème brûlée. It was unbelievably smooth and creamy, and she used brown sugar in place of white sugar traditionally used for the topping.

Mix the egg yolks and granulated sugar. Place the cream and salt in a heavy saucepan. Slice the vanilla bean lengthwise, scrape out the inner portion and add the scrapings to the cream. Heat until scalding. Gradually beat the cream into the egg yolk mixture, then strain through a fine sieve. Pour into 6 to 8 (4-ounce) soufflé cups. Cover with foil, place in a pan of hot water, and bake at 350 degrees for 30 to 40 minutes, or until set.

Remove the foil. Top each serving with 2 tablespoons brown sugar and place under a broiler until the sugar is melted and caramelized. If desired, dry brown sugar slightly by spreading out in a thin layer on a platter, then grind to the consistency of powdered sugar in a food processor.

7 egg yolks
½ cup granulated sugar
3 cups whipping cream
Pinch salt
½ vanilla bean
¾ to 1 cup brown sugar, packed

MAKES 6 TO 8 SERVINGS

RASPBERRY CRÈME BRÛLÉE

Anyone who combines the luscious sweetness of fresh raspberries with a base of crème brûlée has to know her way around the kitchen. Le Chardonnay restaurant on Melrose gave us the recipe after a number of readers requested it.

In a medium bowl, gradually beat 6½ tablespoons sugar into the egg yolks. Whisk constantly until the mixture is light and creamy. Whisk in the cream and vanilla.

Place 7 raspberries in each of 8 6-ounce ramekins. Pour the custard mixture into ramekins. Place in a large baking pan. Add enough warm water to reach halfway up the ramekins. Bake at 350 degrees for 50 minutes or until set. Remove from the pan of water and cool. Refrigerate for a few hours.

Purée the remaining berries in a food processor, then strain. Pour 1 teaspoon purée onto each custard and sprinkle with 2 teaspoons sugar. Set the cups in a baking pan filled halfway with ice and water. Broil about 2 inches from the heat for about 3 minutes, or until the tops are caramelized.

Sugar
8 egg yolks
1 quart whipping cream
1 teaspoon vanilla
1½ baskets fresh raspberries

MAKES 8 SERVINGS

RICE CUSTARD

Clifton's Cafeterias, a small local chain of restaurants, serve true comfort food that is always perfectly prepared.

Blend the eggs, sugar, mace, and salt. Add the milk to the egg mixture and mix well. Stir in the vanilla. Place the cooked rice in an 8-inch square pan. Pour the milk mixture over the rice, filling the pan to within a ½ inch of the top.

Place the pan in a larger pan and pour in hot water to come about halfway up the rice pan. Bake at 400 degrees for 35 to 40 minutes, or until a knife inserted in the center comes out clean. Cut into squares to serve.

MAKES 9 SERVINGS

4 eggs, lightly beaten
½ cup sugar
⅔ teaspoon ground mace
¼ teaspoon salt
3 cups milk
1 teaspoon vanilla
1⅓ cups cooked rice

RICE PUDDING

When word got out that The Grill restaurant in Beverly Hills was serving a mouth-watering rice pudding, we got in line and asked for the recipe. It turned out that chef John Sola had been serving the pudding since 1984, and it was the most popular dessert on their menu. Sola got the original recipe from a cousin in Great Britain. The secret to success? You must use short-grain rice. The pudding simply doesn't thicken properly otherwise.

Place the butter, milk, sugar, rice, vanilla bean, and cinnamon stick in a 4-quart saucepan. Bring to a boil, reduce the heat, and simmer for 8 minutes, stirring every 2 to 3 minutes.

Combine the egg yolk and water, then stir into the saucepan. Simmer 10 minutes longer. Remove from the heat, transfer to a separate container, and chill in the refrigerator. Stir every 8 to 10 minutes to prevent the rice from settling at the bottom.

Simmer the raisins for 3 minutes in water to cover. Cool for 1 hour, drain, and add to the rice pudding. Refrigerate 2 to 3 hours or until as thick as desired. Remove the cinnamon stick. Sprinkle with ground cinnamon to garnish.

MAKES 6 (½-CUP) SERVINGS

2 tablespoons butter
3½ cups milk
¼ cup sugar
½ cup short-grain rice
1 (1½-inch) vanilla bean
1 cinnamon stick
1 egg yolk
2 tablespoons water
¾ cup raisins
Ground cinnamon, for garnish

NEW YORK RICE PUDDING

Rice puddings were all the rage in the mid-eighties. Some were very good; others were totally spectacular. We tasted a lot of rice puddings during that era and came to the conclusion that the best of the lot was from the Coach House restaurant in New York.

Wash the rice in cold water and drain well. Scald the milk in a large heavy saucepan. Add the rice and sugar. Simmer gently, uncovered, stirring often with a wooden spoon to prevent the rice from sticking to the bottom of the pan. Cook for 30 to 35 minutes, or until the rice is tender and most of the liquid is absorbed. Remove from the heat.

Beat the eggs until frothy. Add the cream and continue beating while slowly adding about 2 cups of the hot rice mixture. Return the egg mixture to the remaining rice mixture and cook over medium heat, about 15 minutes, or until the mixture coats a wooden spoon. Do not overcook.

Remove from the heat and stir in the vanilla. Turn the pudding into a 13 × 9-inch baking dish or other large shallow serving dish. Cool 10 minutes, then refrigerate.

Top the chilled pudding with a layer of pistachios, then with hot brittle topping. Refrigerate again. Before serving, crack the topping all over with the back of a large spoon.

MAKES 8 TO 10 SERVINGS

Melt the butter in a large saucepan. Add the sugar and cook, stirring, until the mixture reaches 310 degrees on a candy thermometer. Remove from the heat and pour at once over the chilled rice pudding.

¾ *cup long-grain rice*

7 *cups milk*

¾ *cup sugar*

5 *eggs*

1 *cup whipping cream*

1 *teaspoon vanilla*

1½ *cups chopped pistachios*

Brittle Topping *(recipe follows)*

BRITTLE TOPPING

1 *pound butter*

2½ *cups sugar*

NOODLE PUDDING

This lemony kugel-like dessert recipe was sent to our "My Best Recipe" column in 1985 by Hettie Kram. She grates her own lemon peel and freezes it so it's always on hand.

Cook the noodles and drain. Add the raisins, sugar, and butter. In a large bowl fold the eggs into the sour cream. Add the cottage cheese and lemon peel and mix. Stir in the noodle mixture. Turn into a buttered 10 × 7-inch or 9-inch square baking dish.

Place on a baking sheet and bake at 350 degrees for 30 minutes. Turn off the heat. Leave the pudding in the oven briefly, just until the pudding falls. Serve warm or cold.

MAKES 6 TO 8 SERVINGS

1 (1-pound) package fine egg noodles

½-pound golden or dark raisins

1 cup sugar or to taste

½ cup butter, softened

6 eggs, well beaten

1 pint sour cream

1 pint large curd cottage cheese

Grated peel of 3 medium lemons

LIGHT LEMON MOUSSE TERRINE

The talented chef at Seventh Street Bistro in downtown Los Angeles serves spectacular food, such as this light lemony mousse.

Line a 9-inch loaf pan with foil or plastic wrap, being sure that enough wrap is used to cover and overhang all 4 sides of the pan and top.

Sprinkle gelatin over lemon juice in a saucepan and heat until the gelatin is dissolved. Place in a medium bowl set in a larger bowl of ice. Whip the cream, add the lemon juice, and stir with a rubber spatula until blended. Let stand over the ice for 10 to 15 minutes, or until the mixture is slightly thickened.

Remove the bowl from the ice. Beat the egg whites with sugar to form soft peaks. Fold ¼ of the egg whites into the lemon-cream mixture, then fold the mixture carefully into the remaining egg whites. Spoon into the lined loaf pan. Cover the top with plastic or foil and freeze.

To serve, invert the lemon mousse terrine onto a flat serving platter. Slice off the ends. Cut into slices ¼- to ½-inch thick. Serve with black currant sauce.

MAKES 8 TO 10 SERVINGS

1¾ teaspoons unflavored gelatin
½ cup well-strained lemon juice
¾ cup well-chilled whipping cream
4 to 5 egg whites
¾ cup sugar
Black Currant Sauce *(recipe follows)*

Thaw the currants. Place in a blender with the lemon juice, sugar, and water and blend until smooth.

BLACK CURRANT SAUCE
1 (12-ounce) package frozen black currants
Juice of 1 lemon
¾ cup sugar
½ cup water

CHOCOLATE SOUFFLÉ

The Bistro's chocolate soufflé has been a longtime favorite dessert with Angelenos and tourists alike.

Beat the egg yolks with ½ cup sugar and the vanilla until light and fluffy. Gradually beat in the flour until a paste is formed. Meanwhile, bring the milk to a boil. Add the egg mixture all at once to milk and return to a boil. With a heavy wire whisk, quickly and vigorously beat until the paste is well incorporated into the milk and is smooth. Continue to stir with a wooden spoon until the mixture is thick as light choux paste or pastry cream. Add the melted chocolate and stir until blended. Cool.

Beat 3 egg whites with one-third of the remaining sugar until light and frothy. Add 3 more egg whites and half of the remaining sugar. Continue beating until the sugar is incorporated. Add the remaining 2 egg whites and remaining sugar and beat until the whites are stiff and shiny but not dry. The egg whites should not slide if the bowl is tipped. Fold the egg whites into the soufflé batter. Pipe or spoon into 12 greased and sugared 2-inch soufflé dishes or custard cups, or 2 (5-inch) soufflé dishes.

Bake at 350 degrees for 30 minutes for individual soufflés, or 1 hour or longer for large soufflés. Dust with powdered sugar and serve topped with sweetened whipped cream.

MAKES 12 SERVINGS

5 egg yolks
¾ cup sugar
4 drops vanilla
1 cup flour
2 cups milk
2 ounces unsweetened chocolate, melted
8 egg whites
Powdered sugar
Sweetened whipped cream

Candied Ginger Cheesecake (page 272)

Winter Citrus Cheesecake (page 268)

Chocolate Chestnut Gâteau (page 290)

Strawberries

Opposite: *Chocolate Mousse Torte (page 289)*

Double Chocolate Cake (page 267)

Baseball Bars (page 296)

Crème Brûlée (page 275)

CHOCOLATE MOUSSE TORTE

Don Ferch, chef at Highlands Inn in Carmel, gave us this recipe for a torte so good it's hard to believe it's easy to make. The brownie-like base is topped with a rich chocolate mousse filling and a chocolate glaze tops it all off.

Combine the cocoa and boiling water in a small bowl until smooth. Set aside.

Cream the butter in a large bowl of an electric mixer. Add the vanilla, salt, and sugar. Beat until mixed well. Add the egg, beating until smooth.

Stir the soda into the sour cream in a small bowl. Using low speed, add the flour to the egg mixture in 3 portions, alternating with the sour cream and scraping the bowl with a rubber spatula, beating only until smooth after each addition.

Add the cocoa and walnuts and beat only until smooth. Pour the batter into a well greased and floured 10-inch springform pan. Shake the pan and rotate slightly to level the top. Bake at 350 degrees for 25 to 30 minutes, or until the cake barely begins to shrink from the sides of the pan. Cool in the pan for 1 hour.

Spread the mousse over the cooled cake, still in the springform pan. Level the top and place in a freezer to set at least 2 hours.

Remove the cake from the freezer. Run a paring knife around the sides of the pan and remove the sides. Place the cake on a rack with a pan underneath. Pour the thickened glaze over the mousse, allowing it to run down the sides. Use a palette knife to spread and smooth the glaze around the sides.

MAKES 1 (10-INCH) CAKE

¼ cup sifted cocoa powder
⅓ cup boiling water
¼ cup unsalted butter
½ teaspoon vanilla
Pinch salt
¾ cup sugar
1 egg
½ teaspoon baking soda
½ cup sour cream
1 cup sifted flour
¼ cup walnut pieces
Mousse (recipe follows)
Glaze (recipe follows)

Melt the chocolate in a double boiler over simmering water. Combine the egg yolks, whole egg, and instant coffee powder. Whip until light and creamy. Blend in the melted chocolate.

Whip the cream and powdered sugar until fairly firm peaks form. Fold the chocolate mixture into the whipped cream. Beat the egg whites on high speed until moist and fluffy. Fold them into the chocolate mixture.

MOUSSE

12 ounces semisweet chocolate
4 egg yolks
1 whole egg
1 teaspoon instant coffee powder
1½ cups whipping cream
3 tablespoons powdered sugar
4 egg whites

Break up the chocolate and place in the top of a small double boiler. Add the sugar and water. Place over hot water over moderate heat. Stir occasionally until the chocolate is melted and mixture is smooth.

Remove from the hot water. Add the butter and stir until smooth. Let stand at room temperature, stirring occasionally, until the mixture thickens slightly.

GLAZE

3 ounces semisweet chocolate
3 tablespoons granulated sugar
2 tablespoons water
2 tablespoons unsalted butter, at room temperature

CHOCOLATE CHESTNUT GÂTEAU

When Times *wine writer Dan Berger found out we were doing a story on chestnuts, he raved about the gâteau made by Margaret Clark when she catered for Guenoc Winery in Lake County, north of Napa Valley. It's a fabulous party dessert, particularly at holiday time.*

Line the bottom of an 8-inch cake pan with parchment paper. Butter the sides of the pan and parchment paper.

Melt ¼ cup butter in a small saucepan. Slowly incorporate well into chestnut purée in a medium bowl. Add the honey, brandy, and cream and continue mixing until thoroughly blended.

Melt the chocolate in the top of a double boiler set over simmering water. When melted, but just lukewarm, add a half at a time to the chestnut mixture, mixing well at low speed. Add the eggs and blend well, still at low speed. Stir in the flour, mixing well.

Pour into the prepared pan and bake at 300 degrees for 35 minutes, or until just set in the center. Remove from the oven and cool completely in the pan on a rack.

Unmold onto a plate just before serving. Serve with the honey sauce.

MAKES 16 SERVINGS

Note: If chestnut purée is not available, 1 (8¾-ounce) can chestnut spread (sweetened) may be substituted for 2 cups purée and ¼ cup honey.

Butter

2 cups crumbled canned chestnut purée

¼ cup honey

¼ cup brandy

⅓ cup whipping cream

½ pound bittersweet or semisweet chocolate, chopped

3 eggs, well beaten

2 tablespoons flour

Honey Sauce (recipe follows)

Warm the milk over medium heat until small bubbles appear around the edge. Whisk the honey into the egg yolks, then continuing to whisk slowly add the milk until thoroughly mixed.

Return the mixture to a saucepan and cook over medium-low heat, stirring constantly with a wooden spoon, until slightly thickened. Do not boil. The cooked sauce should coat a spoon.

Remove from the heat and strain into a small bowl. Stir in the orange flower water, cover, and chill thoroughly before serving (sauce will thicken somewhat during cooling).

MAKES ABOUT 1⅓ CUPS

Note: Orange flower water is available at specialty food markets.

HONEY SAUCE

1 cup milk

3 tablespoons honey

3 egg yolks, well beaten

1 teaspoon orange flower water

TIRAMISU

Tiramisu is a cousin of trifle, but made with mascarpone cheese and biscotti rather than whipping cream and pound cake. This recipe came from La Cucina restaurant in Los Angeles.

Beat the egg yolks with powdered sugar and Marsala wine over warm water until light. Cool.

Slowly whip the mascarpone cheese. Beat into the egg yolk mixture. Beat the whipping cream, gradually adding vanilla, until stiff. Fold into the egg yolk-cheese mixture.

Dip the split ladyfingers into espresso, just enough to moisten. Layer the ladyfingers on the bottom of a large bowl. Spoon a layer of the cheese mixture over them. Cover with more ladyfingers. Repeat the layering.

Sprinkle the surface with cocoa powder.

MAKES 12 SERVINGS

Note: Garnish with whipped cream and coffee beans, if desired.

8 egg yolks

1¼ cups powdered sugar

½ cup Marsala wine

1¼ pounds mascarpone or cream cheese

3 cups whipping cream

1 teaspoon vanilla

1 (3½-ounce) package ladyfingers, split, or Italian biscotti

1 cup espresso or strong coffee

1 tablespoon unsweetened cocoa powder

GRANDMOTHER'S BEST BROWNIES

When Danielle Gomez sent us this recipe in 1988, she told us her grandmother made the brownies for the family without icing. For company she added the icing. Either way they're good eating.

Melt the shortening and chocolate in a saucepan (use a saucepan large enough to serve as a mixing bowl) over very low heat. Stir constantly to avoid burning. Remove from the heat.

Add the sugar and mix well. Add the eggs, nuts, and vanilla. Beat thoroughly until well blended. Stir in the flour and salt. Pour into 2 greased (9-inch) square pans. Bake at 325 degrees for 35 minutes. Remove from the oven and spread with frosting.

MAKES ABOUT 24 SERVINGS

Melt the butter and chocolate in a small saucepan over very low heat (or use a double boiler). Stir constantly to avoid burning. Add the powdered sugar, salt, milk, and vanilla. Beat until well blended. Chill 10 to 15 minutes, until of spreading consistency.

1⅓ cups shortening

8 (1-ounce) squares unsweetened baking chocolate

4 cups sugar

8 eggs

2 cups chopped walnuts, optional

4 teaspoons vanilla

2 cups flour, sifted

1 teaspoon salt

Frosting, *optional (recipe follows)*

FROSTING

3 tablespoons butter or margarine

3 (1-ounce) squares unsweetened baking chocolate

3 cups powdered sugar

¼ teaspoon salt

⅓ cup milk

1 teaspoon vanilla

PECAN-CARAMEL-CAKE MIX BROWNIES

We used to call this recipe Turtle brownies, but the candy maker objected so we renamed it. Norma Keen, who sent the recipe to us, said it came from Texas. Wherever it's from, it's a very fudgy, almost gooey brownie. If you prefer a more cake-like brownie, you can cook it a bit longer but it will always be slightly gooey.

Combine the caramels and ⅓ cup evaporated milk in the top of a double boiler. Heat over simmering water, stirring until melted.

Combine the cake mix, remaining ⅓ cup evaporated milk, and soft butter. Mix until the batter holds together. Stir in the nuts. Press half of the cake batter mixture in a greased 13 × 9-inch baking pan. Bake at 350 degrees for 6 minutes.

Sprinkle the chocolate pieces evenly over the top. Pour the melted caramels over. Crumble the remaining cake mix mixture on top of the caramels. Bake another 15 to 18 minutes or until desired doneness (shorter baking time results in a moister brownie). Cool slightly and cut into bars.

MAKES ABOUT 12 BROWNIES

1 (14-ounce) package caramels
⅔ cup evaporated milk
1 (18½ ounce) package German chocolate cake mix
¾ cup butter or margarine, softened
1 cup chopped nuts
1 (12-ounce) package semisweet chocolate pieces

SOFT CHOCOLATE CHIP COOKIES

A wonderful soft chocolate chip cookie recipe toured the town in 1987. It was said that it was Mrs. Fields' recipe, but the company quickly denied that. Served warm and fresh from the oven the way the Mrs. Fields' cookies are, however, it makes a wonderful substitute.

Cream together the butter and both sugars. Add the eggs and vanilla, beating well.

Mix together the flour, oats, salt, baking powder, and baking soda. Place small amounts in the blender and process until the mixture turns into a powder.

Mix the butter-egg mixture with the flour mixture until just blended. Add the chocolate pieces, milk chocolate, and chopped nuts. Roll into balls about the size of golf balls and place 2 inches apart on an ungreased baking sheet. Bake at 375 degrees for 12 minutes.

MAKES 3 TO 4 DOZEN COOKIES

1 cup butter
1 cup granulated sugar
1 cup brown sugar, packed
2 eggs
1 teaspoon vanilla
2 cups flour
2½ cups oats
½ teaspoon salt
1 teaspoon baking powder
1 teaspoon baking soda
1 (12-ounce) package semisweet chocolate pieces
1 (4-ounce) bar milk chocolate, grated
1½ cups chopped nuts

CHOCOLATE CHIP-OATMEAL COOKIES

Even hospitals serve good food in California. A reader who spent some time in Scripps Clinic in La Jolla raved about the hospital's chewy oatmeal cookies. We asked for the recipe, which the hospital graciously supplied.

Beat together the margarine, both sugars, egg, water, and vanilla until creamy. Combine the oats, flour, salt, baking soda, and chocolate pieces. Add to the creamed mixture, blending well. Place about ¼ cup dough per cookie on a greased baking sheet and bake at 350 degrees for 12 to 15 minutes.

MAKES 1½ DOZEN COOKIES

¾ cup margarine
1 cup brown sugar, packed
¼ cup granulated sugar
1 egg
¼ cup water
1 teaspoon vanilla
2½ cups oats
¾ cup plus 2 tablespoons flour
½ teaspoon salt
½ teaspoon baking soda
½ cup semisweet chocolate pieces

FLYING SAUCERS

Sometimes called ranger cookies, these big chocolate cookies filled with raisins and nuts have been favorites with Los Angeles schoolchildren for years. The recipe came originally from the city school system and has been printed many times.

Melt the chocolate in a double boiler over hot water. Sift together the flour, salt, and soda. Cream together the shortening, sugar, egg, and vanilla until light and fluffy. Thoroughly mix in the chocolate and flour mixture. Stir in the milk, oats, and raisins. Chill. Shape pieces of the dough into balls about ¾ inch in diameter and roll in the almonds. Place on a greased baking sheet about 3 inches apart and flatten with the bottom of a glass. Bake at 375 degrees for 10 minutes.

MAKES ABOUT 1½ DOZEN COOKIES

1 (6-ounce) package semisweet chocolate pieces
1½ cups sifted flour
1 teaspoon salt
½ teaspoon baking soda
¾ cup shortening
1½ cups brown sugar, packed
1 egg
1 teaspoon vanilla
¼ cup milk
½ cup oats
1 cup raisins
1 cup chopped almonds

CREAM CHEESE COOKIES

Reader Renee Ketcham found a recipe for a cream cheese cookie in a magazine but decided she could do better. So she did . . . and sent the resulting recipe to our "My Best Recipe" column.

Cream together the butter and cream cheese in a bowl. Add the vanilla, orange peel, coriander, ginger, and mace. Slowly add the honey, beating until smooth.

In a separate bowl, mix together the flour and bran. Stir into the cream cheese mixture. Stir in the nuts and coconut. Drop by teaspoons onto a baking sheet. Bake at 350 degrees for 15 minutes or until lightly browned.

MAKES ABOUT 3 DOZEN COOKIES

1 cup butter or margarine, at room temperature

1 (8-ounce) package cream cheese, at room temperature

1 teaspoon vanilla

1 teaspoon grated orange peel

½ teaspoon ground coriander

½ teaspoon ground ginger

½ teaspoon ground mace

¾ cup honey or light molasses

1¾ cups flour

¾ cup wheat bran or crushed bran flakes

½ cup chopped walnuts and/or 1 cup shredded coconut, optional

VACUUM CLEANER COOKIES

These bar cookies got their name because they disappear with such speed. Connie Hankins's mother in Kansas gave her the original recipe, which has since become a California cookie classic with all who have tried it. Be sure to use a jelly-roll pan with sides at least ½- to ¾-inch high or the batter will overflow the pan as it cooks.

Combine the margarine, cake mix, and 1 egg. Stir together until the dry ingredients are moistened. Pat the mixture into the bottom of a well-greased 15 × 10-inch jelly-roll pan.

Lightly beat the remaining 2 eggs, then beat in the cream cheese and powdered sugar. Stir in the coconut and nuts. Pour over the mixture in the jelly-roll pan, spreading evenly. Bake at 325 degrees for 45 to 50 minutes or until golden brown. Cool the pan on a wire rack to room temperature.

MAKES 4 DOZEN BARS

Note: Use *plain* cake mix, not a mix with pudding added. Do not use whipped margarine.

½ cup margarine (not butter) melted

1 (18.25-ounce) package yellow cake mix

3 eggs

1 (8-ounce) package cream cheese, softened

1 (1-pound) box powdered sugar

½ cup flaked coconut

½ cup chopped walnuts or pecans

BASEBALL BARS

Cindy Guttenplan begged her boss for the recipe for the cookies he would bring to office parties. Then she added some of her own ideas to the basic recipe and our "My Best Recipe" column benefitted from the result in 1986. The bars are very rich and very sweet, so be sure to cut small pieces.

Melt the butter, brown sugar, and corn syrup together. Add the peanut butter and vanilla. Mix well. Stir in the oats. Press the mixture into a greased 9-inch baking pan. Bake at 375 degrees for 15 minutes.

Spread with the hot topping. Sprinkle with chopped nuts. Cool, then refrigerate. If too cold, let stand about 15 minutes for ease in cutting. Cut into bars.

MAKES 16 TO 20 BARS

Mix the chocolate and butterscotch pieces, peanut butter, and nuts in a saucepan. Heat over medium heat, stirring until blended.

⅔ cup butter
1 cup brown sugar, packed
¼ cup light corn syrup
¼ cup chunky peanut butter
1 teaspoon vanilla
4 cups quick oats
Topping (recipe follows)
Chopped nuts, optional

TOPPING

1 (12-ounce) package semisweet chocolate pieces
1 (12-ounce) package butterscotch pieces
⅔ cup chunky peanut butter
1 cup chopped unsalted nuts

INDEX

Photo Credits

Myron Beck, 40, 285; Jeff Burke, 73, 98; Mike Chesser, 76, 210, 215; Steve Dykes, 99; Michael Edwards, 103 top, 186, 281; John Reed Forsman, 97, 104, 192; Rosemary Kaul, 286; Tom Kelsey, 288; Con Keyes, 34, 103 bottom, 284; Carin Krasner, 216; Randy Leffingwell, 35, 36, 37, 38, 39, 75, 100, 185, 188, 191, 211, 282; Jim Mendenhall, 101, 283; Rick Meyer, 189, 209, 212; Anacleto Rapping, 74, 77, 79, 190, 214 top; Teri Sandison, 187; Al Seib, 33, 102; L. Kent Whitehead, 78, 80, 213, 214 bottom, 287.

Stylists

Nona Baer, 40, 210, 215; Lynn Ellen, 104; Janet Miller, 216; Stephanie Puddy, 192; Norman Stewart, 37, 74, 97, 187, 190; Lorraine Triolo, 73, 98; Robin Tucker, 76, 285; Donna Deane and Minnie Bernardino, all other photographs.